COMEDY IN THE WEIMAR REPUBLIC

A Chronicle of Incongruous Laughter

William Grange

Contributions in Drama and Theatre Studies, Number 74

GREENWOOD PRESS
Westport, Connecticut • London

Library of Congress Cataloging-in-Publication Data

Grange, William, 1947–
Comedy in the Weimar Republic : a chronicle of incongruous laughter / by William Grange.
p. cm. — (Contributions in drama and theatre studies, ISSN 0163–3821 ; no. 74)
Includes bibliographical references and index.
ISBN 0–313–29983–8 (alk. paper)
1. German drama—20th century—History and criticism. 2. German drama (Comedy)—History and criticism. 3. Theater—Germany—History—20th century. 4. Germany—Politics and government—1918–1933. I. Title. II. Series.
PT666.G7 1996
832′.052309091—dc20 96–5834

British Library Cataloguing in Publication Data is available.

Library of Congress Catalog Card Number: 96–5834
ISBN: 0–313–29983–8
ISSN: 0163–3821

First published in 1996

Greenwood Press, 88 Post Road West, Westport, CT 06881
An imprint of Greenwood Publishing Group, Inc.

Printed in the United States of America

The paper used in this book complies with the Permanent Paper Standard issued by the National Information Standards Organization (Z39.48–1984).

10 9 8 7 6 5 4 3 2 1

for Leah

Contents

A photographic essay begins on page 92.

Preface

This is a study of comedy, comic playwrights, and comedy production in Germany from 1918 to 1933. To date there has been only inadequate appraisal of plays (and their productions) which were riotously popular in the Weimar Republic but are almost unknown today. These comedies did extraordinarily well at the box office, but they were frequently dismissed by contemporary critics as intellectually insufficient, despite their acknowledged and significant contributions to German popular culture. They constitute a drama that historically suffers from scholarly neglect because many observers, writing both in German and in English, consider them trivial and unworthy of rigorous assessment. Studying them provides valuable insights into the German theatre as a whole and contributes needed perspective on other areas of German drama. Why were there so many performances of these comedies? What made them so popular? Who wrote them, and who performed them? What historical significance did they have? Why were Germans laughing when society around them was crumbling? These are some of the questions this study attempts to answer.

To most casual observers, it may come as a surprise to learn that comedy even existed during the Weimar Republic. The years that spawned National Socialism are seldom regarded as humorous in the public mind. Yet the years between the kaiser's abdication and Adolf Hitler's move into the Reich Chancellery consisted of more than cabarets, hooligans in brown shirts, and *The Threepenny Opera.*This book could in fact be subtitled, "How Comedy Conquered and then Saved the German Theatre." Theatre was one of many German institutions experiencing profound change in the aftermath of World War I. Had not comedy, a peculiar species of comedy in particular, prevailed throughout the turbulent years of the illfated German experiment in democracy, much of theatre as a German institution would have died along with the republic itself. Audiences attended performances of comedies in numbers far surpassing those of any other genre.

Comedy in the Weimar Republic was a culmination of developments begun decades earlier, whose sources were political and economic as much as theatrical. That is what made comedy a cultural phenomenon, for comedy is among all genres the one most closely akin to its immediate environment. The comedies studied here are works that few would recognize, written by men whose names have largely disappeared from the annals of theatre history. Most students of German drama will recognize Georg Kaiser, Carl Zuckmayer, and Walter Hasenclever. But who remembers Franz Arnold and Ernst Bach, the creators of the most popular and well-known comedies of their day? And who would imagine that Avery Hopwood would share pride of place with George Bernard Shaw as the Weimar Republic's most frequently performed contemporary English-language playwright? This book seeks to rectify perceptions and revise commonly held suppositions of German theatre after World War I and, in doing so, provide needed insights into comedy's position within an entire culture.

I witnessed my first "Weimar comedy" in 1969, at Berlin's Schiller Theater, while a college student. In that play, *Der Hauptmann von Köpenick* (The Captain of Köpenick) by Carl Zuckmayer, I saw characters literally spring to life with a vibrancy I had never before experienced. I became convinced that Germany was full of such characters. In college, however, one learns that there are very few comedies in German. Gotthold Ephraim Lessing wrote one, as did Heinrich von Kleist and Gerhart Hauptmann. Bertolt Brecht tried to write one, and before them all Hans Sachs wrote a few short ones, but "German" and "comedy" just do not mix. Or so we were taught. The laughter that night in the Schiller Theater, however, exploded everything I had ever heard about German comedy. I started making inquiries, and nearly thirty years later they led to this book.

I owe debts of gratitude to many people for its completion. The German Academic Exchange Service provided funding for research; without the assistance of that outstanding organization, its staff both in Bonn and New York, along with their confidence in me, this book simply would not have been completed. Johannes-Martin Giesen, then a student with me at Heidelberg and now a professor of art history, provided me with a ticket to that performance of *Der Hauptmann von Köpenick* at the Schiller Theater. Professor Leigh Woods of the University of Michigan provided invaluable personal encouragement and professional insight. To Professor Woods I owe more than I can ever repay. Professor Marvin Carlson of the City University of New York likewise provided expert suggestions for the project. His wide-ranging expertise in all areas of German theatre production would be invaluable to any author. Professor Roswitha Flatz of the University of Cologne provided the first recommendations for research, and Professor Elmar Buck, director of that university's Theatre Collection and Museum, furnished priceless counsel on working with hundreds of playscripts at the Collection. I am likewise indebted to Dr. Jürgen Ohlhoff and Ulrike Münkel-Ohlhoff for their generosity, kindness, and friendship during several sojourns to Germany. Many colleagues furnished proposals for further avenues of inquiry. I am particularly grateful to Professors Thomas Postlewait of Ohio State University, Felicia Londré of the

University of Missouri/Kansas City, and to Steve Goldzwig of Marquette University. Professors Michael J. Price and James Scotton of Marquette provided much needed moral support during some dark days. So did many of my students, who posed questions about the book's premise and helped to clarify numerous topics of discussion. I am especially grateful to Wes Savick and Judy McGeorge for their patience.

My personal thanks, finally and most importantly, are due to Willa, my wife, helpmate, and most enthusiastic audience member. Martin Luther phrased my feelings of gratitude to her better than I can in his translation of Paul's letter to Timothy: *Denn Gott hat uns nicht gegeben den Geist der Furcht, sondern der Kraft und der Liebe und der Besonnenheit.*

Introduction: Comedy for an Industrial Age

Comedy in the Weimar Republic inherited its audience from the Wilhelmine years, during which the German theatre had undergone profound changes. The so-called *Gründerjahre*, or expansionist epoch, had witnessed unprecedented economic growth, beginning with the victorious conclusion of the Franco-Prussian War, the formation of the new German state under Bismarck in 1871, and the collection of billions in war reparations from the vanquished French. The economic wealth created in such circumstances had a profound and lasting effect, but before undertaking an examination of those effects, we need to consider the theatrical conditions and historical forces that led to the expansion of an enormously vast audience for comedy on the German stage.

Economic circumstances in Bismarck's Second Reich benefited theatrical enterprise; between 1871 and 1890, the German economy surpassed that of France and soon thereafter that of Great Britain. German steel production increased eightfold between 1880 and 1910, leading to rapid development in rail, banking, chemical, shipbuilding, and electrical industries. The increase in industrial capacity had a corresponding effect upon both theatre art and theatre construction; a trade law encouraging competition promoted the creation of new theatres and other businesses, and in the 1870s ninety new theatres had been built in Prussia alone.[1] Audiences became more affluent, especially in larger cities, and producers sought new kinds of theatrical fare to please them. A pivotal figure in that search was Theodor Lebrun (Theodor Leinenweber, 1822–1895), who developed a species of comedy that, like a victorious Prussian army, conquered one theatre's repertoire after another.

Lebrun operated the Wallner Theater in Berlin, a building named for its founder, Franz Wallner, who had presented "Berlin comedies" in the 1850s and 1860s similar to the "Viennese comedies" of Nestroy in the 1840s.[2] In these comedies, Wallner audiences encountered familiar Berlin character types like plumbers, carpenters, cooks, coachmen, and chambermaids, all speaking the distinctive dialect of Berlin and its surroundings. The most prolific of the Berlin comic playwrights was Louis Angely (1787–1835), who wrote over 100 Berlin comedies and had a decisive role in transforming the genre from its French prototype into distinctive linguistic and social products of a specific Berlin milieu.[3] Angely's comedies presented optimistic depictions of the city's neighborhoods, a certain contemporary view of the world, of which the audience itself was a part. Such comedies were, however, declining in popularity by the later 1860s. They were too "plebeian," and plebeian audiences could not support a whole season of plays that had large casts, required musicians, and demanded several scene changes. Wallner leased his theatre to Lebrun in 1869, who began to search for plays that would attract, cultivate, and retain a wider and more affluent audience. It was a propitious time for Lebrun to take over the Wallner for the unification of the German Reich, with Berlin as its capital, effected unforeseen changes that helped provide him with the audience he sought.

Berlin had been a rustic garrison town compared with London or Paris throughout most of the nineteenth century. It was notable as the seat of the Prussian military and civil administration, yet by 1800 it could boast a population of only 170,000, sixth in size of the cities on the Continent (behind Paris, Rome, and even Prague). Industrial expansion had increased particularly after the revolution of 1848, however, and by 1870 Berlin had a population of 825,000. The billions of gold French francs flowing into Germany as war reparations came mostly to Berlin where, along with normal business expansion, there was a great deal of real estate speculation. Between 1870 and 1880, Berlin grew by sixty percent, and that produced a concomitant increase in the size of audiences.

In 1872 alone, 175 corporations were founded in Berlin; the city was also the beneficiary of the new Reich's geography. It lay midway between Königsberg in the east, Cologne to the west, and Munich in the south. Rail networks made it, in Mark Twain's apt phrase, "the Teutonic Chicago." It was moreover growing much faster, and much bigger, than Chicago. In 1882 a surface rail system was built to connect the city proper with its suburbs. By 1890 there were already 2 million people living in those outlying towns and villages, and by 1910 the overall population had increased to 3,730,000. In 1911 there was an informal union of the city and its suburbs, and by the beginning of the Weimar Republic, "Greater Berlin" encompassed an area of 340 square miles. In comparison, the five boroughs of New York City covered 309; Paris, 185; and London, 116. Greater Berlin, in 1920, had over fifty working theatres and a population of well over 4 million, making it one of the five largest cities in the world. The explosive growth of Berlin throughout the *Gründerjahre* and the succeeding Wilhelmine years (Kaiser Wilhelm II assumed the throne in 1888) generated an unprecedented demand for entertainment among middlebrow audiences. They were business managers, real estate brokers, professionals, bankers, and entrepreneurs, the most prosperous element in German society and in Berlin particularly. Their taste in theatrical fare proved likewise influential, for despite its governmental importance, Berlin was never a city intellectually dominated by the government as in Vienna. The aristocratic elites of Prussia tended to stay on their estates to the east and did not involve themselves much in Berlin's affairs. Audiences were not attuned to "aristocratic" tastes, nor did they generally prefer intellectual subject matter. They were the *Bürgertum*, the audience that Lebrun wanted to attract.

Theatre business was good in Berlin; not only did theatre buildings proliferate, so did enterprises supplying the needs of theatres such as scenery construction studios, costume studios, and publishers of manuscripts like Felix Bloch, Georg Marton, Drei Masken, and Georg Müller. Lebrun began his regime at the Wallner with plays by Roderich Benedix (1811–1873) and Gustav von Moser (1825–1903), both of whom created comedies with a more sophisticated outlook than the rustic local comedies Wallner had presented. Benedix and von Moser had, in fact, grown up in privileged circumstances (on large country estates, and von Moser was indeed a nobleman); their feel for the middle-class audience and for middle-class taste was adequate, and they both wrote plays that Lebrun's audiences enjoyed. Lebrun was nevertheless looking for a "breakthrough" playwright; he found him in the unlikely person of composer and conductor Adolf L'Arronge (Adolf Aronsohn, 1838–1908), who at the beginning of the Second Reich was the musical director of Berlin's Kroll Opera. L'Arronge's father, however, had been actor-manager Eberhard Theodor L'Arronge (Eberhard Theodor Aronsohn, 1812–1878), from whom the son learned a great deal about the business end of theatre and the technical side of playwriting.

What middle-class audiences in Berlin wanted, L'Arronge surmised, were comedies that portrayed a happy, prosperous bourgeois who, at the same time, was a somewhat beleaguered father and oppressed husband but who regardless was a proud member of the Establishment. He was a man like many in the audience, making his way to the top by himself, under his own power; society provided him with an honorable place within its midst, and therefore he did not engage himself in any kind of political or social discussions. The characters in such comedies were to have no political opinions whatsoever. It was a format derived from August Kotzebue and from the French comédie-vaudeville, a situation comedy first and foremost. Discoveries, reversals, and mistaken identities were its stock in trade and the basic materials of its dramatic content, the essentials of its identity as a comic genre. Its goal was the satisfied laughter of its audience; therefore, it relinquished any attempt at pathos or "deeper significance."

It was an industrial comedy fit for an industrial age. The boulevard theatres of Paris in the Second Empire had been the first mills to produce such comedies; Berlin of the Second Reich became the forge on which they were stamped out with startling precision and regularity. They resembled Eugène Scribe's plays to an extent, but Scribe played mostly for audiences made up of aristocrats and he tended to carry plot tension throughout the play. They did not, for example, depend upon an effect created within individual situations the way industrial comedies did. They more nearly resembled the farces of Eugène Labiche, especially his *Un chapeau de paille d'Itallie* (The Italian Straw Hat, 1851); here was a play that created laughter out of superficial bourgeois dilemmas, allowing the audience to take pleasure in seeing itself positively and humorously portrayed on the stage. In Berlin, David Kalisch had adapted Labiche's *Un notaire à marier* (1853) and turned it into *Otto Bellmann* in 1857; later, Franz von Schönthann transformed Scribe's *Les petits oiseaux* (1862) into *Die Spatzen* (The Sparrows) in 1882 and *Célimare le bien-aimé* (1863) into *Der Vielgeliebte* (The Much Beloved) in 1885. The German-language comedy to establish a workable and imitable pattern for subsequent production, however, was L'Arronge's *Mein Leopold*; L'Arronge wrote it in 1873, and Theodor Lebrun premiered it at the Wallner Theater the same year.

Its success was so substantial that it continued to run for years afterward, performed thousands of times in scores of productions all over Germany. It was a well-wrought, tightly structured mechanism designed to set up comic situations; it established a precedent for thousands of German comedies that were to follow, the popularity of which exceeded *Mein Leopold's*. These were plays closely connected to the German bourgeois world and its accompanying morality; in them, there was great effort made to present affirmative images of middle-class life, one that was relatively secure and prosperous. Prosperity had to be assured, for financial concerns would distract from the major focus, the comic situation. The characters had relationships with each other that went only so deep as to further that situation. They had no previous conflicts with one another; their feelings, their views, and their interests were explored only insofar as complications enabled further comic situations to develop.

The Wallner Theater of the 1870s was the birthplace of the German industrial comedy, where not only L'Arronge enjoyed his first success as a playwright. Following him were actors Franz von Schönthann and Gustav Kadelburg who, as members of the Lebrun ensemble, recognized what techniques were effective with the audiences streaming to the Wallner. Their *Der Raub der Sabinerinnen* (The Rape of the Sabine Women) became a staple of nearly every theatre in Germany after its premiere in 1884. Its popularity far surpassed that of *Mein Leopold*, both in time occupying a place in the Wallner repertoire and in the number of productions through the Wilhelmine years and into the Weimar Republic.

The Wallner Theater was a business enterprise, like nearly all other theatres in the Reich capital. Only the Prussian Hoftheater, or Court Theatre, received government subsidies; it was literally a royal asset of the Prussian kingdom. If comedy appeared on the Hoftheater stage at all, it was never contemporary; the Prussian Hoftheater was almost exclusively reserved for well-known tragedy or comedy, most of it by Shakespeare, Lessing, Goethe, and Schiller. The Hoftheater in Berlin was, in short, a repository; as such it resembled court theatres throughout the country. They were "generally feudal institutions," as John Willett has accurately described them;[4] yet court theatres represented only a portion of the diverse and decentralized German theatre establishment. Prior to unification there had been four general types of theatrical organization in nineteenth century Germany. The court theatres were subsidized by the local nobleman, although they were still open to the public; Stadttheater, or city theatres, were municipal properties usually leased to the highest bidder; private theatres were in most instances self-supporting, managed by entrepreneurs like Lebrun. There were also some remaining "national theatres" in some cities, notably Leipzig, Düsseldorf, and Braunschweig, which retained the idealistic notion that governmental control could maintain high literary standards as an antidote to purely financial concerns. The formation of the German Reich in 1871, with its emphasis upon economic expansion, largely put an end to such utopian attempts. The distinctions among these theatres prior to unification was often blurred anyway because private theatres sometimes became court theatres, and city theatres often became private theatres several times over, depending upon who had available capital to keep the establishment in operation.

Most court theatres had already been built by the time of German unification. As the German Reich became wealthier, investors speculated on theatre construction in cities where curious "cooperative agreements" with local governments were possible. The local government, for example, permitted the newly constructed buildings to be called city theatres. These structures were then leased to an entrepreneur; the city government restricted licensing for dramatic performance to that venue, for which the city received a portion of the business's profits. Such monopolies tied the theatre to city government, just as direct subsidies tied court theatres to their patrons. The court theatres and the municipal theatres combined to form a powerful force of influence. Their repertoires resembled that of the Prussian Hoftheater, although some producers added Kleist, Franz Grillparzer, or Pedro Calderon de la Barca to the aforementioned "standards." Some included translations from such French playwrights like Victorien Sardou and Labiche, and added melodramas by Kotzebue and August Wilhelm Iffland. There was also an operetta or two to be found in the repertoire.[5]

At the end of the Franco-Prussian War there were only eight cities in Germany with a population of more than one hundred thousand; by 1900 there were thirty-three such cities, and in each of them a great deal of theatre construction had taken place. In each of them, theatre enterprises resembling Lebrun's eagerly sought plays to satisfy an increasingly large middle-class audience. In the provincial cities, as noted above government-sanctioned monopolies often restricted the kinds of plays private theatres could do. The Wilhelmine legal structure also had an aesthetic impact on theatre practice. Laws specifically forbade denigration, implied or direct, of the monarchy, the church, the army, the family, or "Christian sexual mores" in plays, literature, or journalism. Though such laws were enforced haphazardly (the Reich had no national police force, and what might have been banned in Bavaria would meet with less resistance in Berlin, for example), plays had to conform to certain guidelines; though they were somewhat ambiguous in Berlin, they remained firmly in place almost everywhere else.[6] Had the laws been more flexible, audiences might have been less cautious; as it was, they expressed a preference for "entertainment and a comic release from a vexatious reality."[7] While enormous in numbers and in influence, such audiences were, as Arnold Hauser described the German middle class generally, "half-cultured [and] often miseducated, essentially uncreative and completely passive."[8]

NOTES

1. Marvin Carlson, *The German Stage of the Nineteenth Century* (Metuchen, NJ: Scarecrow, 1972), 164.

2. Other playwrights closely associated with cities in which they wrote were Karl Malß in Frankfurt am Main and Ernst Elias Nebergall in Darmstadt. Their *Lokalposse*, or "local farces," dealt with local themes and characters, with a liberal admixture of local references, regionally popular songs, and topical allusions.

3. Volker Klotz, *Bürgerliches Lachtheater* (Munich: DTV, 1980), 111.

4. John Willett, *The Theatre of the Weimar Republic* (New York: Holmes and Meyer, 1988), 58.

5. One should recognize the importance of opera in the repertoires of most court and city theatres during the nineteenth century. Opera was extremely popular, especially Wagnerian opera, but it was usually presented in a separate building under an administration distinct from dramatic presentation. Operettas were presented by both administrations.

6. Roy Pascal, *From Naturalism to Expressionism: German Literature and Society, 1880–1918* (New York: Basic Books, 1973), 258.

7. Jürgen Hein, "Das Volkstück: Entwicklung und Tendenzen," in Jürgen Hein, ed. *Theater und Gesellschaft* (Düsseldorf: Bertelsmann, 1973), 10.

8. Arnold Hauser, *The Sociology of Art*, trans. Kenneth Northcott (Chicago: University of Chicago Press, 1982), 550.

1

Comedy and the German-Language Theatre Audience

Comedy has frequently suffered a discredited reputation in the German-language theatre because there is a German tendency to "underestimate comedy as a valid form of artistic expression,"[1] although the one-act *Fastnachtspiele* (Shrovetide Plays) of Hans Sachs (1494–1576) constitute a prominent beginning of comedy as a legitimate, playable species on the German stage. The poet Andreas Gryphius (1616–1664) wrote comedies which likewise were effective in performance, and during the later decades of the seventeenth century his *Peter Squentz* (1658) and the later *Das verliebte Gespenst* (The Ghost in Love) and *Die geliebte Dornrose* (The Beloved Thorn Rose, both 1661) enjoyed inclusion in the repertoires of some ambitious companies. By the 1720s, however, most troupes made their living by improvising comedic routines as a means to capture what audiences they could find. Although England and France had by the same time period established theatre troupes and even well-financed theatre structures in their capitals, Germany was still suffering from the devastating effects of the Thirty Years' War (1618–1648). The war had destroyed most of Central Europe's economic capacity, leaving a demolished infrastructure in its wake and obliterating networks of commercial communication which had taken decades to establish. Germany required decades to rebuild, and that included rebuilding a theatre-going public affluent enough to support uniform performance standards. Even by the 1720s rehearsals were haphazard at best, and performances normally took place on an open-air platform. Actors were judged by their ability to attract and hold an audience's attention in the face of manifold distractions, as there emerged an oddly fashioned commedia dell'arte in which performers were required to be extraordinarily versatile.

The central character in these proceedings was Hanswurst, a kind of Teutonic Harlequin who provided comic commentary as the action proceeded. He ambled in and out of the melodramatic enactments of intrigue in high places known as plays of *Haupt- und Staatsaktionen*, which Lessing described as "complete nonsense, bombast, filth, and mob humor."[2] The exact genealogy of Hanswurst remains in dispute; there is general agreement, however, that he provided abundant (if vulgar and obscene) amusement for his audiences. As such he became an easy target for eighteenth-century reformers like Johann Christoph Gottsched, who envisioned the theatre as a source of popular uplift and education.

Gottsched (1700–1766) proposed giving audiences "not what they liked but what they ought to like."[3] The popular theatre in Gottsched's day resembled carnival shows, during the performances of which actors also sold medicine, pulled teeth, and did juggling acts. The actor Konrad Ekhof (1720–1778) provided a contemporary description of an audience favorite during this period, titled *Adam und Eva*, featuring an overweight Eva whose body was covered by flesh-colored canvas and sported strategically painted-on fig leaves. Adam looked just as ridiculous, Ekhof reported, while God himself appeared in a bathrobe, an enormous wig, and a long white beard. "In summary, it was all repulsive; the stage floor wobbled, the audience never stopped talking, the actors were done up in rags and ill-fitting wigs, and all of them resembled heroically bedecked hired coachmen. In a word, comedy was entertainment for the masses."[4]

Ekhof presumed that actors had no future in pursuing a mass audience because money to support theatre on a long-term basis was available only through the courts and the middle-class authorities in cities. Yet sustaining an audience, once Gottsched and other reformers had cleansed the German theatre, was no mean task. Gottsched sought to build an audience through moral blandishments and a quixotic attempt simultaneously to vaccinate the German theatre against bad taste and to inculcate a new system of aesthetic values within it. In collaboration with actress/manager Caroline Neuber (Friederike Caroline Weissenborn, 1697–1760) he staged his own adaptations of French neoclassical drama and sought to extirpate any vestige of improvisation (including the infamously vulgar Hanswurst). Gottsched represented an intellectual minority that wanted to impose its taste upon audiences and to establish a theatre which satisfied its own moral necessities.

Gotthold Ephraim Lessing (1729–1781) differed with Gottsched as to the model Germans should emulate in the creation of more refined taste among audiences, but he shared Gottsched's notion that theatre should augment decorum and ennoble morality. Those sentiments Friedrich Schiller echoed in his work with Johann Wolfgang Goethe at the Weimar Court Theater between 1798 and 1805; Schiller in particular advocated a theatre as *moralische Anstalt*, or moral institution. Court theatres around the country wanted to project a similar image of "high culture" in the wake of Goethe's success in Weimar, which in the early 1800s had enjoyed a widespread reputation for excellence.

The ideas of Gottsched, Lessing, and Schiller had a powerful impact on the German stage, as theatres on the subsidized basis of a moral institution proliferated. Yet that impact was not powerful enough to eradicate completely the appeal of theatre as an institution for the sake of entertainment. If, for example, "the Hamburg public listened to the London merchant, Mr. Thoroughgood, with delightful approbation, the Viennese found him intolerably prosy."[5] Thanks to Gottsched and Neuber's calls for reform, Mr. Thoroughgood (and upstanding characters like him) largely replaced Hanswurst on German stages in the north. In Vienna, Hanswurst disappeared by imperial decree in 1752, but he persisted in the suburban theatres of Josefstadt and Leopoldstadt. There the decree of 1752 had ironically served to stimulate demand for lowbrow entertainment because troupes had established themselves permanently by performing it exclusively. Anton Joseph Stranitsky (1676–1726), for example, had been in residence at the Kärntnertor Theater (Carinthian Gate Theatre) since 1711; by the time of the 1752 decree, the Kärntnertor had cultivated a loyal audience.

The theatres of the Vienna suburbs continued to thrive into the nineteenth century, producing comedies that remained influential into the twentieth century. Popular comedy in Vienna, indeed, aroused progressively greater enthusiasm than any of the forms that were supposed to supplant it.[6] Popular comedy was distinguished by various genre labels, such as *Lustspiel*, *Schwank*, *Komödie*, *Volkstück*, *Besserungstück*, *Zauberstück*, *Lokalposse*, *Zauberposse*, or simply *Posse*.[7] All of them conspicuously lacked the edifying attributes Gottsched had demanded; the earmarks of Schiller's "moral institution" were also absent. The early nineteenth century saw the appearance in Vienna of playwrights following the Stranitsky tradition; they were Josef Alois Gleich (1772–1841), Karl Meisl (1775–1853), and Adolf Bäuerle (1786–1859). Among them, they dominated the Viennese popular theatre until the 1840s.

Gleich wrote more than 250 plays, most of which parodied recognizable Viennese character types. Meisl's *Das Gespenst auf dem Bastei* (The Ghost on the Bulwark, 1819) proved so successful that the playwright was obliged to write several sequels to it; his most representative was *Orpheus und Eurydice, oder so geht es im Olympus zu* (Orpheus and Eurydice, or That's the Way Things Happen on Olympus, 1816), in which Mount Olympus is ruled by gods in the guise of familiar Viennese characters. Bäuerle was a journalist as well as a playwright, with about seventy plays to his credit; among his most significant was *Die Bürger in Wien* (The Citizens of Vienna, 1814), in which he transformed Hanswurst into a Viennese umbrella maker named Staberl. Staberl was no longer a mere specimen but possessed an individualized personality with contemporary concerns about business and family. *Die Bürger in Wien* also prompted sequels, as Staberl found himself in a series of misadventures all over the Viennese metropolitan area. The plays of Bäuerle, Meisl, and Gleich, while popular with audiences and theatre managers, were formulaic and predictable; that explains part of their popularity, as does the fact that their dialogue was written almost completely in the Viennese dialect. A playwright whose work was almost as popular, yet possessed a greater complexity, was that of actor Ferdinand Raimund (1790–1836).

Raimund had studied Shakespeare and the classical playwrights of Greece and of the Spanish Golden Age. His *Das Mädchen aus der Feenwelt* (The Girl from the Fairy World, 1826) was distinctly different from previous Viennese popular comedy. It had "an honesty and naturalness quite different from [previous] offerings. The interpenetration of fairy and peasant worlds was reminiscent at times of *A Midsummer Night's Dream*,"[8] but what made Raimund distinctive were his efforts to move beyond the established traditions of dialect, local allusions, obligatory songs, and limited range of emotions in Viennese comedy. As a result, his subsequent plays began to appear beyond the boundaries of Vienna and its surrounding suburbs; during the 1820s they were performed in Switzerland, Bohemia, and Germany. His best play was *Der Alpenkönig und der Menschenfeind* (The Alpine King and the Misanthrope, 1827), which featured Viennese types focused on a central character named Rappelkopf, who was "closer to Molière's Alceste or even Shakespeare's Timon. [Raimund's] depiction of an isolated charcoal-maker's hut, where an intolerance of all human society has driven Rappelkopf, [was] a precursor to Naturalism in the German theatre."[9] Despite his contemporary popularity and the esteem his reputation subsequently enjoyed, none of Raimund's plays were published in his lifetime.

The comedies of Gleich, Meisl, Bäuerle, and Raimund are best understood within the historical context of the *Biedermeierzeit*, a term defining the milieu in which they and their audiences lived and worked. The "Biedermeier era" encompassed the decades between 1815 and 1848; the term itself derived from a series of poems surreptitiously written by a certain Gottlieb Biedermeier, said to be a schoolmaster living in Swabia. Biedermeier was in fact the invention of two newspaper editors in Munich, in whose weekly publication *Fliegende Blätter* the poems first appeared. They celebrated "the limited vision and passive acceptance of the *Kleinbürger* (petit bourgeoisie), whose respect for order and authority made for contentment within the confines of such a narrow sphere."[10] The expression "Biedermeier" did not come into vogue until the decades marking the reign of Kaiser Wilhelm II (1888–1918). By then, the years between 1815 and 1848 had a golden glow and in nostalgic comparison seemed in the minds of many people to be the "good old days." Against the backdrop of a turbulent, grasping materialism characteristic of the Wilhelmine years, when economic and political changes dominated the public consciousness, a longing for naïveté and simplicity is understandable. "People will never comprehend our behavior during the expansionist years," Hermann Bahr wrote, "unless one knows that we all came from small towns and as children were carefully tended in bright, quiet rooms with white curtains, enveloped in an artificial world of fidelity and honesty. Now, however, suddenly ejected from the Biedermeier style into life, we screamed in horror."[11]

NESTROY AND BIEDERMEIER

The Biedermeier style also described an attitude in the midst of tumultuous social and economic change, an attitude that reappeared in the comedy of the Weimar Republic. It included a retreat from social problems, combined with an "air of resignation, the concern with the apparently trivial, and the dislike of disturbance."[12] Vienna, in the decades following the Napoleonic wars, was like many German cities in the wake of World War I. A sense of defeat was pervasive, and a revolutionary fervor had unleashed chaos in many quarters. In 1811, for example, Austria officially declared bankruptcy, and the repressive measures of Metternich's regime following the assassination of the playwright Kotzebue in 1819 were intended to preserve order and prevent further disturbances.[13] Thus a historical figure (Metternich) as well as a fictional one (Biedermeier) have lent their names to the same epoch. If the governmental policies of the former were committed to the preservation of order, the latter's instincts for selfpreservation led to a mentality of "small-man coziness."[14]

The most innovative of all Viennese comic playwrights was also the one who most effectively parodied the era's coziness. Johann Nepomuk Nestroy (1801–1862), an opera singer and actor, made his theatrical debut in 1822 as Sarastro in Mozart's *Die Zauberflöte* (The Magic Flute). He began acting in 1827 and by 1831 was a star performer at the Leopoldstädter Theater, where he began writing plays.[15] His plays resembled those of his predecessors (though his sources were often adapted English or French models), and on the surface they seemed outwardly frivolous and jocund. They employed predictable plot structures and their conventions were nearly transparent; they included daughters arbitrarily engaged by fathers, secret marriages, lost wills, duels, mysterious letters, rich uncles who suddenly appear, and "a perpetual round of mistaken identities [facilitated] with side doors, trap doors, folding partitions, draperies, and convenient closets."[16]

What made Nestroy unique were his characters and the dialogue he gave them to speak. He endowed the north German with appropriate stolidity, the Frenchman with affectation, the Jewish moneylender with rapaciousness, and the Hungarian shopkeeper with irascibility. These were recognizable types from the Viennese milieu, but they were not always the cheerful inhabitants one met in plays written by Gleich, Meisl, or Bäuerle. Nestroy's Viennese were "sometimes bitterly poor, the children snotty, and not everyone resigned to his station;"[17] they were "charming and amusing perhaps, but also somewhat pitiful and unregenerate."[18] Nestroy furthermore used language more effectively than did his predecessors, using shadings of dialect to rank social, economic, and cultural class; his plays feature an entire spectrum of the Viennese from streetsweeper to seamstress, from sausage merchant to nobleman, all of whom spoke in the patois of their social and economic circumstances. Nestroy also used language to heighten social and political irony; he would portray a pair of lovers, for example, who at the moment of high emotional ardor would burst into rapturous bureaucratic jargon.

The most conspicuous feature of Nestroy's comedies were the central characters he created for his own performance. In *Der Zerissene* (The Man Full of Nothing, 1844) he played the title role, a bored millionaire named Herr Lips who one day decides on a whim to marry the first woman he encounters. As Nebel in *Liebesgeschichten und Heiratssachen* (Love Affairs and Wedding Bells, 1843) he played an unemployed valet who facilitates three love affairs while juggling the pretensions of a parvenu sausage maker against the antiquated class distinctions of a gullible marquis. In *Der Talisman* (The Talisman, 1840) he played Titus Feuerfuchs, a red-haired outcast who, with the help of various hairpieces, advances from gardener to the prospective bridegroom of a noblewoman. In these and in many of his other comedies, the "Nestroy roles" functioned within an atmosphere of apparent peace, stability, and order; but soon the "hero" turns a cozy world upside down, exposing the shifting sands upon which other characters have built their assumptions. In the end, Nestroy allowed the values of simplicity, decency, and honesty to win out even while he satirized aspects of Viennese life; his audiences were, after all, largely made up of coach builders, silk weavers, metal craftsmen, government bureaucrats, glove makers, and piano tuners. They came to the Leopoldstädter (later the Carl) Theater with certain expectations, as did their German counterparts in both the Wilhelmine and the Republican eras.

COMEDY IN WILHELMINE GERMANY

The theatre culture of Wilhelmine Germany resembled that of Metternich/Biedermeier Austria, and theatre audiences shared similar instincts for self-preservation. Governmental misgivings about artistic freedom were also similar, while a policy of censorship and police supervision suppressed the production of any play that questioned establishment viewpoints. Bismarck's government, for example, restricted artistic freedom through the *Sozialistengesetz*, or Socialist Law of 1878. That legislation had several inhibiting features; it authorized local police to ban public assembly of "Socialists, Social Democrats, or Communists," or of anyone else deemed suspicious. It restrained the publication and distribution of printed matter considered objectionable, thereby encouraging the censorship of plays. It denied employment in the public sector to any "socialist agitator," thereby restricting job opportunities to any artist who might be considered unorthodox.[19] Such policies fostered the growth of a drama concentrating on bourgeois life and its new-found economic significance, one that turned the theatre into an advocate for a progressively striving middle class. It justified the behavior it flatteringly presented and made no revolutionary pronouncements.

Bismarck's policies ironically aroused curiosity among some middle-class theatre audiences, especially in Berlin; a demand for the plays of Henrik Ibsen increased there until a means was created to present them. That was the fundamental task of Otto Brahm (1856–1912) and the Freie Bühne organization in Berlin, who in 1889 presented Ibsen's *Ghosts* and Gerhart Hauptmann's *Vor Sonnenaufgang* (Before Sunrise) before an invited audience on Sunday afternoons at the Lessing Theater, to avoid confrontation with police. When Bismarck left office a year later, Brahm's task was made easier, but the government regime without Bismarck was no more enlightened. Wilhelm II had cashiered the "Iron Chancellor" but continued a policy of police censorship, the repression of dissident viewpoints, and the patronage of Ferdinand Bonn's theatre in Berlin, which specialized in comic puffery and detective mysteries.[20] Rarely were plays written by Benjamin Franklin Wedekind or Carl Sternheim produced, and when they were it was in abridged versions, again before invited audiences. Ibsen and Hauptmann were, thanks to the efforts of Brahm, performed more frequently; yet Wilhelm "took it as a personal insult" when the Berlin High Court reversed a police ban on Hauptmann's *Die Weber* (The Weavers) and allowed its public performance. Wilhelm soon thereafter canceled the Schiller Prize, which Hauptmann was to receive for his *Die versunkene Glocke* (The Sunken Bell).[21] Hauptmann had contented himself with "making misery more repulsive than reality," Wilhelm said. If art did that, it was "committing treason against the German people. The outstanding task of culture is to foster the ideal."[22]

For these and other reasons, the kaiser's taste reflected that of a growing theatre audience in the Second Reich; only a numerically small segment of the German audience displayed much interest in Ibsen and Hauptmann. While industrialization stimulated the growth of political consciousness and a tiny but intellectually acute audience, it also produced, as we have seen, a much larger one based on "industrial" theatre production. Germany was becoming a mass society, and producers realized that if they could assemble a product with a broad appeal to an ever increasing market, the potential for monetary return was enormous. Such a producer was the aforementioned Theodor Lebrun; the commodity he manufactured was a comedy combining both escapism and felicitous self-mockery. The commodity his actors Franz von Schönthann and Gustav Kadelburg created (*Der Raub der Sabinerinnen*) is an example of stock merchandised (and remerchandised in various guises) on the Wilhelmine theatrical market—stock that later overwhelmed the theatrical market of the Weimar Republic.

An actor employed by Otto Brahm named Max Reinhardt (1873–1943) was keenly aware of the changing theatrical marketplace in Germany, and when he got the opportunity to cultivate an audience for his own directorial efforts in 1902, he began by recognizing the realities of that marketplace. "[Reinhardt's] audiences, if they are going to fill the house," said actress Tilla Durieux, "did not come to solve riddles."[23] They came instead to see stars in nicely designed costumes on well decorated stages; Reinhardt gave them plenty of both. From 1902 to 1905 at the Kleines and at the Neues Theater in Berlin he produced commercial properties by Gustav Holländer and Lothar Schmidt, Leo Feld, and Paul Adolf, while interlarding his seasons with less overtly commercial plays like George Bernard Shaw's *Candida*, Oscar Wilde's *Salomé*, and Wedekind's *Erdgeist* (Earth Spirit) in order to attract the intelligentsia Brahm had cultivated. When he took over the Deutsches Theater lease from Brahm, he continued the practice; from 1905 to 1914, he produced Herbert Eulenberg's *Der natürliche Vater* (The Natural Father), Heinz Ruderer's *Wolkenkuckkucksheim* (Cloud Cuckoo Land), Erich Schmidtbonn's *Hilfe, ein Kind ist von Himmel gefallen* (Help, a Child has Fallen from Heaven), along with more than a dozen French boulevard farces written by Sacha Guitry, Gustave Mirbeau, and others in German translation.

The theatre marketplace in Berlin during the Wilhelmine years was solidified in large measure by Austrians, including Schönthann, Reinhardt, and Rudolf Bernauer. Bringing with them a distinct feel for comedy inherited from Nestroy and the Viennese, they hoped to establish themselves in the north German metropolis "among the blue eyes," as Bernauer called Berliners. They believed that the German economic juggernaut could support their artistic ambitions. They were themselves capable of becoming "genuine Berliners" in a very short period of time—a phenomenon that was ironically the theme of Bernauer's 1909 hit, *Einer von unser Leut* (One of Our Kind), which he had adapted from an old Viennese comedy. He got his first job working as an extra for Brahm in 1900, but he started earning real money as a performer for the novelist Ernst von Wolzogen, who wanted to start a cabaret in Berlin like the ones he had seen in Paris. He called it Das Überbrettl, or "super stage," in conspicuous mockery of Friedrich Nietzsche's notion of *Der Übermensch*, or "superman." Wolzogen hired a composer-pianist to write satirical songs for his cabaret and hired Bernauer to write sketches parodying works by Ibsen, Wedekind, Hauptmann, Hermann Sudermann, Shaw, Wilde, Maxim Gorky, and Maurice Maeterlinck. Das Überbrettl proved to be a huge attraction from its opening night, and Reinhardt's cabaret, Schall und Rauch ("noise and smoke," which he started when, like Bernauer, he was still working for Brahm), was based on the Überbrettl model. They attracted the audiences who had gone to see authentic material presented by Brahm, then came to see the same material parodied. Many of the great Berlin actors, Bernauer claimed, got their start in Berlin as comedians in such cabarets.[24]

Brahm himself had been the personification of the German theatre as a moral institution. He was the first German director to espouse "the theatre of modern life" and had cultivated an audience for it; he had furthermore built a distinguished reputation on his introduction of Ibsen and Hauptmann to the German theatrical mainstream. Yet even Brahm recognized the importance of industrial comedy when in 1908 he directed a production of *Der Raub der Sabinerinnen* at the Lessing Theater, which he had leased after giving up the Deutsches Theater. At the Lessing he had staged his much acclaimed Ibsen cycle with many of the actors who had worked for him with the Freie Bühne and later at the Deutsches Theater. One of the best actors in his ensemble was Albert Bassermann (1867–1952), whom Brahm assigned the leading role of Martin Gollwitz—to the surprise of many critics in Berlin.[25] The best joke in *Raub* was that he was directing it, Brahm noted; his decision to stage the play, however, was based on economics. It played through its scheduled run of the 1908–1909 season and played a total of eighty-five times at the Lessing in the 1909–1910 season.

COMEDY IN PROVINCIAL PLAYHOUSES OF THE WEIMAR REPUBLIC

While Bismarck had centralized political power with its administrative nucleus in Berlin, the lesser political entities making up the Second Reich were left to administer their cultural institutions autonomously. Thus the tradition of decentralized regional theatre stayed strong through the remainder of the Second Reich, the war years, and the final collapse of the old order. Economic pressures on provincial playhouses became insurmountable after 1919, however, and the cost of remaining moral institutions in a republican era threatened their very existence.

The Reischstag had declared that provincial court theatres were to become state theatres; local jurisdictions were furthermore required to reimburse the noble families for their property. Theatres were not simply to be expropriated. In 1920, the Reichstag terminated the policy of leasing theatres to the highest bidder and advocated placing theatre personnel on governmental payrolls. In other words, the national government socialized theatre; these measures were idealistically intended to ensure that theatre in Germany would remain preserves of uplift and education.[26] Yet the national government had placed the onus of such expenditures on local governments—"despite the fact that local government was virtually bankrupt."[27]

In order to finance their operations, and sometimes in order merely to survive, many provincial theatre administrations turned to productions of Expressionist plays which would have been suppressed before or during the war. They hoped that curiosity, if nothing else, would attract an audience; members of provincial audiences comprised individuals who, like many soldiers in the trenches, had undergone a kind of transformation. The sense of betrayal they felt attracted them to plays that pilloried the military, the nation's hierarchy, or its economic system. These plays called for a "new man," a new order, or a new Germany. Expressionism, however, was not economically feasible in the repertoires of most theatres. Audiences in Berlin and Frankfurt am Main during the immediate postwar years enthusiastically attended productions of Georg Kaiser, Reinhard Johannes Sorge, Ernst Toller, Fritz von Unruh, and Walter Hasenclever, but even there the fervor for revolution had begun to fade by the early 1920s. The provincial theatres meanwhile found themselves in worsening financial straits.

Local theatres turned to industrial comedy to attract audiences; never before had such comedies been produced on so widespread a scale, and never before had they been so popular. The result was an explosion in the number of comedy productions and performances throughout the Weimar Republic; over 900 comedies premiered between 1919 and 1933, far outnumbering the premieres of all other genres combined. Some were performed over a thousand times in one season alone, and the numbers of their performances over the life of the Weimar Republic were in the scores of thousands. In the Weimar Republic, no longer was the industrial comedy merely a commercial triviality; in many cases, it became the German theatre's lifeblood.

What exactly was the nature of a drama which came to play such an important part in the survival of many German theatres? As we have already seen, it owed a great deal to Kotzebue in the early nineteenth century, to French prototypes of the Parisian boulevard theatres, and to the popular comedies of Vienna; they were a staple of the commercial playhouses in Berlin during the Wilhelmine period. None of these facts, however, explains their epidemic popularity in Weimar Germany.

For that explanation we must look to the structure of the plays themselves.

The cast of most industrial comedies rarely exceeded a dozen characters. Since the average provincial playhouse could afford to contract only that number of actors for a season, the play made no extraordinary financial demands upon the theatre's personnel budget. Few industrial comedies required more than three playing areas. There is usually no change of location between acts, and certainly none between scenes. Such changes would disrupt the tempo. These comedies avoid pauses as the action courses along in a rapid, ever-peaking series of situations. The industrial comedy makes few demands upon the technical capacity of a theatre either, so even the smallest playhouse could accommodate it. Extraordinary scenery would moreover distract the viewer from focusing on the comic situation. Most of the comedies take place in a single room somewhere in a provincial city or town. In that spot characters meet their comic misfortune; the same doors always open, and through them come ever more surprises. No unusual lighting effects were necessary; most costumes were contemporary clothing, and no peculiar or expensive props were required.

The scene designer had the somewhat unimaginative job of providing a "general" playing area with necessary entrances, levels, and exits. The design could be simple, indeed primitive, and still be effective. Many playwrights in the Weimar period provided ground plans with the script, recommending that it be adhered to as closely as possible for the greatest effect. Any additional decorative effects were to be avoided, as they would distract from the "closed environment" in which the central character usually found himself. It was a milieu that offered the "hero" no means of escape from the impending catastrophes facing him. He anticipated nothing and suddenly through the door the next catastrophe confronted him. Situations broke in on him within this narrow sphere. Yet this was not an imaginary place; it was to be concrete and recognizable, though not so detailed as to recall a specific location.

A good example of such dynamics at work is *Zwangseinquartierung* ("forced emergency housing" is a rough approximation of the title's meaning) by Franz Arnold and Ernst Bach. It premiered at the Berlin Lustspielhaus on April 30, 1920, and went on to become the most frequently performed play of both the 1920–1921 and the 1921–1922 seasons. The comedy's central character is Anton Schwalbe, a rich, middle-aged businessman; the exposition provides enough information about him in the opening scenes to inform the audience of his basic goals. He wishes first of all to retire from his business, and second to leave his business to his nephew. From that point onward several complications frustrate both goals. His nephew has studied music (against his uncle's wishes) and knows nothing about business. The nephew wishes to marry a beautiful Hungarian soprano, who may be Anton's illegitimate daughter. Anton's servants go on strike, and a government official has taken it upon himself to find shelter for homeless people in Anton's house (hence the play's title).

The audience knows little else about Anton Schwalbe or any of the other characters; there is no hint what kind of business Schwalbe was in, why he never married, what kind of relationship he has had with his nephew, or what exactly led to the firing of his valet and cook. He admits to a brief encounter twenty years earlier in a Berlin elevator with an exotic cleaning lady, but he has no idea that the result may have been an illegitimate daughter. The audience experiences a series of situations that test his patience. There is also a veiled satire of government housing schemes in the exertions of the well-meaning but intrusive housing official. The housing shortage in Germany after World War I was particularly acute. The satirical aspects surface periodically as the play surges along in a rapid series of humorous personal challenges for Anton Schwalbe.

His response to the calamities cascading upon him is the repeated cry, "Anton, zieh die Bremse an!" ("Anton, hit the brakes!"). The phrase is completely incongruous and is a misplaced metaphor, but it is typical of dialogue effects used in comedies by Arnold and Bach, as well as by other writers of industrial comedies. These are not comedies of manners nor "conversational comedies" in the style of Wilde or Coward; the dialogue was always clear and uncomplicated, a flat, nonmetaphorical idiom without ambiguity, because it almost exclusively dealt with topics of everyday life. The emphasis in performance was not upon speech anyway, but rather upon mimicry and gesticulation. They were demonstrative, not rhetorical. In fact, when a character like Anton Schwalbe gets to the point where he cannot find the "right" word, the intended comic effect is at its strongest.

The play demanded a master of comic timing for the role of Anton because the actor had to be flexible enough to make the action believable, yet inflexibile enough to make it funny. All characters had to retain a degree of inflexibility, since they were closely associated with a social system of norms and conventions, and that system determined their inward being and outer behavior. The effect was comparable to Georg Wilhelm Friedrich Hegel's understanding of humor; we laugh at the tasteless and at the superficial in the same way we laugh at the refined and significant, according to Hegel. All that is needed is to place the quotidian within a contradictory set of circumstances, so that laughter becomes simply "an expression of the audience's pleasing sense of cleverness, a sign that they are wise enough to recognize such a contrast."[28] Characters intend to obey the rules but unintentionally collide with them. Ordinarily confident and self-assured figures are reduced to ridiculous simpletons.

Most industrial comedies were assembled by playwriting "teams," based on the partnership paradigm of Schönthann and Kadelburg in 1884. The most successful playwriting enterprise in the Weimar Republic was that of Arnold and Bach, who began their work together in 1913 with *Die spanische Fliege* (The Spanish Fly), whose popularity persisted well into the 1920s. By that time, the "firm of Arnold and Bach" (as it was popularly known) had produced several other hits dominating the Weimar comedy market until Bach's death in 1929. Their competitors included Anton "Toni" Impekoven and Carl Mathern, authors of *Die drei Zwillinge* (The Three Twins); Rudolph Presber and Leo Walter Stein, whose "historical" comedy *Liselotte von der Pfalz* (Liselotte of the Palatinate) had a place in the repertoire of almost every German provincial playhouse in the 1920s; Max Reimann and Otto

Schwartz, whose *Der Sprung in die Ehe* (The Leap Into Marriage) dominated repertoires during the inflation years of the early 1920s; and the two Rudolfs, Bernauer and Österreicher, whose plays enjoyed hundreds of performances in the later 1920s.

Significant attempts were made by individual playwrights to create alternatives to the industrial comedy during the Weimar Republic; the first (and most profitable) resembled the bedroom farce of Georges Feydeau and the conversational comedy of Noel Coward. The most successful of these were Curt Goetz and Max Mohr. Mohr's *Improvisationen im Juni* (Improvisations in June) was the second most frequently performed play of the 1922–1923 season, and Goetz's *Sturm im Wasserglas* (Tempest in a Teacup) was the leading play of the 1930–1931 season. A less successful model was the literary comedy, which retained characteristics of the Expressionist period, best understood as a "grotesque" comedy.[29] The most sensational of these were Arnolt Bronnen's *Die Exzesse* (The Excesses, 1923), which attracted attention because it featured sodomy on the stage. Robert Musil's *Vinzenz und die Freundin bedeutender Männer* (Vincent and the Girlfriend of Important Men) of the same year attracted less sensation but shared a similar fate at the box office. Hugo von Hofmannsthal's *Der Schwierige* (The Difficult Gentleman, 1921) and *Der Unbestechliche* (The Incorruptible Man, 1923) were moderately successful in Berlin, but they resembled Musil's echoes of a lost Viennese milieu and found little resonance among provincial audiences. The most striking attempt to create a literary alternative was Bertolt Brecht's effort to formulate a "new humor."[30] Brecht subtitled his *Trommeln in der Nacht* (Drums in the Night) and *Mann ist Mann* (A Man's a Man) "comedies" in a conscious assault on the prevailing idea of what "comedy" really meant in German. The central characters in both plays parallel constructions like Arnold and Bach's Anton Schwalbe, but their experiences are grotesque inversions of any dilemma found in an industrial comedy.

THE "CRITICAL" COMEDIES

The most distinguished alternatives to industrial comedy in the Weimar Republic were those that retained a critical stance while simultaneously endorsing middle-class predilections for escapism. The plays of Georg Kaiser (1878–1945), written before World War I, were the Expressionist dramas for which he remains best known; they included *Von Morgens bis Mitternacht* (From Morn to Midnight, 1916), *Gas* I & II (1918), *Die Koralle* (The Coral, 1917), and *Die Bürger von Calais* (The Citizens of Calais, 1914).[31] Kaiser recognized by 1921 that most German audiences longed for a return to nonrevolutionary normalcy, or better still, "to complacency. They rejected Expressionism's enthusiasm, intensity, and call to revolt. . . . It had become too abstract, too subjective, and too idealistic."[32] When he began to concentrate on comedy, Kaiser became the single most successful playwright during the Weimar period. His plays enjoyed more premieres, namely forty; his *Nebeneinander* (Side by Side) led the 1923–1924 season in numbers of performances; and the following season his *Kolportage* (Pulp Fiction) was even more popular, with over 800 performances. Yet Kaiser's intention in both these comedies was to retain a critical edge, something missing from industrial comedies. His favorite targets had been capitalists; but capitalists like Anton Schwalbe in *Zwangseinquartierung* were almost lovable. Aristocrats in plays like Impekoven and Mathern's *Die drei Zwillinge* were parodied—especially if they needed money. In *Die drei Zwillinge* vain, rigid aristocrats wear false pride to go with the clichéd monocle. They functioned as comic foreground, putting the bourgeois world into stronger, more colorful contrast. Count von Rabenklau performed a similar function in Otto Schwartz and Georg Lengbach's *Der blaue Heinrich* (Blue Blood Henry, 1922), whom the playwrights described as an "old, elegant, quirky aristocrat; dressed in morning coat, spats, and monocle; white haired, feudal, stiff gaited."[33]

When Kaiser created both capitalists and aristocrats in *Kolportage* he did more than parody them; he criticized their faith in money and promoted the value of individual integrity. The aristocrat Erik has grown up as a cowboy in America, where he emerged selfless and capable of loving a bourgeois girl. Kaiser did not create intellectual juxtapositions, however. He avoided the pitfalls of making his audience think, and he was "careful not to confront an audience bent on enjoying its new prosperity with problems," an audience who "wanted to see the clichéd, arrogant aristocracy, a wealthy and open-handed uncle from America, a wiry cowboy, a young couple in love, and a good-hearted proletarian mother on stage."[34] Some of Kaiser's comedies veered too far in the critical direction, and he undertook frequent revisions to make them more palatable. His 1925 hit *Margarine* was a revision of *Konstantin Strobel*, which was itself a revision of *Der Zentaur* (The Centaur) in like manner his popular *Die Papiermühle* (The Paper Mill) of 1927 was a remake of his pre-war *Der Austauschprofessor* (The Exchange Professor). Walter Hasenclever was another former Expressionist. He wrote *Der Sohn* (The Son) in 1914, which was frequently performed in the immediate postwar period, but he became uncommonly successful when he turned his hand to comedy. His *Ein besserer Herr* (A Better Sort of Gentleman) was among the most frequently performed plays of the 1927–1928 season.

The most prominent, and perhaps most successful, of all the critical playwrights in the Weimar Republic was Carl Zuckmayer. He, like Kaiser and Hasenclever, sought wider appeal for his plays in the provinces, recognizing (as he himself stated) that he was not "an instigator of a literary movement" but a playwright responding to the "actualities of the day."[35] That meant, for practical playwriting purposes, a return to a neorealistic format which scholars and critics have come to call *neue Sachlichkeit*. Critic Alfred Kerr recognized the new trend as a replacement for Expressionism when he declared, "Sic transit gloria expressionismi" in response to Zuckmayer's comedy *Der fröhliche Weinberg* (The Merry Vineyard).[36] Herbert Ihering, a critic who rarely agreed with Kerr about anything, echoed similar sentiments when he said that *Der fröhliche Weinberg* "had blown Expressionism off the stage in a gale of laughter."[37]

Zuckmayer's comedy did not achieve the overwhelming popularity of Kaiser's *Kolportage* or of Hasenclever's *Ein besserer Herr* (though it was performed nearly 700 times between 1925 and 1927), perhaps because it was a curious instance of being predictably commercial and provocative at the same time. After making its provincial debut in Frankfurt am Main in 1925, it went on to more than seventy productions in provincial locales in 1926; there it encountered numerous campaigns to censor it or to halt performances altogether. There were some instances of street demonstrations against the play; even in Zuckmayer's home town of Mainz, protests delayed the planned opening at the subsidized municipal playhouse for nine months. Zuckmayer claimed to have been totally surprised by the reaction of the home folks, although he later acknowledged that the controversy surrounding *Der fröhliche Weinberg* promoted ticket sales. More important, he noted, it had "enlightened" an entire new generation of German audience members with its satire on nationalists and its advocacy of free love. When it did open in Mainz it convinced audiences as it had elsewhere of its "affirmative realism which renounced all revolutionary tendencies and sought to come to terms with the actualities of the Republic."[38] Zuckmayer's greatest popular, commercial, and critical success came five years later with *Der Hauptmann von Köpenick* (The Captain of Köpenick). It proved to be one of the most frequently performed and longest running comedies in the history of the Weimar Republic, even though it openly flouted accepted conventions for successful comedies: it had a cast of seventy-three people, it took place in over twenty separate locations, and it candidly (though with a masterful comedic hand) presented political conflict.

Ödön von Horváth's comedies formed still a third strategy of appeal to German audiences, while retaining a somewhat critical stance. Horváth's subject, in nearly every case, was the Austro-Bavarian *Kleinbürger*, or petit-bourgeois. The playwright's comic effect lay in his ability to view this species as one "restricted in his intellectual horizon, but with some cultural pretensions, fearful for his pension, and jealous of the encroaching proletarian mass beneath him."[39] Horváth himself stated that since ninety percent of the German population was petit-bourgeois, he could not address his comedies to the remaining ten percent. "I'm a serious observer of my times," he said, "so I have to look at the majority."[40] Like Zuckmayer, Horváth wanted his comedies to reveal an earthiness he felt was missing in industrial comedies. His plays appealed to the audience's instincts and not to its intellect, but they did so in a remarkably stylized way. Horváth's work is indeed among the most uniquely patterned of any comic playwright's. He subtitled his comedies *Volkstücke* to recall nineteenth-century Viennese traditions, and in most instances they featured the "verbal juggling, stock figures, dual situations, folk-songs, and musical accompaniment" of their Viennese forebears.[41] The distinguishing twentieth-century mark of Horváth, however, is his characters' use of *Bildungsjargon*, or "cultured patois." It is an artificial, acquired idiom, a language of convention, riddled with hollow clichés, banalities, and aphorisms—in other words, a façade. The characters do not speak a language authentic to their own existence because there is nothing authentic about them. They instead repeat phrases picked up on radio, in advertisements, from political party propaganda, and from sermons they have heard. These are primitive people, Martin Esslin has observed, and their language "mirrors [their] archetypal non-authentic false consciousness." In an ordinary nineteenth century *Volkstück*, these people would express their primitive ideas in a primitive dialect, but Horváth replaced dialect with "ready made and very bad literary language of the leading articles in popular newspapers."[42] A good example of such jargonistic inauthenticity one finds in *Geschichten aus dem Wienerwald* (Tales of Vienna Woods), when a man is overheard saying to a woman, "Frau Ulrike, you are indeed lovely as a petunia, lovely as a petunia e'er blooming;" in *Italienische Nacht* (Italian Night) a proto-Nazi character attempts to rape a woman, but in the midst of his labors, fireworks illumine a statue of the kaiser, whose head some hooligans have painted red. The rapist buttons up his trousers and starts spouting Nazi party slogans, such as "The God who made us, made us strong as iron!" and "Revenge! God be with us! Germany awake!"

There were extremely conservative elements in the German audience who were unconvinced that playwrights like Kaiser, Hasenclever, Zuckmayer, and Horváth were composing plays merely to satisfy audiences; they realized that, unlike industrial comedies, these critical comedies had the potential to challenge an audience's assumptions. The National Socialists asserted that their plays subverted "real" German values. As they gathered strength politically, the Nazis resolved to "cleanse" German theatre of "decadent" and "un-German" tendencies. Their attacks on Zuckmayer and others were not a mere reecho of Wilhelmine prejudice, philistinism, and prudery. They were instead part of a carefully wrought agenda constructed to appeal to antimodernist prejudices.

The roots of antimodernism, which National Socialism successfully nurtured, likewise lay in the nineteenth century, although there is not adequate space here to elaborate upon the background of Nazi cultural ideology. Fritz Stern has done that already in his excellent study of the subject; treatments of "the politics of cultural despair" subsequent to Stern's concur with his main thesis— that Hitler and the Nazis were philosophical heirs to a "Germanic" strain of extreme antimodern, elitist idealism. It espoused a mystical faith in the Germans and their moral purity which qualified them to purge their culture and to instigate a new order. They saw themselves as "heroic vitalists," but they were in reality "cultural Luddites, who in their resentment of modernity sought to smash the whole machinery of culture."[43] Yet the Nazis were not just another reactionary force in German politics eager to impose their authoritarian will on the nation. They saw themselves as saviors of a cherished legacy; their duty was to engage in the struggle to preserve it. In some important ways, the Nazi perception of the nation's cultural legacy found resonance among audiences in the Weimar Republic who cherished the industrial comedy and would have continued attending even as the Nazis tightened their grip on German culture. The Nazi regime furthermore had no ideological objections to comedies by Arnold and Bach, Bernauer and Österreicher, Max Mohr, Heinz Gordon, Hans

Sturm, Bruno Frank, and many others. The Nazi regime banned them because they were Jewish, homosexual, leftist, or otherwise objectionable.

What follows in this volume is a chronicle of how comedy, and which comedies in particular, formed an important cog in the machinery of German theatre culture during the Weimar Republic. Its goal is to discern which comedies premiered where and when; to provide a historical context allowing the reader more easily to comprehend why certain comedies appeared when they did; and finally to discover which comedies were popular with audiences and what their popularity might articulate about the Weimar Republic as a whole. An investigation of the plays themselves will provide some insight into the "collective psyche," as Fritz Stern called it, of an audience suffering intense anxiety, under unprecedented economic and political stress.

Stern asserted that such stresses made an enormous impact upon the collective psyche of the Germans, and in the worsening economic climate after 1929, Nazi claims of saving German culture began to take precedence over most other considerations, especially among middlebrow theatre audiences. Yet the Nazi leadership was itself made up of avid theatregoers, many of whom had close personal ties to the theatre community. They endorsed a form of comedy that made no intellectual demands upon its audience, their clamor for a "Germanic revitalization of art" notwithstanding.[44] Such claims found wide appeal among theatre audiences. Thus the student of German theatre and drama should not regard the Nazis as just another reactionary force in German politics eager to impose their authoritarian will on the nation. The Nazis saw themselves as saviors of a cherished legacy; in struggling to preserve it, they drove out many of the men who had created it.

NOTES

1. Laurance Harding, *The Dramatic Art of Raimund and Nestroy* (The Hague: Mouton, 1974), 31.

2. Quoted in W. E. Yates, *Nestroy* (Cambridge: Cambridge University Press, 1972), 15.

3. Betsy Aikin-Sneath, *Comedy in Germany in the First Half of the 18th Century* (Oxford: Clarendon, 1936), 96.

4. Friedrich Reden-Esbeck, *Caroline Neuber und ihre Zeitgenossen* (Leipzig: Barth, 1881), 37–38.

5. Warren H. Bruford, *Germany in the 18th Century* (Cambridge: Cambridge University Press, 1965), 296. Lessing admired George Lillo's *The London Merchant* (1731) as an example of "domestic tragedy," and the play's eponymous Mr. Thoroughgood was regarded in Germany as an outstanding example of a stage figure suitable for emulation.

6. Aikin-Sneath, *Comedy in Germany*, 96.

7. The term *Schwank* best describes the form of comedy whose popularity was established with *Der Raub der Sabinerinnen* and which proliferated so extensively in the Weimar Republic. It derived from the Middle High German word *swanc* meaning originally *Schwung*, connoting vitality, buoyancy, or animation.

8. Marvin Carlson, *The German Stage in the Nineteenth Century* (Metuchen, NJ: Scarecrow, 1972) 72.

9. Ibid., 73.

10. M. J. Norst, "Biedermeier," in James M. Ritchie, ed., *Periods in German Literature* (London: Dufour, 1967), 149.

11. Hermann Bahr, *Glossen zum Wiener Theater* (Berlin: Fischer, 1907): 408

12. Ibid., 164.

13. The Carlsbad Decrees provided for strict press censorship, unrestricted police surveillance of "suspicious persons," and close supervision of universities, especially of student organizations. The decrees remained in force until 1848. The repressive measures taken by the "revolutionary government" in Germany after the assassination of Rosa Luxemburg and Carl Liebknecht in 1919 contained an extraordinary echo of postrevolutionary events in 1811. They included the bloody suppression of numerous independence movements in Germany.

14. Ilsa Barea, *Vienna* (New York: Knopf, 1966), 112.

15. Nestroy is notable even in twentieth- century American musical theatre; his *Einen Jux will er sich machen* (adapted from the 1835 one-act in English by John Oxenford titled *A Day Well Spent*; it premiered at the Theater an der Wien in 1842 and was published in 1844) is the basis of *Hello, Dolly!*. Thornton Wilder (1897–1975) revised the Nestroy play and set it in upstate New York, titling it *The Merchant of Yonkers* in 1938; he revised it again, adding the character of Dolly Levi, in *The Matchmaker* (1954); Michael Stewart adapted it for Jerry Herman's music, and *Hello, Dolly!* opened at the St. James Theatre in New York in 1964. It ran there for a total of 2,844 performances.

16. Harding, *Dramatic Art*, 72.

17. Barea, *Vienna*, 171.

18. Carlson, *The German Stage*, 130.

19. Gordon Craig, *Germany 1866–1945* (New York: Oxford University Press, 1980), 147.

20. Ferdinand Bonn (1861–1933) was among the first Berlin actor-managers to produce the fiction of Arthur Conan Doyle on the German stage. His 1907 production of *The Hound of the Baskervilles* was particularly popular.

21. Michael Balfour, *The Kaiser and his Times* (New York: Norton, 1972), 161.

22. Ibid., 162.

23. Quoted in Heinz Kindermann, *Theatergeschichte Europas*, vol. 8 (Salzburg: Müller, 1968), 306.

24. Rudolf Bernauer, *Das Theater meines Lebens* (Berlin: Blanvalet, 1955), 110.

25. Bassermann's career began with the Meininger troupe, and he was well established before he began working with Brahm. His range was extraordinary, which is perhaps one reason Brahm assigned him the role of Gollwitz. He had played heroic leads in Schiller's *Don Carlos* and the *Wallenstein* trilogy, Shylock in *The Merchant of Venice*, and Mephisto in Goethe's *Faust* before he began playing the realistic roles of Ibsen and Hauptmann under Brahm. In the 1920s Bassermann was awarded the Iffland Ring as the German-language theatre's outstanding male performer; in 1933 he emigrated to the United States, where he appeared in several Hollywood films.

26. Institut für Theaterwissenschaft der Universität Köln, *Theater in der Weimarer Republik* (Berlin: Kunstamt Kreuzberg, 1977), 694.

27. Detlev J. K. Peukert, *The Weimar Republic*, trans. Richard Deveson (New York: Hill and Wang, 1992), 137.

28. Georg Wilhelm Friedrich Hegel, *Vorlesungen über die Aesthetik* II (Frankfurt: Europäische Verlagsanstalt, 1966), 552.

29. Robert Musil, *Tagebücher, Aphorismen, Essays, und Reden*, ed. A. Frisé (Reinbek: Rowohlt, 1968), 270.

30. Reinhold Grimm, "Neuer Humor? Die Komödienproduktion zwischen 1918 und 1933," in Wolfgang Paulsen, ed., *Die deutsche Komödie im zwansigsten Jahrhundert*, (Heidelberg: Lothar Stiem, 1976), 131.

31. Kaiser's Expressionist plays were never performed very frequently. *Gas* I played 151 times in the 1919–1920 season, but his others played no more than two dozen times.

32. Ernst Schürer, *Georg Kaiser* (Boston: Twayne, 1971), 129.

33. Otto Schwartz and Georg Lengbach, *Der blaue Heinrich* (Berlin: Drei Masken, 1922), 4.

34. Schürer, *Georg Kaiser*, 129.

35. Carl Zuckmayer, *Als wär's ein Stück von mir* (Frankfurt: Fischer, 1966), 398.

36. Günther Rühle, *Theater für die Republik* (Frankfurt: Fischer, 1966), 671.

37. Ibid., 135.

38. Jost Hermand and Frank Trommler, *Die Kultur der Weimarer Republik* (Munich: Nymphenberger, 1978), 169.

39. Alan Best, "Ödön von Horváth: the Volkstück Revisited," in Alan Best, ed., *Modern Austrian Writing* (London: Wolff, 1980), 46.

40. Ödön von Horváth, "Gebrauchsanweisung," in *Gesammelte Werke*, vol. 4, ed. Traugott Krischke, (Frankfurt: Suhrkamp, 1973), 662.

41. Best, "Ödön von Horváth," 112.

42. Martin Esslin, "Horváth's Language," in *Symposium on Ödön von Horváth* (Ödön von Horváth Archive, Akademie der Künste Berlin), 23.

43. Fritz Stern, *The Politics of Cultural Despair* (Berkeley: University of California Press, 1961), xiii.

44. "German art of the next decade will be heroic, it will be steely romantic, it will be factual without sentiment, it will be national with great pathos, and it will be mindful of its communal duty," Goebbels informed theatre directors in 1933, "or it won't exist at all." In Joseph Goebbels, "Rede des Propagandaministers vor den Theaterleitern, 8. Mai 1933," *Das deutsche Drama in Geschichte und Gegenwart*, vol. 5 (1933), 36.

2

The 1918–1919 Season

German theatres found themselves in peculiar circumstances during the 1918–1919 season. Soon after the season began, Austro-Hungarian, Bulgarian, and Turkish allies capitulated, exposing Germany to the south. By the end of October, there were mutinies aboard German naval ships in Bremen and Kiel, followed by popular uprisings in Munich, Hamburg, Bremen, and other cities. In early November, leaders of the Social Democratic party called for the kaiser's abdication; he left the city on November 9. Almost immediately a general strike took effect in Berlin, and in nearly every other major German city "revolutionary councils" seized temporary control of governmental authority. Most theatres suspended operations, although the Lessing Theater in Berlin continued its run of *Charley's Aunt*.[1]

Revolutionary councils in Bavaria, Baden, Hessia, Saxony, and Württemburg attempted to declare independent republics, and among their first items of business was the transformation of the former Hoftheaters (court theatres) into Staats- or Landestheaters (state or provincial theatres)—although there were no productions being performed in them at the time. By the third week in November, most private and municipal theatres resumed "normal" operations. The Nuremberg Municipal Theatre, for example, gave Georg Kaiser's *Der Brand im Opernhaus* (Fire in the Opera House) its world premiere, while in Berlin Max Reinhardt gave Walter Hasenclever's *Der Sohn* (The Son) its first large-scale production. At the Berlin Volksbühne, Friedrich Kayssler staged Schiller's revolutionary drama *Wilhelm Tell*.[2] A largely overlooked premiere took place in Stuttgart amidst the chaos; it was Rudolf Presber and Leo Walter Stein's *Liselotte von der Pfalz* (Liselotte of the Palatinate), a "historical comedy" about King Louis XIV's German sister-in-law. This play was important for several reasons, not the least of which was its immense popularity. It was performed hundreds of times in dozens of productions throughout the succeeding decade and was the basis of a popular film of the same title.

That comedy's anti-French bias proved particularly seductive when French troops occupied major German cities along the Rhine. German leaders petitioned President Woodrow Wilson to hinder what they considered "a determined [French] policy of hatred towards Germany," but Wilson ignored the petitions, while supporting German unity and refusing to recognize the legitimacy of "Soviet republics" declared in several German provinces. The strategy of maintaining the German Reich in its previous, but now republican, form led to several internecine confrontations.[3] Anarchy prevailed in the streets of several cities, culminating in numerous tragic flash points. In Berlin, the "Spartacus" revolt of January ended with the murder of the revolt's leaders, Karl Liebknecht and Rosa Luxemburg. A month later the "Soviet Republic of Bremen" was overthrown by Freikorps (volunteer militia) troops. In Munich, Bavarian provincial president Kurt Eisner was murdered, and later government troops overthrew the "Bavarian Soviet Republic." They arrested and killed the Communist minister, Gustav Landauer, and other leaders (including the playwright Ernst Toller) were subsequently put on trial and received long prison terms. One was sentenced to death for treason and hanged.

Some attempts were made to capture revolutionary fervor in drama and present it on the stage. These included *Der Minister* (The Minister) by Roda Roda (pseudonym for Sandor Friedrich Rosenfeld) at the Munich Schauspielhaus, *Freie Knechte* (Free Servants) by Hans Franck at Kleines Theater in Berlin, and *Der gerettete Alkibiades* (Alcibiades Saved) by Georg Kaiser in Munich. All of these productions failed, however, to find favor with audiences or critics. The most revolutionary event taking place in a theatre during the 1918–1919 season was the gathering of the National Assembly in the Neues Theater of Weimar, where elected representatives framed a republican constitution and accepted the terms of the Versailles Treaty.

Given the uncertainty of the times, it is hardly surprising that German audiences attended comedies in numbers far larger than those of other genres. Comedy by its nature has a social imperative, and laughter is said to have healing properties. Critic Siegfried Jacobssohn, having just seen Reinhardt's production of Shakespeare's *As You Like It*, took note of his own "distinct reluctance to leave this delicate fantasy world and return to bleak reality outside."[4] The Germans' need for collective recuperation was nearly palpable, and comedy was an indispensable balm in the healing process.

The most popular play during this season was *Die spanische Fliege* (The Spanish Fly) by Franz Arnold and Ernst Bach, which had premiered in May 1913 at the Viktoria Theater in Magdeburg and had been a staple in many repertoires throughout the war. During the "revolutionary" season of 1918–1919 it was performed more than 400 times in more than seventy German theatres. It was followed by Otto Ernst's *Flachsmann als Erzieher* (Flachsmann as Educator), Hans Reimann's *Die Familie Hannemann* (The Hannemann Family), and Hans Sturm's *Das Extemporale* (The Ad-libber, which was also performed under the title of *So ein Mädel*, Such a Girl).

Die spanische Fliege was a farce treatment of a serious topic, namely a woman's exploitation of a man by claiming his paternity of her child. The man in this instance was the owner of a mustard factory named Ludwig Klinke, who is beset by two women. He chafes under the moralistic pontifications of his wife Emma, an officer in the local League of Decency. Many years prior to their marriage Klinke was, unbeknownst to Emma, involved with a dancer. The dancer (known in the popular press as "The Spanish Fly") claimed that Klinke fathered her illegitimate son, and to the present day he has paid the dancer restitution to keep her quiet. Complicating the situation is the arrival of a young man named Heinrich Meisel, whom Klinke suspects may be his son. He expends a great deal of energy trying to get rid of Meisel until he learns that Emma has actually invited this upstanding, moral young gentleman to be a guest in their home. He has meantime fallen in love with Emma's equally upstanding niece. Klinke is ashamed of himself for suspecting Meisel of blackmail, and his shame is compounded at the end of the play when he learns that the "Spanish Fly" has no children at all but has for years extorted money from "fathers" like Klinke all over the country.

The other (nearly as popular) comedy of this revolutionary season was also a favorite from past seasons. Otto Ernst's *Flachsmann als Erzieher*, which had premiered in 1900, was a forceful parody on the German school system, concentrating on Flachsmann the school principal. Flachsmann's nemesis is Herr Flemming, a popular and effective teacher in the school. The play follows Flachsmann's numerous and often unethical attempts to fire Flemming, concluding with the surprise revelation that Flachsmann is indeed a scoundrel, having forged his pedagogical credentials.

Other popular comedies in this tumultuous season included perennial favorites like Wilhelm Meyer-Förster's *Alt-Heidelberg* (Old Heidelberg, which had premiered in 1901), Franz von Schönthann and Gustav Kadelburg's *Der Raub der Sabinerinnen* (The Rape of the Sabine Women, premiered in 1884), and Roderich Benedix' *Die Hochzeitsreise* (The Honeymoon, premiered in 1871), all of which had dominated the repertoires of several theatres since their premieres in the Wilhelmine years. Carl Sternheim's *Bürger Schippel* (Citizen Schippel) had been written in 1912, but performances of it had been rare due to the wartime censorship imposed by the Army High Command. When censorship was lifted, this and other comedies by Sternheim experienced a surge in popularity. Comedy productions far outnumbered those of straight plays during this season; the removal of censorship permitted the run of plays that would previously have been impossible to produce. They included Hasenclever's *Der Sohn*, Wedekind's *Frühlings Erwachen* (Spring's Awakening) and the Lulu plays, Sternheim's *Die Hose* (The Underpants) and *1913*, and Fritz von Unruh's *Ein Geschlecht* (One Generation). Hasenclever was very popular among audiences in Frankfurt and Kassel; Wedekind in Hamburg, Königsberg, Nuremberg, Magdeburg, Lübeck, Regensburg, Berlin (at Reinhardt's Deutsches Theater), and Dresden. Kaiser had numerous performances in Hannover, Leipzig, and Mainz.

COMEDY PREMIERES of 1918–1919

PLAYWRIGHT(S)	PLAY TITLE	CITY and THEATRE	DATE
Arnold, Franz, and Ernst Bach	*Jubiläum, Das*	Hannover Residenz-theater	06/12/19
Boldt, Johannes	*Vertrauer, Das*	Cottbus Stadttheater	11/19/18
Bonn, Ferdinand	*Jäger aus Kurpfalz, Der*	Berlin Walhalla Theater	04/02/19
Brennert, Hans	*Von fünf bis sieben*	Hamburg Thalia Theater	11/26/18
Burg, Eugen and Otto Härting	*Wo die Liebe hinfällt*	Berlin Theater des Wes-tens	05/05/19
Eger, Rudolf	*grosse und die kleine Welt, Die*	Munich Volkstheater	11/30/18
Frank, Paul, and Siegfried Geyer	*Feuerzauber*	Hamburg Thalia Theater	11/30/18
Friedorf, Hans	*Badereise wider Will-en*	Hannover Staatstheater	01/02/19
Fuschs-Liska, Ro-bert, and Oskar Engel	*Chlodwig, der Wahr-haftiger*	Spandau Stadttheater	07/15/19
Gans, Hans	*Ich, Theobald Blaschke*	Guben Stadttheater	02/08/19
Gordon, Heinz, and Curt Goetz	*Rutschbahn, Die*	Berlin Deutsches Künst-lertheater	06/01/19
Greef, R. Bauer	*Umzug, Der*	Berlin Volksbühne	05/19/19
Gross, Hans	*Mann mit 100 Köpfen, Der*	Hannover Schauburg	01/01/19
Hagen, Wilhelm	*Erben, Die*	Munich Deutsches Theater	11/23/18
Härtling, D.	*ewige Lampe, Die*	Hannover Schauburg	02/16/19
Herwig, Franz	*Kaiser Karls Schwert*	Thale Harzer Bergtheater	07/12/19
Hoffmann, Arthur	*Fabrikgeheimnisse*	Elberfeld Stadttheater	11/11/18
Impekoven, Toni, and Carl Mathern	*Liselotte von der Pfalz*	Frankfurt/M Schauspiel-haus	05/4/19

Kaiser, Georg	*Konstantin Strobel*	Munich Schauspielhaus	07/15/19
Kirchfeld, Ludwig	*Dame ohne Beruf, Die*	Berlin Theater der Friedrichsstadt	04/12/19
Kraatz, Curt, and Richard Kessler	*Kabarettdiva, Die*	Potsdam Schauspielhaus	04/30/19
L'Arronge, Hans	*Bettys Talent*	Celle Union Theater	06/15/19
Liebmann, Robert	*ewige Braut, Die*	Munich Volkstheater	05/01/19
Löffel, Willy	*Handelsleutnant, Der*	Bremen Volkstheater	07/19/19
Lorenz, Emil	*Sohn der Excellenz, Der*	Hamburg Thalia Theater	01/16/19
Löser, Franz	*Herrgottsbrücke, Die*	Würzburg Stadttheater	06/20/19
Matthei, Albert	*Um ein Kind*	Chemnitz Thalia Theater	12/25/18
Meiergräfe, Julius	*Heinrich der Beglücker*	Frankfurt/M. Schauspielhaus	11/27/18
Neidhard, August	*G'schamige, Die*	Berlin Theater der Friedrichsstadt	04/12/19
Rittner, Thomas	*dumme Jakob, Der*	Hannover Deutsches Theater	02/14/19
Römer, Alwin, and Rolf Römer	*Freien zu Dreien, Das*	Dresden Albert Theater	02/28/19
Rosenhah, Paul and Erich Köhrer	*Mann von Morgen, Der*	Dresden Albert Theater	05/01/19
Stein, Leo Walter	*Ihr Papa*	Hannover Schauburg	12/25/18
Sternheim, Carl	*1913*	Frankfurt/M. Schauspielhaus	01/23/19
Sternheim, Carl	*Tabula rasa*	Berlin Kleines Theater	01/25/19
Sturm, Hans	*So ein Mädel*	Berlin Lustspielhaus	07/03/19
Sudermann, Hermann	*hohere Leben, Das*	Berlin Residenztheater	02/01/19
Thoma, Ludwig	*Gelähmte Schwingen*	Munich Residenztheater	10/24/18
Tressler, C.K.M.	*freudige Ereignis, Das*	Düsseldorf Stadttheater	02/15/19
Wangenhoff, Franz	*grosse Vergangenheit, Die*	Wiesbaden Residenztheater	05/10/19

Warmer, Richard	*rotte Korah, Die*	Gera Reußliches Landes-theater	01/29/19
Wedekind, Frank	*König Nicolo*	Leipzig Schauspielhaus	01/15/19
Wolff, Franz	*Sündenbock, Der*	Hannover Deutsches Theater	11/07/18
Wolff, Willi, and Morton Zickel	*verschwundene Pauline, Die*	Potsdam Schauspielhaus	03/07/19

NOTES

1. The popular comedy by Brandon Thomas had its German premiere in 1898. This particular production, which ran throughout the tumultuous 1918–1919 season, celebrated its 1,000th performance on July 14, 1919.

2. This production employed a then little-known singer in the chorus named Maria Magdelena von Losch, later known as Marlene Dietrich.

3. Labor unrest contributed to internal strife. There were over 500 extended work stoppages during the 1918–1919 season, economic activity slowed nearly to a standstill, and the German currency rapidly began to lose its value.

4. Quoted in Günther Rühle, *Theater für die Republik* (Frankfurt: Fischer, 1967) 156.

3

The 1919–1920 Season

During the 1919–1920 season, an attempt was made to reestablish regular and uninterrupted presentations of plays throughout the country, and to a large extent it was successful. Several comedies from previous seasons continued to realize high numbers of performances: *Die spanische Fliege* (The Spanish Fly), *Der Raub der Sabinerinnen* (The Rape of the Sabine Women), and *Charley's Aunt* each enjoyed about 300 presentations. Two newcomers, premiered the previous season, however, were the most notable. *Die drei Zwillinge* (The Three Twins) by Toni Impekoven and Carl Mathern led all genres with over 700 performances; *Liselotte von der Pfalz* (Liselotte of the Palatinate) was performed 298 times, but its importance lay in its significance as a cultural emblem of German national identity.

As noted earlier, the eponymous heroine is the historical Elisabeth Charlotte, sister-in-law of King Louis XIV. She was the daughter of the Elector Palatinate, whose residence was the Heidelberg Castle. That is where the first act takes place, when an ambassador from the French court arrives to ask for the hand of the teenaged Liselotte in marriage to Louis's brother, the Duke of Orleans. In this act the playwrights struck the humorously derisive stance toward France that prevailed throughout the play. When the French ambassador bows gallantly to kiss her hand, Liselotte tells him that boys in the neighborhood have tried the same thing. If she denied them, she was not about to "let a painted-up Frenchman do it!" Liselotte is the embodiment of German honesty, forthrightness, earthiness, and candor.

The French court at Versailles, in juxtaposition, is portrayed as totally decadent. Liselotte's husband slavishly imitates his brother, while Liselotte herself remains jovial and perceptive. She mildly rebukes Louis's bastard daughter for being anemic, noting that German girls are healthy, robust, and vivacious—all of which describe Liselotte. The play projects a historical atmosphere, with convincing dialogue peppered with courtly expressions and turns of phrase. By the play's end, Liselotte is a matron, France has gone to war with Germany, and French armies have taken her childhood friends prisoner. King Louis agrees to release them if Liselotte will agree to a marriage between her son and his bastard daughter. The confrontation between Liselotte and the girl's mother (Louis's mistress) reveals Liselotte's wisdom in accepting that both young people love each other—a non-subtle plea for common sense between France and Germany in the postwar period.

The success of *Liselotte* ran parallel to difficult and sometimes violent confrontations between Germans and the French occupying forces along the Rhine. French troops had marched in as soon as the cease-fire had taken effect; their presence was a galling reminder to Germans of their national humiliation. The French insisted in all dealings with the new German government that Germans take responsibility for starting World War I; they likewise demanded confiscatory reparation payments amounting to trillions of dollars and were intended to colonize the German economy. Besides its economic provisions, the Versailles Treaty, which had taken effect on January 10, 1920, exacted the forfeiture of German territories abroad and the loss of German border domains, where Germans still lived and were now subject to foreign governments.

The most popular play of the season, Impekoven and Mathern's *Die drei Zwillinge* was an equally unsubtle (but more farcical) treatment of a subject likewise on the minds of many postwar audiences, namely the now-defunct German aristocracy. The new government had been careful not to expropriate the properties of noble houses, and settlements for their former holdings totaled hundreds of millions of marks, all paid from public tax coffers. This play offered Germans a chance to laugh at aristocrats, along with the spectacle of parvenus trying to imitate the ancien régime.

Die drei Zwillinge is a comedy of mistaken identities taken to extremes. It concerns the Falkensteins, a distinctly minor branch of German nobility who, through a mix-up at birth, discover they must admit a new member to their family. That new member is the "third twin" of the title. Eberhard von Falkenstein, elder twin brother and heir to the Falkenstein estate on the Rhine, has been reared by his father Count Oktavio von Falkenstein according to the strict customs of their illustrious family. Eberhard is supposedly a few minutes older than his brother Krafft (they look nothing at all alike), although no one really knows for sure; the hospital in which they were born burned to the ground soon after their birth and all records were lost. The nurses had supposedly tied a red ribbon on the older twin's ankle, but in the confusion that ribbon was lost. A wine merchant named Knäblein from the nearby town of Bonn arrives to take his orders for Count Oktavio's favorite beverage, the sweet Rhenish white wine of the region. Knäblein is a charming bumbler, but servants notice a stunning similarity between him and the younger twin Krafft (stage directions call for the same actor playing Krafft to play Knäblein).

When the servants introduce Knäblein to Oktavio, the count in dazed agreement says the merchant looks enough like Krafft to be his twin brother. Knäblein reveals that he was born in the same hospital as the Falkenstein twins. "Look," he says, "I've still got the red ribbon that was tied onto my leg when I was a baby!"

Everyone now realizes that Knäblein is in fact the "third twin" of the Falkenstein family. The Falkensteins go into emergency session; they decide that Krafft must become the heir and that Eberhard will have to settle for a lesser title. They swear among themselves to reveal nothing to Knäblein. But the affable Knäblein finds out anyway, and he is delighted at the prospect of owning a castle; even the dispossessed Eberhard is won over. He observes that being bourgeois will be easier than being an aristocrat: no more getting up at 6:00 a.m. to ride the horses and inspect the estate; no more sitting through hours of lessons in "noble behavior" with his father; and he'll earn 60,000 marks a year as a wine merchant, far more than he ever would have had as Count von Falkenstein! But with middle-class life come middle- class responsibilities, including a wife, a father-in-law, and twin sons named Max and Moritz. Such complications arrive with breathtaking speed as the play gallops toward its conclusion.

The characterization is two dimensional, bordering on caricature, but the play's figures are all appealing. In some ways they resemble the characters in Oliver Goldsmith's *She Stoops to Conquer*, and the character of Knäblein is as memorable as Tony Lumpkin. He also closely resembles Titus Feuerfuchs in Johann Nepomuk Nestroy's *Der Talisman.*

The social satire works effectively, as Knäblein tries unsuccessfully to learn aristocratic ways. In his equestrian attempts he has fallen off so many times he has trouble walking straight. The Falkensteins meanwhile are horrified that they must associate with such people. The effective novelty in this play is the dual casting of Krafft and Knäblein. Krafft disappears in the first act, facilitating Knäblein's appearance. The play masterfully contrasts dual worlds, as the now defunct aristocracy appear eccentric yet unselfish, temperate, and wholesome. The now preeminent middle class is portrayed as naive, wealthy, ill-mannered, and optimistic. The play's humor derives from such contrasts but also from finely drawn personalities. Two repeated gags, which consistently draw a laugh, are the young countess's despairing cry, "Ich bin so betrüüüüüübt!" ("I'm so-oooo-oooooooo upset!") and Count Oktavio's continual request for advice from the portrait of his sixteenth-century forefather Count Cunibert von Falkenstein, which hangs high above the fireplace.

Franz Arnold and Ernst Bach's *Das Jubiläum* (The Class Reunion), which had premiered the previous June in Hannover, was a nostalgic look at "the good old prewar days," when students sang songs, drank beer, and fell in love. Arnold and Bach reconstructed those clichés by presenting formerly young men at the twenty-fifth reunion of their class at a German university. Three levels of society appear in the form of servants, middle classes, and nobility. They contrast but do not conflict with one another. A student choir sings songs of wistful melancholy, husbands and wives argue about careers, and an aunt warns her niece about "going too far" (allowing a young man to kiss her hand). The characters are distinct from one another by virtue of their eccentricities.

A comedy curious by virtue of its failure was Hans Müller-Schlösser's *Eau de Cologne*. It was an skillfully constructed chronicle of the chimney sweep

Dominicus Donnerstag (he got his name from being left on a Thursday, "Donnerstag" in German, near the steps of Saint Dominicus's church in Cologne). It is best described a comedy of proletarian manners. Dominicus got into the chimney sweeping business, he says, because he enjoyed "looking down on people." He uses the famous perfume Eau de Cologne to cover the smell of chimneys whose soot often covers his clothing; he has become fond of the perfume, and he figures that his parents must have been extremely cultured people to have endowed him with such a sensitive nose. Since his arrival "at the top" within his community, Dominicus has been chairman of the Chimney Sweepers' Guild, has joined Konrad Adenauer's political party,[1] and has recently been nominated to run for city council. In the end, Dominicus discovers that his mother is actually the pitiful old lady in the neighborhood whom he has for years ridiculed for her poverty and shabby clothing. Dominicus undergoes a change of heart, now knowing his parentage; he even learns that his dim-witted apprentice is actually his brother, who has recently fallen off a roof and landed in a manure pile. The remedy: ample portions of Eau de Cologne.

Several premieres and productions of straight plays during this season attempted to capture the "revolutionary spirit" still discernible in Germany. Among them were Karlheinz Martin's premiere of (the now incarcerated) Ernst Toller's *Die Wandlung* (The Transformation) at the Tribüne in Charlottenburg, with Fritz Kortner in the role that made him famous. "I played myself," he said later, "a young German Jew and rebel, in conflict with my surroundings."[2] Critics agreed it was "ingenious demagoguery," and although the play attracted attention in Berlin, it had little resonance elsewhere. Ernst Barlach's *Der tote Tag* (The Dead Day) premiered in Leipzig to lukewarm critical reception; only when this remarkable sculptor/playwright's work encountered the director Jürgen Fehling did Barlach receive nationwide attention. Georg Kaiser's expressionist *Hölle-Weg-Erde* (Hell-Road-Earth) premiered in Frankfurt, leaving critics divided.[3] The most significant political production of the entire season was director Leopold Jessner's *Wilhelm Tell* by Friedrich Schiller at the Prussian State Theater in Berlin, with Albert Bassermann in the title role and Fritz Kortner as the villainous Gessler. Street riots frequently ensued outside the theatre after performances concluded, and the production stirred controversy (along with vituperative condemnation in nationalist newspaper editorials) throughout the country. Jessner and Kortner were accused of "Jewifying" German culture, while others despaired of the control that left-wing intellectuals had gained in other Prussian theatres.

COMEDY PREMIERES of 1919–1920

PLAYWRIGHT(S)	PLAY TITLE	CITY and THEATRE	DATE
Arnold, Franz, and Ernst Bach	*Zwangsein-quartierung*	Berlin Lustspielhaus	04/03/20

Bahr, Hermann	*Unmensch, Der*	Munich Residenztheater	11/19/19
Balbo, Enrico	*Glas der Jungfrau, Das*	Berlin Lessing Theater	06/12/20
Berg, Hans	*Knorpsselige Witwe*	Berlin Casino Theater	08/14/20
Bittrich, Max	*Adams Heimkehr*	Freiburg I/B. Stadttheater	04/14/20
Bodenstedt, A. R.	*Buchbinder Schwalbe*	Dresden Central Theater	05/22/20
Braun, Wilhelm	*bessere Leben, Das*	Berlin Weissensee Volkstheater	08/24/19
Brentano, Anna	*Drei Frauenhute*	Berlin Theater in der Friedrichstraße	11/29/19
Burg, Eugen, and Otto Härting	*unvermählte Ehepaar, Das*	Munich Volkstheater	03/17/20
Burg, Eugen, and Fritz Wilding	*Erholungsreise, Die*	Düsseldorf Stadttheater	02/13/20
Cahan, Richard M.	*Brandl*	Berlin Staatsschauspielhaus	11/22/19
Drechsler, Hermann	*Wer ein böses Weib hat*	Gera Reussisches Theater	12/03/19
Düsnel, Paul	*Stammvater, Der*	Eisenach Stadttheater	03/05/20
Eichler, Rudolf	*Mann auf Vorrat, Der*	Hamburg Thalia Theater	06/01/20
Engel, Oskar, and Georg L'Orange	*Tieffenbachs*	Gotha Landestheater	03/01/20
Ernst, Otto	*Herr Bummerlunder*	Hamburg Deutsches Schauspielhaus	11/01/19
Eulenberg, Herbert	*Pansanabum*	Frankfurt/M. Schauspielhaus	12/05/19
Fleischmann, M.	*Kampf gegen das Küssen, Der*	Hamburg Kammerspiele	03/09/20
Friedmann, Arnim, and Ludwig Nerz	*Doktor Stieglitz*	Berlin Theater in der Friedrichstraße	10/17/19
Fulda, Ludwig	*Wundermittel, Das*	Hamburg Thalia Theater	10/25/19
Gal, Hans	*Arzt der Sobeide*	Breslau Stadttheater	11/02/19

Goldstein, Moritz	*Gabe Dottes, Die*	Berlin Staats-schauspielhaus	02/17/20
Haas, Rudolf	*Schelm von Neu-berg, Der*	Eger Stadttheater	01/16/20
Hannemann, Adolf	*Madame Favart*	Reichenberg Stadttheater	03/19/20
Hartenau-Thiel, Gert	*Punktum, streu Sand darauf*	Brandenburg Stadttheater	02/10/20
Heller, Ludwig, and Ferdinand Kahn	*alten Junglinge, Die*	Hamburg Deutsches Schauspielhaus	02/21/20
Kadelburg, Gustav, and Heinz Gordon	*ehemalige Leut-nant, Der*	Breslau Lobe Theater	09/01/19
Kahn, Harry	*Krach*	Berlin Kleines Schau-spielhaus	09/23/19
Kanter, Waldemar	*Tanz auf dem Vul-kan, Der*	Leipzig Schauspielhaus	11/29/19
Kaufmann, Willy	*Liebes-schlummer*	Hannover Deutsches Theater	03/31/20
Kaula, Ludwig	*steinerne Gast, Der*	Zwickau Stadttheater	02/17/20
Kurpium, Robert	*Einbruch m .b. H.*	Beuthen Stadttheater	08/28/20
Kurth, Adolf, and Vik-tor Laverrenz	*schwarze Hoheit, Die*	Erfurt Reichshallen-theater	04/30/20
Legal, Ernst	*Ja, ja, und ja*	Barmen Stadttheater	02/29/20
Lenz, Leo	*Bettinas Verl-obung*	Dresden Central Theater	06/19/20
Matthaei, Albert	*Ex-Herzog, Der*	Chemnitz Stadttheater	11/01/19
Misch, Robert	*Kuckucksei, Das*	Hannover Residenz-theater	08/10/20
Möller, Alfred, and Hans Lorenz	*Jugendpächter, Der*	Hamburg Thalia Theater	01/30/20
Mosenthal, Salomon	*Auf'm Sonnenwendehof*	Mannheim Neues Theater	09/27/19
Müller-Schlösser, Hans	*Eau de Cologne*	Düsseldorf Schau-spielhaus	06/13/20
Neal, Max, and Ferd-inand Kahn	*Bett der Pom-padour, Das*	Arnstadt Landestheater	05/09/20

Neiße, Max-Hermann	*Albine und August*	Berlin Kleines Theater	11/14/19
Neumann, Siegmund, and Erich Kuhn	*Aber Hoheit!*	Hamburg Thalia Theater	04/27/20
Nonnenbruch, Robert, and Carl Traut	*Braune Lappen*	Krefeld Stadttheater	10/08/19
Okonkowski, Georg	*Großstadtkava-lier, Der*	Berlin Lustspielhaus	10/31/19
Overweg, A.	*Instanzenkind, Das*	Berlin Komödienhaus	12/01/19
Paetzold, Kurt	*Kunstkritik, Die*	Gotha Landestheater	08/30/19
Pfeiffer, Heinrich	*letzten Ritter, Die*	Berlin Deutsches Künstlertheater	09/13/19
Presber, Rudolf	*Rumpelstilzchen*	Meiningen Landestheater	10/05/19
Rehse, Bernhard	*Köpfe der Hydra, Die*	Dresden Schauspielhaus	06/03/20
Reicke, Georg	*Sie*	Berlin Komödienhaus	11/22/19
Rosendahl, Wismar	*Lied der Liebe, Das*	Berlin Rose Theater	04/01/20
Rossem, C. P. van	*Femina*	Brünn Stadttheater	09/01/19
Rossem, C. P. van	*Kokette Phyllis, Die*	Schwerin Landestheater	01/08/20
Rossem, C. P. van	*Pomarius*	Munich Lustspielhaus	10/14/19
Schmazov, Alfred	*Ein alter Sünder*	Berlin Casino Theater	03/27/20
Schmitt, Heinrich	*Excellenz*	Hamburg Deutsches Schauspielhaus	01/30/20
Sebrecht, Friedrich	*Frau XY und ihre goldene Kalber*	Plauen Stadttheater	12/26/19
Seeliger, Ewald	*Peter Voß, der Millionendieb*	Hannover Deutsches Theater	02/07/20
Siener, Joseph, and Hans Kempner	*lockere Zeisig, Der*	Cologne Metropol Theater	06/01/20
Skovronek, Richard	*gute Auskunft, Die*	Hamburg Thalia Theater	09/23/19
Spener, Wilhelm	*Er kann nicht befehlen*	Berlin Kleines Theater	10/11/19

Staudte, Fritz	*Drei Wege zur Frau*	Breslau Thalia Theater	11/01/19
Stayton, Frank	*schwache Geschlecht, Das*	Munich Residenztheater	08/31/20
Stockhausen, Otto	*Trostpreis, Der*	Darmstadt Landestheater	04/24/20
Strecker, Karl	*Erbsohn, Der*	Nuremberg Stadttheater	04/18/20
Stroemveld, Harro	*Bade zu Haufe*	Hamburg Schiller Theater	08/14/20
Traut, Carl	*tote Schuster, Der*	Bad Salzschlirf Kurtheater	07/30/20
Umrhein, Franz	*Liebhaberin, Die*	Meissen Stadttheater	10/02/19
Weidt, Richard	*Onkel Shellberrys Tochter*	Hannover Schauburg	02/21/20
Wiegand, Johannes	*Hans im Glück*	Bremerhaven Stadttheater	10/15/19
Wilde, Richard	*Recht der Jungen*	Landshut Stadttheater	03/30/20
Wittmaack, Adolf	*Lump, Der*	Hannover Deutsches Theater	04/22/20
Ziersch, Walter	*Dämon Schievelbein*	Stuttgart Landestheater	05/06/20
Zinn, Adelbert Alexander	*Schlemihl*	Düsseldorf Stadttheater	03/05/20
Zoder, Paul	*feste Rad, Das*	Altona Stadttheater	09/23/19

NOTES

1. Konrad Adenauer (1876-1967) is best known as Chancellor of the post-World War II Federal Republic of Germany, but he was influential in the Weimar Republic as well. He served as mayor of Cologne during those years and was frequently mentioned as a candidate for Chancellor of a Weimar government.

2. Fritz Kortner, *Aller Tage Abend* (Munich: Kindler, 1969), 224.

3. Kaiser's *From Morn to Midnight* had its London premiere during this season, but audiences and critics found it incomprehensible. Karlheinz Martin did a film version of the play later in the year. Other notable film premieres during this season included *Das Cabinett des Dr. Caligari* (The Cabinet of Dr. Caligari) directed by Robert Wiene, and *Madame Dubarry*, directed by Ernst Lubitsch, both of which subsequently enjoyed worldwide popularity.

4

The 1920–1921 Season

The road of return to normalcy, to paraphrase an American presidential nominee in 1920,[1] met with unanticipated detours during the 1920-1921 German theatre season. The German currency continued its downward slide against the American dollar[2] and political unrest continued as nationalist and other right-wing elements consistently called for the government's overthrow. The abortive Kapp Putsch during the previous March convinced President Ebert and the Weimar cabinet that only repressive measures against dissidents could provide necessary stability. A young vagrant with a distinguished war record named Adolf Hitler was one such dissident; he made speeches in Munich demanding the removal of all Jews from government office. Hitler and others also demanded a suspension of the Versailles "Edict" (as they had begun to call the treaty). The reparation provision of the treaty imposed an intolerable burden on the German economy, and the new government simply refused to make the assigned payments. In response, French troops occupied three more cities on the Rhine (Düsseldorf, Duisdorf, and Ruhrort), which made the Reich government look even weaker in the eyes of its own citizens and an easy target for criticism from the right. The right also condemned the Reich government for failing to assist German freedom fighters in Silesia. That former German province, now a part of Poland, had witnessed several insurrections in September against Polish authorities, who had brutally subdued them. A referendum the following March gave majority consent for a return to German rule, but the Polish ignored it.

Meantime the left did not remain idle. Communist uprisings in Saxony resulted in successive rounds of government militia encounters with German citizens. Similar uprisings in Hamburg rendered the port of that city defunct for weeks, further clouding the economic picture in Germany.[3] Left-wing agitators were active in the German theatre, too. Karlheinz Martin gave Georg Kaiser's *Europa* its world premiere at Max Reinhardt's Grosses Schauspielhaus and followed it with a "cycle of revolutionary dramas" at the same theatre with Gerhart Hauptmann's *Florian Geyer* and his *Die Weber* (The Weavers), Friedrich Schiller's *Die Räuber* (The Robbers), and Johann Wolfgang Goethe's *Götz von Berlichingen.* Erwin Piscator opened his "Proletarian Theater" in Berlin with *Der Krüppel* (The Cripple), while Fritz von Unruh's *Louis Ferdinand, Prinz von Preussen* (Louis Ferdinand, Prince of Prussia) premiered in Darmstadt. None of these productions attracted a wide following, but Leopold Jessner's *Richard III* at the Prussian State Theater in Berlin certainly did; the director compared Shakespeare's tyrant with ambitious politicians obsessed with seizing power. Traditionalists, accustomed to *Richard III* as "a study in psychopathology," were outraged.[4]

The play with performances than any other during this season was Franz Arnold and Ernst Bach's *Zwangseinquartierung* (Forced Emergency Housing). It was so popular, in fact, that its number of performances was nearly triple that of its closest rival (the previous season's leader, *Liselotte von der Pfalz*, or Liselotte of the Palatinate). Arnold and Bach's comedy had opened the previous April at the Berlin Lustspielhaus and from there proceeded through the repertoires of over 100 theatres throughout the 1920–1921 season. Audiences relished its humorous treatment of the catastrophic housing shortage in Germany during that season, a shortage that began with the return of the defeated German army. Yet this was not a trivialized "returning soldier" play; its focus was instead the trivial consequences of a serious question. The personification of that focus was Anton Schwalbe, the play's central character. A retired industrialist and owner of a comfortable villa within a large German city, Schwalbe's nemesis is an overzealous government housing official named Dr. Hans Hellwig, whose efforts upend the household's domestic tranquility. These two characters represented opposing mentalities in the immediate postwar period, as Schwalbe passionately desires an ordered calm within his villa, while Hellwig (like many in the republican government) is determined to enforce amelioration of suffering. To that end, he delivers several unfortunate homeless individuals to the villa; Schwalbe's servants go on strike for higher wages; and Schwalbe himself is threatened with bankruptcy.

The playwrights skillfully interlarded the principal conflict with predictable romantic intrigues, mistaken identities, and a contrivance borrowed directly from their first big success (*Die spanische Fliege*, or The Spanish Fly, in 1913), the putative fatherhood of illegitimate offspring. When Schwalbe learns he may have to support a child he has never known, his reaction is similar to that of most Germans when contemplating reparation payments dictated in the Versailles Treaty: initial stupefaction, followed quickly by outrage. Yet this was a comic treatment of outrage, indeed an affectionate portrayal of one, which made it extraordinarily palatable to audiences.

When he meets the young woman who may be his daughter (a Hungarian violinist named Etélka), Schwalbe gingerly inquires about her father. "I never knew him," she replies. "My family is full of tragedies—almost like Strindberg." "I don't know that family," says Anton. "Who are the Strindbergs?" This conflict, along with all the others, is peaceably resolved by the final curtain. The villa returns to normal, young lovers are united, servants return to work with a new sense of respect (in fact, the household maid turns out to be Schwalbe's daughter), and the intrusive government official is censured.

The popularity of Rudolf Presber and Leo Walter Stein's *Liselotte* continued this season (as noted above), followed by Arnold and Bach's "perennial" *Die spanische Fliege* with about 250 performances. There were other notable, though less frequently performed, comedy productions in 1920–1921. The premieres of Ernst Barlach's *Die echten Sedemunds* (The Genuine Sedemund Family), Rudolf Bernauer's *Die Sache mit Lola* (The Business with Lola), Toni Impekoven's *Luderchen* (The Tart), and Theodor Tagger's one-acts *Harry* and *Annette* had little impact upon this season directly, but these playwrights were marked for subsequent success. Barlach and Tagger[5] ceased writing comedy but had substantial success with straight dramas in the mid- and late 1920s; Bernauer's comedy became a performance leader the following season.

Impekoven's work, as we have previously noted, had already had a considerable impact on Weimar theatre culture. His *Luderchen* of this season did not duplicate the success of his and Carl Mathern's *Die drei Zwillinge* (The Three Twins), but it is worth considering as an example of a local success; indeed, it generated perhaps too much controversy to make it acceptable on a widespread basis.

Luderchen was a comic Weimar variant of *Camille*, with La Traviata in this case not a whore with a heart of gold but a completely unrepentant exploiter of male emotions. She unashamedly makes her living off men who keep her as their mistress—a dramatic type neither unique nor original—but here she is handed up from son to father, all in the name of propriety. Marion Bergmann (known as Marion de Merville) is an engaging personality, one blithely able to maximize her resources while also remaining capable of intense passion.

The aristocracy is again portrayed as corrupt and witless, but the middle class has few redeeming features as well. Marion's desire for independence and her amiable disposition are sincere, but her defining traits are acquisitiveness and a cheerful willingness to prostitute herself. She is the reason the play was condemned as degenerate when *Luderchen* opened in 1920 at Frankfurt's Neues Theater, though audiences flocked to it there. It had relatively few productions elsewhere.

COMEDY PREMIERES OF 1920–1921

PLAYWRIGHT(S)	PLAY TITLE	CITY and THEATRE	DATE
Aldermann, Antonius	*leere Wohnung, Die*	Bad Ischl Kurtheater	08/03/21
Altheer, Paul	*Don Juans Freund*	Breslau Lobe Theater	09/11/20
Bahr, Hermann	*Ehelei*	Berlin Kleines Schau-spielhaus	12/07/20
Bahr, Hermann	*Selige, Der*	Berlin Kleines Theater	12/17/20

Barlach, Ernst	*echten Sedemunds, Die*	Hamburg Kammer-spiele	03/23/21
Berges, Heinrich	*grüne Lapislazuli, Der*	Hamburg Thalia Theater	04/19/21
Bernauer, Rudolf, and Rudolph Schanzer	*Sache mit Lola, Die*	Berlin Komödienhaus	10/23/20
Björnson, Björn-stjerne	*durstige Kamel, Das*	Bochum Stadttheater	05/18/21
Blunck, Hans	*heilige Hannes, Der*	Hamburg Kammer-spiele	05/10/21
Eger, A. P.	*Im Gasthof zum Schwanen*	Bremen Schauspielhaus	11/07/20
Eisenlohr, Friedrich	*Skandal, Der*	Munich Schauspielhaus	12/11/20
Engel, Alexander	*Eheringe*	Hanau Stadttheater	01/12/21
Engel, Alexander	*ewige Braut, Die*	Munich Volkstheater	03/02/21
Feuchtwanger, Lion	*Amerikaner, Der*	Munich Kammerspiele	12/09/20
Gaßmann, Hans	*weisse Lämmchen, Das*	Berlin Komödienhaus	02/12/21
Gehr, Theodor	*goldene Freiheit, Die*	Berlin Theater in der Kommandantenstraße	06/02/21
Golz, Emil and Os-wald Golz	*unwiderliche Max, Der*	Kattowitz Stadttheater	09/19/20
Hagedorn, Viktor	*Großstadtgeheim-nisse*	Cleve Stadttheater	01/30/21
Harlan, Walter	*In Kanaan*	Hannover Deutsches Theater	02/12/21
Heiseler, Henry	*magische Laterne, Die*	Hamburg Kammer-spiele	05/30/21
Himmelmann, Weich	*Yankee-Dudler, Der*	Munich Münchner-theater	11/27/20
Hirschfelder, A.	*Schieber & Co.*	Grünberg i/S. Stadt-theater	01/01/21
Hoffmann, Arthur	*Paragraph-Koller*	Krefeld Stadttheater	03/11/21
Impekoven, Toni	*Luderchen*	Frankfurt/M. Neues Theater	12/04/20

Kästner, Leo	*Ihr Glücksjunge*	Bremerhaven Stadttheater	02/23/21
Knopf, Julius	*Flucht vor der Frau*	Neustrelitz Landestheater	02/12/21
Kraatz, Curt	*falsche Note, Die*	Bad Salzschlirf Kurtheater	07/31/21
Lothar, Rudolf	*Casanovas Sohn*	Hamburg Thalia Theater	12/11/20
Mathern, Carl	*Ehezauber*	Frankfurt/M. Neues Theater	04/07/21
Metzger, Max	*Nichts als Überraschungen*	Lübeck Stadttheater	12/19/20
Mittermayer, Carl	*letzte Fahrt, Die*	Darmstadt Schleierseer Bauerntheater	03/23/21
Mosse, Erich	*Himmel auf Erde*	Bonn Stadttheater	07/02/21
Müller-Heym, Georg	*pieschener Frechdachs, Der*	Dresden Volkstheater	07/16/21
Müller-Schlösser, Hans	*Rangierbahnhof, Der*	Düsseldorf Schauspielhaus	02/19/21
Neal, Max, and Max Ferner	*doppelte Adele, Die*	Munich Lustspielhaus	02/17/21
Norrie, Wilhelm	*Zwischen zwei Stühlen*	Hamburg Thalia Theater	11/18/20
Pietschel, Oskar	*Wohltätigkeitsverein, Der*	Berlin Lichterfeldtheater	12/02/20
Prechtl, Robert	*Nacht der Jenny Lind, Die*	Munich Schauspielhaus	08/14/20
Rößler, Carl	*pathetische Hut, Der*	Berlin Kammerspiele des Deutschen Theaters	01/21/21
Rudolf, Werner	*Erfindung des Dr. Lux, Die*	Landsberg Stadttheater	04/19/21
Sachs, Lothar	*Peterle*	Nuremberg Stadttheater	09/09/20
Schmidt, Lothar	*Man von 50 Jahren, Der*	Hannover Deutsches Theater	12/15/20
Schmidtbonn, Wolfgang	*Schauspieler, Die*	Berlin Lustspielhaus	9/24/21

Speyer, Wilhelm	*Rugby*	Berlin Theater in der Königgrätzerstraße	03/26/21
Sternheim, Carl	*entfesselte Zeit-genosse, Der*	Darmstadt Hessisches Landestheater	02/17/21
Strecker, Karl Alfons	*Krokodil, Das*	Harburg Stadttheater	02/03/21
Sturm, Hans, and Hans Bachwitz	*Liebe und Trompetenblasen*	Altenburg Landestheater	05/11/21
Sturm, Hans, and Hans Bachwitz	*Mausefalle, Die*	Berlin Lustspielhaus	02/18/21
Tagger, Theodor	*Harry*	Halle Stadttheater	12/23/20
Tietsch, Karl	*Perücke, Die*	Guben Stadttheater	11/27/20
Unger, Hellmuth	*grosse Augenblick, Der*	Gotha Landestheater	11/29/20
Zellmut, Hans	*Meine Frau, das Fräulein*	Baden-Baden Stadtschauspielhaus	01/01/21
Zinn, Adelbert Alexander	*Polar-Reise, Die*	Hamburg Thalia Theater	01/04/21

NOTES

1. Warren Gamaliel Harding (1865–1923) used the phrase "a return to normalcy" in his successful campaign of 1920 as a promise of social and economic conditions under his administration. He of course had little of the German theatre season of 1920–1921 in mind when he used the phrase, yet his campaign terminology bore an odd parallel to the desires of most German producers and audiences.

2. The exchange rate during this season averaged about 62.5 Reichsmarks (M) for one U.S. dollar.

3. The federal government rang up huge expenditures during this period as well. The deficit by the end of 1921 totaled $640 million, according to then-prevailing exchange rates.

4. Fritz Kortner, *Aller Tage Abend* (Munich: Kindler, 1969), 235. Kortner also claimed much of the credit for this production's notoriety at the expense of its director. At his insistence, he stated, actors no longer spoke in the familiar declamatory style which German audiences at Shakespeare productions had come to expect. "Everything was subject to Richard's lust for power. It was in every sentence."

5. Theodor Tagger (1891–1958) assumed the name Ferdinand Bruckner during this season and soon thereafter assumed leadership of the Renaissance Theater in Berlin, though under his legal name.

5

The 1921–1922 Season

Trends of the previous season continued into the 1921–1922 season. Franz Arnold and Ernst Bach maintained their domination throughout the season with productions of *Zwangseinquartierung* (Forced Emergency Housing) and *Die spansiche Fliege* (The Spanish Fly) outnumbering all others. In second place was Toni Impekoven and Carl Mathern's *Liselotte*, followed by a newcomer, *Die Sache mit Lola* (The Business with Lola) by Rudolf Bernauer and Rudolph Schanzer.[1] Bernauer himself, however, was hardly new to the German theatre. He had worked as an actor for Otto Brahm and by this season was (with his longtime partner, Carl Meinhard) the owner of several Berlin theatres. He had become so wealthy, in fact, that he "retired" to Italy after this season; the rampant inflation afflicting the German economy was doubtless a large factor in his decision.

The German currency began its catastrophic decline during the 1921–1922 season, losing 400 percent of its value against the American dollar in little less than ten months. The net effect of such inflation was the destruction of liquid assets; Germans who held shares in common stock, pension plans, or savings accounts were wiped out. Entrepreneurs like Meinhard and Bernauer, Max Reinhardt, or Arnold and Bach (who now held partial ownership of several theatres) were somewhat protected by their investments in real estate; indeed, such theatres as the Berlin Lustspielhaus (where Arnold was the director) and the Munich Volkstheater (where Bach was in charge) remained prosperous. The business of comedy was so prosperous, in fact, that during this season new theatres devoted entirely to comedy were established.[2]

Political violence took an ominous turn for the worse during this season, although even before it began Matthias Erzberger was murdered in Baden. Erzberger, who had served as Reich finance minister and vice-chancellor, had initialed the cease-fire between Germany and its enemies on November 11, 1918, and had endured the resulting vilification by nationalists. He had been closely associated with other "November criminals" by accepting the Versailles Treaty, and he had led German delegates to the first assembly of the League of Nations. His murder was seen as justifiable vindication for "German honor" and a blatant warning to other parliamentary politicians "collaborating" with Allied intentions to keep Germany weak for the remainder of the twentieth century. Soon after Erzberger's murder, members of an armed private militia set off a bomb near the newly renovated Munich Lustspielhaus; their leader was the thirty-two-year-old Adolf Hitler, who later claimed that such acts were merely displays of the militia's "battle strength." He called the militia the *Sturm-Abteilung* (Storm Troop) of the newly formed National Socialist German Workers' party (NSDAP).[3]

Just as the current season "opened" with a politically motivated murder, so it "closed" with another, this time that of Foreign Minister Walther Rathenau. His death was greeted with particular glee among Hitler's followers, since Rathenau had been Jewish. The foreign minister's killers were tried, convicted, and given long prison terms. When they committed suicide in prison, Hitler (along with other right-wing politicians) hailed them as "martyrs" to a noble cause.

Given the profound economic and political unrest within the country, it is small wonder that audiences turned to comedy for escape. That describes *Die Sache mit Lola* (The Business with Lola), although the play's title is at first misleading. The "business" in which Lola is involved is a small corset shop in Berlin. The real business is escape, as the central character (Sebastian Otterbein) tries repeatedly to get away from Zenobia (his wife of twenty years) for brief sexual dalliances. Sebastian is without question among the most henpecked of husbands in all of German dramatic literature. Sebastian and Zenobia travel to Berlin for the engagement of their daughter; but after only four hours in the big city, Sebastian causes so much confusion that the engagement is nearly called off, Lola's corset business is virtually ruined, and Sebastian almost goes to prison. By play's end, he and Zenobia agree to beat a retreat to Zenzenbach, the little town where they run an "artificial honey" business.

This season, while promoting the work of previously successful playwrights, also saw the premieres of works by playwrights who in subsequent seasons were to do very well indeed. Chief among them was Max Mohr, whose *Improvisationen im Juni* (Improvisations in June) opened in Munich to universally positive reviews and popular acclaim. It was to be among the performance leaders for the next two years. Ludwig Fulda's *Des Esels Schatten* (The Shadow of the Ass) premiered in Mannheim and remained popular there for the next several seasons.[4] Arnold and Bach's *Der keusche Lebemann* (The Virginal Playboy) premiered (as was Arnold and Bach's usual custom) on Christmas Day and went on (as they almost always did) to stupendous success in hundreds of performances all over the country. Heinz Gordon, whose career began in Milwaukee, Wisconsin, at the Pabst Theater, also saw his play premiere on Christmas Day: *Der fromme Lügner* (The Pious Liar). Although moderately successful, it did not enjoy the acclaim of the Arnold and Bach comedy—but then, few other plays of any kind did.

The 1921–1922 season witnessed the German premiere of what was to become the most popular of any American comedy during the Weimar Republic. Avery Hopwood's *Fair and Warmer* had opened November 6, 1915, at the Eltinge Theatre in New York (it later moved to the Harris) and ran for 377 performances. Nine road companies performed the play in the United States from 1916 to 1920; it opened in London on May 14, 1918, and ran 497 performances. A film version was shot in 1919 by Screen Classics, Inc., with May Allison, and it, too, was successful. Its German publishers gave it the title *Der Mustergatte* (The Model Husband) and for reasons not entirely clear it proved far more popular than a German comedy with an analogous plot by Willy Kaufmann titled *Liebesschlummer* (Slumber of Love), which premiered in Hannover during March 1920. Hopwood's achievement, according to New York reviewers, was that his characters are "not wicked but merely mischievous."[5] Their added disingenuousness may also have appealed to German audiences.

COMEDY PREMIERES OF 1921–1922

PLAYWRIGHT(S)	PLAY TITLE	CITY and THEATRE	DATE
Alexander, Paul, and Willi Berndt	*Recht der Jugend, Das*	Hamburg Thalia Theater	10/29/21
Arnold, Franz, and Ernst Bach	*keusche Lebemann, Der*	Munich Volkstheater	12/25/21
Berend, Fritz	*Schöne Seelen finden sich*	Kassel Staatstheater	04/27/22
Berr, Georges, and Louis Verneuil	*Beverley*	Hamburg Thalia Theater	10/06/21
Born, Erich	*Tip, Der*	Cleve Stadttheater	11/27/21
Brandt, Ludwig	*Tragende Wolken*	Halberstadt Stadttheater	11/26/21
Chiarelli, Luigi	*Furcht von Lächer-lichkeit, Die*	Leipzig Schauspielhaus	05/28/22
Ellis, Walter	*Jonnys Busenfreund*	Berlin Komödienhaus	09/07/21
Frohwein, Ludwig	*Schleier, Der*	Dresden Neustädter Schauspielhaus	11/27/21
Fulda, Ludwig	*Esels Schatten, Des*	Mannheim National Theater	01/14/22
Fulda, Ludwig	*Vulkan, Der*	Dresden Neustädter Schauspielhaus	12/25/21
Geifrig, Walther	*Liebesfrühling*	Eisenberg Stadttheater	01/27/22

Goetz, Curt	*Ingeborg*	Berlin Theater am Kurfürstendamm	10/08/21
Gordon, Heinz	*fromme Lügner, Der*	Frankfurt Stadttheater	12/25/21
Heim, Fritz	*Familienbad, Das*	Ulm Stadttheater	11/24/21
Hesse, Otto Ernst	*Bigamist, Der*	Düsseldorf Schauspielhaus	06/16/22
Hofmannsthal, Hugo von	*Schwierige, Der*	Munich Residenztheater	11/08/21
Hopwood, Avery	*Mustergatte, Der*	Hamburg Thalia Theater	04/16/22
Kahn, Harry	*Ring, Der*	Berlin Kleines Schauspielhaus	02/03/22
Kaiser, Georg	*David und Goliath*	Minden Stadttheater	03/18/22
Kaufmann, Willy	*Glückspinscher, Der*	Hannover Deutsches Schauspielhaus	01/21/22
Lagerhöf, Selma	*Onkel Theodor*	Meiningen Landes-theater	12/31/21
Lenz, Leo	*Frauenkenner, Der*	Annaberg Stadttheater	12/27/21
Lorcher, Jens	*Soll mann—soll man nicht?*	Braunschweig Landes-theater	04/07/22
Lothar, Rudolf	*Frau mit der Maske, Die*	Hamburg Thalia Theater	03/21/22
Mack, Fritz	*Flucht aus dem Himmel, Die*	Altenburg Landes-theater	03/30/22
Mohr, Max	*Improvisationen im Juni*	Munich Residenztheater	03/24/22
Möller, Alfred, and Lothar Sachs	*Ehebarometer, Das*	Hamburg Thalia Theater	11/04/21
Molo, Walter von	*Till Lausebums*	Bonn Stadttheater	03/17/22
Müller-Schlosser, Hans	*Loch in der Hecke, Das*	Suttgart Landestheater	10/03/21
Nagel, J. L.	*Schellenkönig, Der*	Neiße Stadttheater	02/04/22
Neal, Max	*zweite Jugend, Die*	Dresden Schauspielhaus	10/30/21
Neubauer, Wilhelm	*Hühnerhof, Der*	Leipzig Schauspielhaus	11/12/21
Neumann, Siegmund	*Sprung ins Paradies, Der*	Hamburg Thalia Theater	11/15/21

Rehfisch, Hans-José	*Erziehung durch Kolibri, Die*	Düsseldorf Schauspielhaus	11/13/21
Rößler, Carl	*Stiefel, Der*	Munich Kammerspiele	07/05/22
Schmidtbonn, Wolfgang	*Schauspieler, Die*	Berlin Lustspielhaus	09/24/21
Schönherr, Karl	*Vivat Academia*	Hamburg Thalia Theater	04/01/22
Schönlank, Herbert	*Napoleon mit der Warze*	Hamburg Thalia Theater	12/06/22
Schurek, Paul	*Stratenmusik*	Hamburg Nieder-deutsche Bühne	10/24/21
Schwartz, Otto, and Georg Lengbach	*blaue Heinrich, Der*	Frankfurt/M. Stadt-theater	05/20/22
Sternheim, Carl	*Mamon und Tschu*	Berlin Theater in der Königgrätzerstraße	10/23/21
Unger, Hellmuth	*Mammon*	Mühlhausen Schauspielhaus	01/14/22
Urias, Siegfried	*Verlobte Ehemänner*	Bonn Stadttheater	02/24/22
Verneuil, Louis	*Der Vertrag von Nizza*	Munich Schau-spielhaus	10/15/21
Walter, Robert	*Große Moritz und die kleine Justine, Der*	Hamburg Komödienhaus	09/03/21
Weigand, Wilhelm	*Lolas Onkel*	Dresden Neustädter Schauspielhaus	02/07/22
Willner, A. M., and Arthur Rebner	*Heilige Ambrosius, Der*	Berlin Deutsches Künstlertheater	11/03/21

NOTES

1. *Die Sache mit Lola* (The Business with Lola) had premiered the previous season in Berlin at the Komödienhaus (House of Comedy) with the popular star Max Pallenberg in the central role of Sebastian Otterbein.

2. During this season, the Munich Lustspielhaus (Comedy Theatre) was completely renovated, refurbished, and enlarged.

3. The NSDAP had been formed the previous season, based on a party called the German Workers' party (DAP). It had been a regional organization, confined mostly to Munich. Hitler's political career began as its director of propaganda. He soon assumed its leadership, based on his appeal and his extraordinary effectiveness as a public speaker—an activity in which he had no previous experience. His first speech as leader of the new NSDAP took place in August 1920, soon after his honorable discharge from the army. It was titled, "Why We are Anti-semitic."

4. Fulda had been a figure of long standing during the Wilhelmine period; his other comedy of this season, *Der Vulkan* (The Volcano), premiered in Dresden but was not successful. Fulda had spent substantial time in America, observing and reporting on Broadway theatre seasons for German-language newspapers; his *Des Esels Schatten* has much in common with then-popular American comedies on Broadway.

5. Review of *Fair and Warmer*, *New York Times*, 8 November 1915, 13.

6

The 1922–1923 Season

Monetary inflation raged out of control during the 1922–1923 season, and theatre (along with every other German institution) bore indelible scars from the experience for the remainder of the Weimar Republic's life. Theatre became much more market-driven than it had been previously, although the trend away from elitist segregation of audiences had been under way for some time. In previous years, a large portion of the middle-class audience had been able to live comfortably off returns from investments. Artists like Max Reinhardt in Berlin, Otto Falckenberg in Munich, and Luise Dumont in Düsseldorf had prospered by catering to the educated bourgeoisie, finding ready capital for their theatre ventures—but this audience greatly diminished during the inflationary period.[1] Thus theatre artists, along with most other artists, became totally dependent for their livelihood on selling their work to bidders who could afford it. The frenetic output characterizing Weimar culture was a result of such economic facts of life. Artists of all kinds were compelled to recognize that they were now working within a market society to create products for a mass culture.

The ruinous inflation of this period had its origins in the reparation payment scheme imposed on Germany by the victorious Allies. When Allied troops occupied industrial regions immediately after the war, the Reich government encouraged a policy of "passive resistance."[2] It even paid wages to workers who refused to work in those formerly productive districts. Those payments, however, were financed by printing money unconnected to gold reserves. German gold reserves meantime steadily dwindled, since the Allies demanded reparation payments in gold. The Allies had insisted that Germany was to pay compensation not only for the war damage the German army had caused, but also for "the costs of the war as a whole." Because the conflict had turned into a total war requiring mobilization of entire economies, costs were so staggering that nobody could comprehend them in economic, social, or political terms.

In the face of these difficulties, several German actors attempted to make a living by forming their own troupes[3] and passing the hat after performances just to keep up with daily expenses. The German mark lost unimaginably large portions of value against the dollar every day; at the beginning of the season, for example, one dollar would buy 1,658 marks; by season's end, it required one hundred times that amount to purchase the same dollar. A loaf of bread cost 2,400 marks, which had been the average *yearly* wage of a factory worker before the war. Other actors, especially those who could sing and dance, formed cabarets during this season in the larger cities.[4] Berlin alone could boast nearly forty such establishments; Hamburg, Munich, and Cologne had at least a dozen each.

The "firm," as it was now called, of Franz Arnold and Ernst Bach led this season with *Der keusche Lebemann* (The Virginal Playboy), a play which enjoyed over one thousand performances. It followed a plot pattern fairly predictable by now, but its premiere in Berlin featured Guido Thielscher in the title role. Thielscher was to become closely associated with the works of Arnold and Bach for the remainder of the Weimar Republic. He was a 300-pound, extraordinarily acrobatic performer whose talent in achieving the "naturalness" of behavior and ease with Arnold and Bach dialogue made him indispensable for premiere productions. Arnold and Bach credited him with generating the leading roles they conceived for him, since theirs were not comedies of manners nor "conversation pieces" in the mode of Oscar Wilde or even Avery Hopwood. Their dialogue was completely without polish or elegance; it was unsentimental and uncomplicated. It was a flat idiom without ambiguity and completely unmetaphorical, because it almost exclusively dealt with current (though wholly frivolous) complications.

Thielscher had begun his career at Berlin's Belle-Alliance Theatre in 1877. His breakthrough came in 1893 when he played the title role in *Charley's Aunt* in 1893; Otto Brahm engaged him for the 1898–1899 season, playing the father in Friedrich Schiller's *Die Räuber*. But when he came on in a nightshirt as the old man, the audience was reminded of his success in *Charley's Aunt* and fell into uncontrollable laughter. He left Brahm in midseason and joined the Metropol Theater's ensemble to play musical reviews. The next year at Berlin's Thalia Theatre he enjoyed his greatest Berlin success to date, playing the lead role of *Die Hochtouristen* (The Tourists in High Season) by Curt Kraatz and Max Neal. He continued playing the role in several productions through 1916, when he rejoined the Metropol ensemble. He remained with Arnold and Bach for the remainder of his career, and in 1928 he marked his two-thousandth performance in an Arnold and Bach role.

Thielscher played the title role in *Der keusche Lebemann*, the shy and virtuous Max, whose business partner Julius wants him as a son-in-law. Julius's daughter wants nothing to do with a man her father's age, who is painfully shy in the bargain. To convince her, Julius concocts a preposterous personal history for Max as a gigolo gambler and squire of myriad movie stars. Max reluctantly plays the role of "playboy in disguise" and ends up beguiling everyone in the play, including the daughter and a "real life" movie star.

The second most popular comedy of this season was Max Mohr's *Improvi-*

sationen im Juni (Improvisations in June), which consisted of equal parts murder mystery, comedy, romantic love story, political satire, and in the opinion of one critic, a resemblance to plays by Frank Wedekind.[5] It had some noteworthy metaphorical significance as well. The "old order" of the German state (represented by an elderly couple who commit suicide) destroyed itself and in its place came a managerial class concerned mostly with materialism; in this play, the "new order" have bought the couple's ancient manor house and set about refurbishing it. The contrast between them and the genteel aristocracy corresponded to Toni Impekoven and Carl Mathern's *Die drei Zwillinge* (The Three Twins), but youthful idealism is the central focus of the play. Its personifications are Olga, one of the "improvisors" brought in to entertain Jan, the melancholy son of the new owner; and Tomkinov, a Russian revolutionary on the run from the Bolsheviks. These three young people accept the responsibilities of adulthood through the course of the play and close on a note of hope for German reconciliation.

Avery Hopwood's *Fair and Warmer* was the third most frequently performed comedy of this season, and the previous chapter alluded to its appeal among German audiences. Within the context of this season, its popularity is best explained by its similarity to *Der keusche Lebemann* since Hopwood's central character is also a virtuous gentleman constrained by circumstance to masquerade as a libertine. The controlling difference between this and an Arnold and Bach play is tempo; Hopwood's pace is much slower, largely because it concentrates on character and depends less upon plot complication.

The complication in *Der Mustergatte* (The Model Husband, as it was titled in German) is the eponymous character's lack of complications. Billy Bartlett is so agreeable that his wife Laura threatens to divorce him on grounds of boredom. He gets drunk one night with a neighbor's wife and both pretend that "something" may have occurred between them. But nobody is convinced, and Laura realizes that being married to Billy means enduring days that are predictably "fair and warmer," and that is preferable to stormy weather.

COMEDY PREMIERES OF 1922–1923

PLAYWRIGHT(S)	PLAY TITLE	CITY and THEATRE	DATE
Arnold, Franz, and Ernst Bach	*kühne Schwimmer, Der*	Munich Volkstheater	12/23/22
Brecht, Bertolt	*Trommeln in der Nacht*	Munich Kammerspiele	09/23/23
Brod, Max	*Klarissas halbes Herz*	Königsberg Schauspielhaus	11/18/22
Cahen, Henry	*Eine glatte Sache*	Neiße Stadttheater	03/01/23
Ernst, Otto	*Herr und der Mann*	Schwerin Mecklenburg-isches Landestheater	10/07/22

Eulenberg, Herbert	*Wie man's macht ist richtig*	Danzig Stadttheater	07/01/23
Feldhaus, Erich	*Günstling wider Willen*	Magdeburg Stadttheater	02/22/23
Förster, Henriette	*Gustav Adolfs Brautfahrt*	Berlin Theater am Nollendorfplatz	04/22/23
Frank, Bruno	*Henne und Korb*	Berlin Komödienhaus	10/11/22
Fulda, Ludwig	*Geliebte, Die*	Hamburg Thalia Theater	11/25/22
Geyer, Siegfried	*Lissi die Kokette*	Berlin Trianon Theater	09/07/22
Goetz, Curt	*Lampenschirm, Der*	Leipzig Altes Theater	12/25/22
Griboyedov, A. G.	*Verstand schafft Leiden*	Mainz Stadttheater	12/01/22
Heintze, Karl	*Brücke, Die*	Dortmund Stadttheater	03/02/23
Impekoven, Toni, and Carl Mathern	*Mohrenwäsche, Die*	Frankfurt/M. Schauspielhaus	12/01/22
Johst, Hanns	*Wechsler und Händler*	Leipzig Schauspielhaus	05/05/23
Kornfeld, Paul	*ewige Traum, Der*	Frankfurt Schauspielhaus	01/20/23
Lenghi, Otto	*Tittis Ferien*	Rostock Stadttheater	12/15/22
Lothar, Rudolf, and Hans Bachwitz	*kritsche Jahr, Das*	Hamburg Thalia Theater	10/01/22
Lothar, Rudolf	*schwarze Messe, Die*	Hamburg Thalia Theater	12/09/22
Maugham, W. Somerset	*Frauen der Cheyneys, Die*	Frankfurt/M. Neues Theater	01/13/23
Mohr, Max	*gelbe Zeit, Die*	Cologne Schauspielhaus	03/03/23
Neal, Max, and Carl Mittermayer	*starke Veronika, Die*	Schleierseer Bauerntheater	01/13/23
Philipp, Hugo W.	*glühende Einmaleins, Das*	Mainz Stadttheater	11/17/22
Poeck, Wilhelm	*göttliche Molli, Die*	Göttingen Stadttheater	03/15/23
Ricco, Dario	*Tageszeiten der Liebe*	Munich Kammerspiele	01/11/23
Römer, Alwin	*Tibania*	Dresden Neustädter Schauspielhaus	02/13/23
Roßegger, Hans	*Cagliosto*	Wißmar Stadttheater	12/01/22

Schmidt, Lothar	*Unmoralischen, Die*	Berlin Kleines Theater	11/20/22
Sternheim, Carl	*Nebbich, Der*	Darmstadt Landestheater	10/09/22
Streng, Karl	*siamesischen Zwillinge, Die*	Sondershausen Landestheater	10/22/22
Trebitsch, Siegfried	*Geliebte, Der*	Deutsches Volkstheater	01/27/23
Ungermayer, Fred	*Reliquien*	Weimar Residenztheater	07/14/23
Walter, Robert	*Liebhaber von Saturn, Der*	Königsberg Neues Schauspielhaus	12/02/22
Weiß, Ernst	*kleine Heilige, Die*	Hamburg Kleines Schauspielhaus	03/01/23
Wilde, Richard	*drei Grazien, Die*	Bonn Stadttheater	05/04/23
Zerlis, Hans	*parfümierte Braut, Die*	Hannover Deutsches Theater	04/25/23

NOTES

1. Detlev J. K. Peukert, *The Weimar Republic*, trans. Richard Deveson (New York: Hill and Wang, 1992), 167.

2. There were 80,000 French and 7,000 Belgian troops stationed in the Ruhr district during this season; unrest in the district caused ninety-two deaths among German protesters. The most notorious among them was Albert Leo Schlageter, whom the French executed for "terrorist activities." He became the eponymous subject of a popular play by Hanns Johst, who was an avid follower of Hitler.

3. They gave themselves serious sounding names like "Gruppe junger Schauspieler" (Young Actors' Group), "Das Schauspielertheater" (The Actors' Theatre), or simply "Die Truppe" (The Troupe).

4. The German cabaret, especially the kind operating during the Weimar Republic, has since the success of the Kander and Ebb treatment on Broadway and in film become a practical cliché for Weimar culture itself. There have been several serious studies of the genre, and the most recent is found in the superb essay by Alan Lareau in *Theatre Journal* 43, 4 (471–90).

5. Peter Scher, review of *Improvisationen im Juni*, *Münchener Neueste Nachrichten*, 29 March 1922, 8.

7

The 1923–1924 Season

This season marked the breakthrough of Georg Kaiser into the ranks of successful comic playwrights. His Expressionist dramas *Von Morgens bis Mitternachts* (From Morn to Midnight), *Die Koralle* (The Coral), *Hölle-Weg-Erde* (Hell-Road-Earth), and *Gas* were well known, at least among the intelligentsia. His comedy *Nebeneinander* (Side by Side) was a humorous—some said "Hogarthian"[1]—depiction of life in Berlin during the crisis of inflation. The play presented vignettes "side by side" of "average" Berliners in their desperate attempts to survive. Featured was the unrequited love of a young pawnbroker for a girl who decided to marry a war profiteer;[2] in response, the pawnbroker committed suicide. His downfall parallels the improbable rise of a street peddler to film mogul. The fates of both are presented in the gritty atmosphere and "out-of-breath" dialogue style typical of Kaiser's Expressionist works. The appeal of *Nebeneinander* for provincial audiences was its confirmation of Berlin's reputation as an asphalt jungle, the very seat of corruption and moral decay. It made sense to most provincial Germans that someone could be sweeping floors in a soup kitchen one night and the next day find himself producing motion pictures. It made so much sense, in fact, that *Nebeneinander* was the most frequently produced comedy of the 1923–1924 season, marking the first time a Kaiser play had found widespread appeal and national popularity.

Kaiser's comedy is a social satire, a term likewise applicable to *Bürger Schippel* (Citizen Schippel) by Carl Sternheim. His plays, like many of Kaiser's "precomedic" works, had premiered during the Wilhelmine years in private, nonpublic productions. During the first years of the Weimar Republic, Sternheim and Kaiser benefited from the easing of censorship. *Bürger Schippel* proved to be Sternheim's most popular play throughout the Republic, and this season it received more performances (over 200) than anything Sternheim had hitherto written. Its spoof on Wilhelminian manners and morals concentrated on Paul Schippel, a penurious workman eager to join the middle class. First he had to prove himself as a tenor in a quartet consisting of government officials and successful businessmen. After his singing helps them win first prize in a local competition, Schippel gets into an argument with one of the quartet members over a woman; he slightly wounds his "rival" and is thus admitted with full honors into *Bürgertum* (the middle class). Sternheim targets both the pretensions of the middle class and the aspirations of the lower class, and during this season he hit both marks with consistent accuracy.

The other leaders during this season were last season's favorite by Max Mohr, *Improvisationen im Juni*, and *Der Sprung in die Ehe* (The Leap into Marriage) by Max Reimann and Otto Schwartz. Reimann and Schwartz constructed a superb piece of farce machinery tooled along lines of Franz Arnold and Ernst Bach. Its subject was Max Wendland, a textile manufacturer who makes the mistake of propositioning his wife's best friend. The best friend (named Charlotte von Arnstaedt) has the most dynamic role in the play, around whom several mistaken identities revolve. The innovation here is that three cases of mistaken identity operate simultaneously. The playwrights also spotlight the subject of money and its complete devaluation. Max has a brother who needs to borrow ten billion marks, and that small amount of cash (worth perhaps two dollars when the play premiered) proves to be the bridge for Charlotte's "leap" of the title.

Money and its mutable value were very much on the minds of Germans during this season, since at the season's onset a Reich Currency Committee had authorized the issuance of new legal tender, based on the economy's potential to produce cereal grains. That potential formed the basis by which the Reich government could secure international credit. The new currency did not appear until mid-November, by which time citizens were hauling billions of old Reichsmarks in wheelbarrows merely to purchase a loaf of bread.[3] The economy, however, did not respond well at first to the new currency; unemployment continued to rise and strikes multiplied. Crime rates escalated, and suicide reached historically high levels.[4]

The Reich government's policies were responsible for much of the ensuing disorder. Germany's difficulty in securing loans from abroad in 1923 and 1924 stemmed from social legislation that had created "a new clientele of 'superior' welfare recipients. Servicemen's relatives, widows, orphans, and disabled soldiers . . . were granted benefits based on their 'previous standard of living' and not, as previously, upon 'basic subsistence.'"[5]The Reichstag supplemented those provisions by passing more entitlement laws for the benefit of the disabled and the unemployed. Foreign creditors were unwilling to underwrite such expenditures, so Berlin continued to raise taxes; as a result, productivity plummeted.

The government meanwhile enacted measures to mollify French and Belgian occupation authorities in the Ruhr district. It declared an end to passive resistance because 132 Germans had been killed in clashes with French and Belgian troops, and eleven more had been executed by firing squads. The French and Belgians continued a punitive policy toward Germany, confiscating natural resources, supporting unrest along the Polish border, and deporting "troublesome" German nationals in occupied territories.

Among the most troublesome Germans on the domestic front were separatists in the Rhineland, who declared "independent republics" and challenged President Ebert to dislodge them. Revolutionaries in Munich, led by Adolf Hitler, staged a street demonstration on November 9, the fifth anniversary of the kaiser's abdication. They called for a seizure of power and declared a "provisional German national government." Local militia fired on the demonstrators, killing or wounding several. Hitler was arrested two days later and imprisoned. He was tried in February and given a five-year sentence in Landsberg prison on April 1; he was released after serving nine months of his sentence. The abortive putsch became an occasion for memorial remembrance among Hitler's followers. The devotees who died on November 9 became the "Sixteen Immortals," and the Nazi banner they carried became the "Blood Flag" Hitler used at Nazi rallies to anoint other flags, memorabilia, and hagiographic relics. Every year thereafter Hitler and Hermann Goering (who was wounded in the fracas) made a pilgrimage to Munich and retraced their steps toward the place where their comrades fell. And every year, thousands more German men claimed they had marched with Hitler on that fateful day in 1923.[6]

COMEDY PREMIERES OF 1923–1924

PLAYWRIGHT(S)	PLAY TITLE	CITY and THEATRE	DATE
Angermayer, Fred Antoine	*Komödie von Rosa*	Aussig Stadttheater	03/25/24
Apelt, Ulrich	*Herbst in Stolpen*	Zittau Stadttheater	02/23/24
Arnold, Franz, and Ernst Bach	*vertagte Nacht, Die*	Breslau Thalia Theater	02/04/24
Bacmeister, Ernst	*Barbara Stoßin*	Gotha Landestheater	01/31/24
Bock, Emilia	*Duellen der Heiligen Helene, Die*	Essen Schauspielhaus	02/29/24
Britting, Georg	*Stubenfliege, Die*	Munich Residenz-theater	09/22/23
Burg, Eugen, and Louis Taustein	*Ein Fehltritt*	Kattowitz Deutsches Theater	12/2/23
Davis, Gustav	*An der Barriere*	Hamburg Kleines Lustspielhaus	09/01/23
Eisenlohr, Fried-rich	*Pirat, Der*	Hamburg Thalia Theater	05/10/24
Feld, Leo	*verschnorkelte Gitter, Das*	Chemnitz Stadttheater	01/16/24

Freiburger, Kurt	*Braut des scharlachroten Tieres, Die*	Ulm Stadttheater	04/24/24
Fulda, Ludwig	*Gegenkandidaten*	Hamburg Deutsches Schauspielhaus	03/14/24
Haensel, Carl	*Menschen ohne Tragödie*	Heidelberg Stadttheater	11/13/23
Hahn, Erwin	*Jungfernvater, Der*	Greifswald Neues Stadttheater	03/26/24
Handtwarden, Bruno	*gefesselte Prometheus, Der*	Plauen Stadttheater	01/03/24
Hoffmann, Aaron	*Herzlich Wilkommen*	Hamburg Thalia Theater	05/26/24
Jonen, Hans	*Kumedemacher*	Cologne Freie Volksbühne	12/01/23
Kaiser, Georg	*Kolportage*	Berlin Lessing Theater	03/27/24
Kaiser, Georg	*Nebeneinander*	Berlin Lustspielhaus	11/17/23
Kihn, Alfred	*Meiseken*	Hamburg Thalia Theater	10/01/23
Klutmann, Rud	*Recht auf dem Vater, Das*	Hamburg Thalia Theater	03/26/24
Kornfeld, Paul	*Palme, oder der Gekränkte*	Berlin Kammerspiele des Deutschen Theaters	03/11/24
Lichtenberg, Wil-helm	*Schießbude, Die*	Kattowitz Deutsches Theater	02/10/24
Lothar, Rudolf, and Alfred Hahn	*Verführer, Der*	Altenburg Land-estheater	11/21/23
Marsen, Erich	*Dachvögel*	Wismar Stadttheater	11/30/23
Merz, Hans Otto	*Heimatstück, Das*	Bonn Stadttheater	06/20/24
Milne, A. A.	*Mr. Pim Passes By*	Berlin Charlottenburg Tribüne Theater	01/23/24
Mohr, Max	*Arbeiter Esau, Der*	Cologne Schau-spielhaus	10/31/23
Mohr, Max	*Karawane, Die*	Braunschweig Landestheater	05/28/24
Mohr, Max	*Still am Wrack*	Frankfurt/M. Neues Theater	10/17/23

Möller, Alfred	*silberne Kaninchen,Das*	Hamburg Thalia Theater	12/25/23
Müller-Schlösser, Hans	*Barbier von Pampelfort, Der*	Hamburg Thalia Theater	10/01/23
Musil, Robert	*Vinzenz, oder die Freundin bedeutender Männer*	Berlin Lustspielhaus	12/04/23
Niccodemi, David	*heilige Untreue, Die*	Berlin Deutsches Künstlertheater	03/16/24
Radatz, Hedwig	*Lew gegen Lew*	Rostock Städtische Bühne	05/01/24
Rademacher, Hanna	*Utopia*	Königsberg Neues Schauspielhaus	12/25/23
Rasquin, Jakob	*En brav Frau*	Cologne Metropol Theater	02/27/24
Rehfisch, Hans-José	*Wer weint um Juckenack?*	Leipzig Schauspielhaus	02/27/24
Reimann, Max, and Otto Schwartz	*Sprung in die Ehe, Der*	Frankfurt/M. Neues Theater	10/06/23
Robs, Fred	*Mein Vetter Eduard*	Berlin Komödienhaus	09/13/23
Rumpf, Fritz	*Liebestrank, Der*	Munich Kammerspiele	04/23/24
Sakatos, Ladislas	*eheliche Verhältnis, Das*	Hamburg Thalia Theater	06/21/24
Schein, Robert	*Aal, Der*	Reichenberg Stadttheater	03/13/24
Sloboda, Carl	*Wette, Die*	Hamburg Thalia Theater	03/22/24
Smirnoff, Karin	*Mächte*	Hamburg Deutsches Schauspielhaus	03/08/24
Stayton, Frank	*schwache Geschlecht, Das*	Hamburg Thalia Theater	04/05/24
Strecker, Karl	*Tybke*	Berlin Deutsches Künstlertheater	10/27/23
Tolstoy, Alexei	*Liebe, Die*	Frankfurt/M. Schauspielhaus	11/03/23
Vischer, Melchior	*Börse, Die*	Königsberg Neues Schauspielhaus	10/27/23
Wolf, Friedrich	schwarze Sonne, Die	Oldenburg Lan-destheater	01/22/24

Zerlitt, Hans H.	*Skandal mit Molly, Der*	Hamburg Kleines Lustspielhaus	03/15/24

NOTES

1. Ludwig Sternaux, quoted in Günther Rühle, *Theater für die Republik* (Frankfurt: Fischer, 1967): 483.

2. This was a theme shared by Brecht's *Trommeln in der Nacht* (Drums in the Night), which had premiered the previous season in Munich. Brecht's *Baal* made its world premiere during the 1923–1924 season in Leipzig to vociferous criticism. After a brief run, the mayor of Leipzig ordered the production closed.

3. On November 15, 1923, when the new Rentenmark was issued, one dollar would buy 4.2 billion old marks; the new mark was worth one billion old marks. The most arresting account of the ruinous inflation in Germany and its affect on the average citizen can be found in Erich Maria Remarque's novel *Der schwarze Obelisk* (The Black Obelisk).

4. By the end of 1923, unemployment totaled an unprecedented 1.47 million (nearly 28 percent of the unionized workforce), and nearly 2,000 strikes had interrupted production and delivery.

5. Detlev J. K. Peukert, *The Weimar Republic*, trans. Richard Daveson (New York: Hill and Wang, 1992), 137–141.

6. Jay Baird, *To Die for Germany* (Bloomington: Indiana University Press, 1990), 68.

8

The 1924–1925 Season

Georg Kaiser continued his rise within the ranks of popular comic playwrights during this season; his *Kolportage* (Pulp Fiction) topped the list of most frequently performed comedies of 1924–1925. It was followed by Franz Arnold and Ernst Bach's *Die vertagte Nacht* (It Happened One Night), and *Der Sprung in die Ehe* (The Leap Into Marriage) by Max Reimann and Otto Schwartz.

Kolportage was a parody of plays popular in previous Weimar seasons ridiculing the aristocracy; it also borrowed narrative elements of pseudohistorical dramas and plot devices from melodrama. Kaiser dedicated his "comedy with a prologue and three acts taking place twenty years later" to "the welfare of children and to the contemporary theatre," which was Kaiser's derisive slap at popular theatrical taste. He recognized, according to Ernst Schürer, that the audience for his Expressionistic dramas had disappeared. An appeal to a larger audience was necessary if he were to survive as a playwright, so he presented a cliché-ridden piece of kitsch featuring "decadent aristocrats, a wealthy uncle from America, a wiry cowboy, a young couple in love, and a good-hearted proletarian mother."[1]

Critic Herbert Ihering described Kaiser's clichés as *Stichwörter* ("catch words"), meaning the playwright loaded his dialogue with more than empty jargon. This comedy's significance, he said, lay in his choice of words with *Übertragungs-fähigkeit*, or words with an ability evoke a certain response in audiences before developing an ideological structure for the response.[2] A good example is the dialogue between the young Count Stjernenhö and the Countess Barrenkrona. The idea is the giddiness of young love, but they talk about "hitting bull's eyes," "getting off a good shot," and "being on target," while in fact they evade talking about their true feelings. Kaiser's dialogue techniques were copied in the early 1930s by Ödön von Horváth with similar effect, although von Horváth made remarkable use of character types borrowed from the traditional German folk play.

As noted earlier, Kaiser used character types familiar to audiences from comedies with proven popularity and box-office appeal. The plot stressed the efforts of the bourgeois wife of the elder Count Stjernenhö to preserve the inheritance rights of her son. She "bought" a child from a peasant woman, disguised him as the heir, and allowed him to be kidnaped by the Count's agents. She then departed with her son for a farm in Kansas. Her estranged husband reared the false heir in the family estate, but on the eve of the true heir's twenty-first birthday mother and son arrive to claim rightful legacy. The play had predictable instances of aristocratic decadence, but featured American innocence (personified by the true heir, who has become a cowboy in Kansas), the inherent goodness of the false heir (who eventually marries a countess anyway), and notable sudden reversals of fortune. It was indeed a melodramatic and "trashy" story—but one German audiences liked immensely. One of Kaiser's most popular plays, it enjoyed numerous revivals throughout the 1920s.

Arnold and Bach presented what was by the 1924–1925 an almost patented formula, one which they alone seemed able season after season to repeat successfully. *Die vertagte Nacht* (It Happened One Night) featured familiar characters and situations. Once again a dancer (not the "Spanish Fly" this time, but one almost identical to her named Elli Ornelli) poses a threat to the domestic tranquility of a solid bourgeois family. The singularity here is that the wives of the family (a mother and her two daughters) mistakenly assume that their husbands (the father and his two sons-in-law) all are having affairs with her. The women indeed have nearly irrefutable proof of spousal waywardness, because the play's second act contrives to have each gentleman discovered in bed with Miss Ornelli. Arnold and Bach managed to make each instance both innocent yet plausible, since they so cleverly arranged the incidents leading up to each discovery. Audiences found their cleverness charming, but most engaging was the father of the family (played by Guido Thielscher), who is dedicated to helping his sons-in-law rehabilitate their relationships with his daughters. In the process he nearly destroys his own marriage.

At first glance, this domestic farce seems like an agreeable piece of escapism. On closer examination it emerges, as Bernd Wilms has demonstrated, as an extension of everyday German life. It fashions the cares and tensions of an average bourgeois and exaggerates them to the point of "elasticity."[3] At that point, Wilms argues, the audience's is disengaged and their passivity is so reinforced as to allow the pleasant sensation of personal acquaintance with the central character. He is furthermore a man everyone recognizes because his tribulations are so familiar. He is a model for the audience to follow, since he never ruminates on war or on political crisis—and yet he survives. Somehow he made it through 1918, he will make it through the inflation catastrophe of 1923, and he will make it through the crisis he now faces with his wife and daughters. "He's like the balloon figure children punch, and who keeps bouncing back."[4]

Audience identification with a character who could "bounce back" was understandable during this season, one which saw for the first time, since the war's end, a faint glimmer of hope for a return to prosperity and order. Germany received a loan of $50 billion from a consortium of American banks, based on the convertibility of the new German currency. Germany and the Soviet Union concluded a pact which provided reliable delivery of crude oil to German refineries, and the Reich government was able to negotiate reparation payments in the form of raw materials like coal, coke, and iron ore. Production in several industries began to increase.

German hopes for stability were sorely tested in February of this season, however, when Reich President Friedrich Ebert died at the age of fifty-four of complications following an appendectomy. His death was completely unanticipated, and it precipitated an unseemly contest for succession. It also set off a vulgar debate within the Reichstag over the responsibility of costs for Ebert's funeral. Even before he was buried, Communist leaders labeled Ebert a "helper's helper of International Capital," while Nazi politicians accused Ebert of impotence.[5] The presidential voting that followed resulted in the narrow election of Field Marshal Paul von Beneckendorff und Hindenburg to a five-year term. Hindenburg was seventy-eight years old at the time of his election. He had already spent sixty of those years in uniform; he was a Prussian aristocrat and Germany's only heroic wartime strategist. He had defeated the Russians at Tannenberg, but he was completely unprepared for a political career, as he himself admitted. "I can fulfill this task more easily," he intoned at his inaugural address to members of the Reichstag in 1925, "if the parties of this esteemed house will not indulge in petty quarrels about advantages for a party or economic group but will compete with each other in serving our hard-pressed people faithfully and effectively."[6] His appeal, like those of the men found with Elli Ornelli, fell on deaf ears.

COMEDY PREMIERES OF 1924–1925

PLAYWRIGHT(S)	PLAY TITLE	CITY and THEATRE	DATE
Arnold, Franz, and Ernst Bach	*wahre Jakob, Der*	Berlin Lustspielhaus	12/20/24
Bachwitz, Hans	*Göttin auf der Balz, Die*	Hamburg Kleines Lustspielhaus	01/03/25
Backer, William	*Heimliche Ehen*	Hamburg Thalia Theater	09/25/24
Bacmeister, Ernst	*Schlange, Die*	Constance Stadttheater	01/24/25
Bang, Ole	*alte Erich, Der*	Halberstadt Stadttheater	03/03/25
Berger, Ludwig	*goldene Schnitt, Der*	Königsberg Städtisches Schauspielhaus	03/14/25
Birabeau, Georges	*Zurück zur Schule*	Berlin Komödie	02/18/25
Braun, Hanns	*Abenteuer in Moll*	Darmstadt Landestheater	03/12/25
Deval, Jacques	*Armer Kleiner*	Munich Schauspielhaus	03/26/25

Dreyer, Max	*Gust Botefuer*	Hamburg Thalia Theater	01/20/25
Eckehard, Gabriele	*Liebeskonzert*	Berlin Intimes Theater	09/21/24
Eisenzahn, Hans	*Frau von Klasse, Die*	Hannover Deutsches Theater	04/25/25
Engel, Georg	*Diplomaten*	Hamburg Thalia Theater	10/24/24
Erler, Otto	*Galgenstrick, Der*	Dresden Staatliches Schauspielhaus	03/03/25
Evans, Will	*Geld wie Heu*	Berlin Lustspielhaus	11/05/25
Fauchois, Rene	*sprechende Affe, Der*	Berlin Komödie	04/08/25
Fischer, E. F.	*Am Tisch der Liebe*	Reichenberg Stadttheater	02/27/25
Franck, Hans	*Martha und Maria*	Dortmund Stadttheater	11/30/24
Galsworthy, John	*Fenster, Das*	Königsberg Neues Schauspielhaus	11/22/24
Goetz, Curt	*tote Tante, Die*	Berlin Kammerspiele des Deutschen Theaters	10/01/24
Grötsch, Robert	*Lächeln der Frau Staatsanwalt, Das*	Dresden Neues Theater	10/25/24
Händel, Carl	*Gummizeit*	Darmstadt Landestheater	03/28/25
Hahn, Paul Edmund	*Familie Krull, Die*	Stuttgart Schauspielhaus	07/27/25
Harlan, Walter	*Frühstück in Genoa, Das*	Bremen Schauspielhaus	04/25/25
Hesse, Otto Ernst	*Maske, Die*	Frankfurt /M. Neues Theater	03/21/25
Hopwood, Avery	*Amerikanische Frauen*	Karlsruhe Landestheater	05/24/25
Ibele, Maria	*dritte Tasse, Die*	Constance Stadttheater	10/12/24
Ilges, F. W.	*weiße Kätchen, Das*	Krefeld Stadttheater	05/08/25
Impekoven, Toni and Carl Mathern	*Otto der Treue*	Frankfurt /M. Neues Theater	11/26/25
Jensen, Thit	*Ihre königliche Hoheit*	Hamburg Thalia Theater	02/03/25
Johst, Hanns	*Ausländer, Der*	Baden-Baden Städtisches Schauspielhaus	05/15/25
Josty, Felix	*blaue Stunde, Die*	Berlin Trianon Theater	06/03/25
Kempner-Hochstadt, Max	*Phryne*	Hamburg Thalia Theater	10/22/24
Kisch, Egon	*gestohlene Stadt, Die*	Stuttgart Schauspielhaus	07/00/25

Klabund (Alfred Henschke)	*Hannibals Brautfahrt*	Breslau Lobe Theater	11/08/24
Klarß, Sophie, and Elisabeth Albrecht	*Vadder Kmack*	Schwerin Landestheater	04/24/25
Krohn, Ernst	*Onkel Sam*	Hamburg Thalia Theater	09/20/24
Lenergke, W. von	*Fräulein du Portail, Das*	Leipzig Schauspielhaus	11/08/24
Lenz, Leo	*heimliche Brautfahrt, Die*	Hamburg Deutsches Schauspielhaus	10/08/24
Lissauer, Ernst	*Gewalt*	Frankfurt /M. Neues Theater	11/15/24
Lothar, Rudolf, and Oskar Franz Winterstein	*Herzogin von Elba, Die*	Hamburg Thalia Theater	02/28/25
Lothar, Rudolf	*schöne Melusine, Die*	Hamburg Kleines Lustspielhaus	01/19/25
Lothar, Rudolf	*sprechende Schuh, Der*	Hamburg Thalia Theater	11/15/25
Manz, Richard	*Keuschheits Konkurrenz*	Stuttgart Bauerntheater	12/22/24
Maugham, W. Somerset	*China*	Bochum Stadttheater	09/30/24
Mayer, Wilhelm	*Scheidungsessen, Das*	Munich Residenztheater	03/07/25
Milne, A. A.	*romantische Alter, Die*	Berlin Renaissance Theater	03/11/25
Milne, A. A.	*Weg nach Dover, Der*	Hamburg Thalia Theater	12/23/24
Müller, Hans	*Tokaier, Der*	Berlin Theater in der Königgrätzerstraße	11/28/24
Neal, Max, and Otto Franck	*wertbeständige Tante, Die*	Munich Volkstheater	10/31/24
Paul, Adolf	*Sie läßt sich nicht verkaufen*	Berlin Trianon Theater	12/06/24
Pirandello, Luigi	*Besser als früher*	Berlin Kleines Theater	09/05/25
Pirandello, Luigi	*Heinrich IV*	Hamburg Thalia Theater	03/25/25
Pirandello, Luigi	*Lebende Maske*	Hamburg Thalia Theater	03/25/25
Pirandello, Luigi	*Wollust der Ehrlichkeit, Die*	Darmstadt Lustspieltheater	01/15/25
Raff, Franz	*Expedition ins Innere, Die*	Stuttgart Schauspielhaus	08/29/25

Rickelt, Gustav	*Glückspilz, Der*	Guben Stadttheater	11/12/24
Roland, Frank	*Sam Fox, amerikanischer Milliardär*	Kiel Schauspielhaus	10/04/24
Romains, Jules	*Dr. Knock*	Cologne Schauspielhaus	05/05/25
Scheffer, Herbert	*Cagliosto*	Halberstadt Stadttheater	01/18/25
Schiff, Bert	*Bankkrach*	Halle Stadttheater	5/29/25
Schmidt, Lothar	*Okkulte Geister*	Magdeburg Wilhelminisches Theater	03/03/25
Schmitt, Heinrich	*große Erlebnis, Das*	Schwerin Landestheater	05/26/25
Schulz, Franz	*Esther Labarre*	Stuttgart Schauspielhaus	07/04/25
Schwartz, Otto, and Max Reimann	*Durch den Rundfunk*	Frankfurt /M. Neues Theater	01/10/25
Shaw, George Bernard	*Borkampf*	Frankfurt/M. Stadttheater	01/08/25
Shaw, George Bernard	*St. Joan*	Dresden Schauspielhaus	10/13/24
Smith, Winchell, and Mapes, Viktor	*Bumerang der Liebe, Der*	Schwerin Landestheater	02/13/25
Stayton, Frank	*Große Pause*	Frankfurt /O. Alberti Theater	12/02/24
Stücklen, Melchior	*Orientalin, Die*	Berlin Lustspielhaus	12/01/24
Theis, Geert	*Meister oder Meister*	Flensburg Stadttheater	09/25/24
Thomson, Fred	*Bräutigamswitwe, Die*	Kiel Stadttheater	05/17/25
Trebitsch, Siegfried	*Geliebte, Der*	Frankfurt /M. Neues Theater	04/04/25
Trenck-Ulrici, Ulrich von	*Lustspielprobe, Die*	Karlsruhe Badisches Lustspieltheater	09/04/24
Unger, Hellmuth	*beliebte Beifu, Der*	Mainz Stadttheater	10/10/24
Urban, Hans	*Fünf Minuten vor der Ehe*	Schwäbisch Hall Kurtheater	02/12/25
Vajda, Ernst Ennö	*Harem, Der*	Berlin Komödientheater	03/26/25
Verneuil, Louis	*Kusine aus Warschau, Die*	Berlin Komödienhaus	03/17/25
Warmbold, Alice	*Bildungsdame, Die*	Göttingen Stadttheater	01/15/25
Wrack, Otto	*weiße Weste, Die*	Berlin Neues Theater am Zoo	02/20/25

NOTES

1. Ernst Schürer, *Georg Kaiser* (Boston: Twayne, 1971), 129–130.

2. Quoted in Günther Rühle, *Theater für die Republik* (Frankfurt: Fischer, 1967), 515.

3. At one point, Elli Ornelli and the younger daughter exchange places with each other three times in succession, stretching Klaus Reiling's credulity to the point of near hysteria.

4. Bernd Wilms, "Der Schwank: Das Trivialtheater 1880–1930" (Ph.D. diss., Freie Universität Berlin, 1969), 90–91.

5. The Nazi leader, Adolf Hitler, had been given early release from Landsberg prison and placed on probation. He was banned from speaking in all German provinces—including even Bavaria, where his party headquarters were located and where he drew much of his support.

6. Andreas Dorpalen, *Hindenburg and the Weimar Republic* (Princeton, NJ: Princeton University Press, 1964), 88.

9

The 1925–1926 Season

Franz Arnold and Ernst Bach followed their success of *Die vertagte Nacht* (It Happened One Night) with *Der wahre Jakob* (The Real Jacob), which once again featured plot complications centered around a dancer. "Why even bother with critical analysis?" asked one critic from a Berlin newspaper. "This comedy is the 100th variant on a familiar theme; the only difference is that [Guido] Thielscher sweats through three collars and the ladies in loge seats go through three hankies drying their tears of laughter."[1] The "familiar theme" was that of a moralist (named Peter Struwe, played by Thielscher) who uses a business trip to Berlin as an excuse for backsliding into sinful adventure. In the big city he poses as "Jakob" and arranges a tête-a-tête with a cabaret dancer named Yvette. Unbeknownst to Jakob is the unsettling fact that Yvette is his stepdaughter. Yvette follows him back to his local town, where he engages in several hilarious feats of chicanery to hide his "sins" from Yvette's mother and to maintain his position as a pillar of rectitude in society.

Sins of the flesh portrayed by Arnold and Bach usually remained sins of intent, shrouded by mistaken identity, misunderstandings, or transparent plot twists. Carl Zuckmayer imitated their plot techniques in his *Der fröhliche Weinberg* (The Merry Vineyard) but created characters with unprecedented earthiness who openly effected their sexual compulsions. Zuckmayer's record as a playwright had been inconsequential to date, having written two dramas in the Expressionist manner. The first closed after four performances and the other after only one. *Der fröhliche Weinberg* had been refused by all major Berlin producers, as no one familiar with Berlin's theatre business expected a popular comedy from Zuckmayer—no one, that is, except critic Paul Fechter, who in November awarded him the Kleist Prize for the comedy. The award attracted the attention of producer Heinz Saltenburg, who agreed to a limited run in his Theater am Schiffbauerdamm.

Zuckmayer's comedy became one of the most frequently performed of the

1925–1926 season, as well as its most controversial. There were public demonstrations against it in sixty- three cities, ironically mimicking efforts of the hypocritical Peter Struwe portrayed in the Arnold and Bach comedy.[2] At least one local court indicted Zuckmayer for blasphemy, but the play's theme was less blasphemous than it was impious.[3] Its central character was a vintner from the Rhineland who insisted that his daughter first become pregnant before marrying the man of her choice. Since her dowry included one-half of his prosperous vineyard, she had no shortage of potential suitor/sires. The vintner himself copulates with a local girl forty-five years his junior in a neighboring barn during the play, so the sense of moral indignation felt by sixty-three provincial communities was perhaps understandable.[4] The comedy also included debates about preferred size of the male organ, a comparison of fertility rates between women and brood sows, and an unapologetic assertion that wine consumption fostered male potency.

Zuckmayer's characters, unlike those of Arnold and Bach, were full of *Kraft und Saft* (strength and juice) in the colorful metaphor of critic Alfred Kerr; most other critics agreed with him (especially those in Berlin), and *Der fröhliche Weinberg* established Zuckmayer as one of the German theatre's most successful playwrights. He was not successful, however, among Nazi critics; they noted that most of the theatre critics in Berlin were Jews[5] and that Zuckmayer himself was partly Jewish. The Nazi press claimed that Berlin critics were thus inclined to favor "this unbelievable swinery," as they termed Zuckmayer's comedy. They said the playwright had "made a mockery of the Christian viewpoint, of German morals, [and] of German women."[6]

The Nazi reaction was an extreme one at the time, but Nazi viewpoints began to find wider acceptance as Hindenburg's presidency began to move cultural perspectives in more traditional, conservative directions. Lengthy and impassioned quarrels beset the 1926 Reichstag debate of the proposed "Gesetz zur Bewahrung der Jugend vor Schund- und Schmutzzeitschriften" (Protection of Youth against Indecent and Obscene Publications Act), a bill prompted by plays like Zuckmayer's, nude dancing in Berlin cabarets, fiction that celebrated deviant sexual behavior, and by questionable films and radio broadcasts. Sergei Eisenstein's film *Battleship Potemkin*, for example, was banned in Bavaria, Hessia, Württemburg, and Thuringia as "a danger to public safety." Novelist Hans Fallada was sent to prison for two and one-half years; Ernst Toller had been in prison for most of the decade; Georg Kaiser and Erwin Piscator had spent time in jail, the actor Rolf Gärtner had been sentenced to fifteen months on a morals charge. In response, leading figures of German arts, letters, and culture convened at the Theater am Nollendorf Platz in Berlin to discuss government and judicial attacks upon German cultural life. Several actors, playwrights, publishers, critics, and even scientists (including Albert Einstein), along with politicians, all of them left-leaning, signed a 1926 declaration titled "For the Freedom of Art."

COMEDY PREMIERES OF 1925–1926

PLAYWRIGHT(S)	PLAY TITLE	CITY and THEATRE	DATE
Adelt, Leonhardt	*Dohle, Die*	Dortmund Stadttheater	12/12/25
Armont, Paul	*Liebling der Familie, Der*	Hamburg Thalia Theater	03/16/26
Arnold, Franz, and Ernst Bach	*Stöpsel*	Berlin Neues Theater am Zoo	01/21/26
Bachwitz, Hans, and Fritz Jacob-stetter	*Jennys Bummel*	Karlsruhe Landestheater	05/30/26
Baudoyer, J. L.	*venezianische Kloster, Das*	Darmstadt Landestheater	03/24/26
Becker, Julius Maria	*Wundermann, Der*	Dessau Friedrich Theater	04/23/26
Berger, Ludwig	*Kronprinzessin Luisa*	Berlin Deutsches Künstlertheater	01/15/26
Bergman, Hjalmar	*Nobelpreis, Der*	Berlin Deutsches Künstlertheater	07/31/26
Bernauer, Rudolf, and Rudolf Öster-reicher	*Garten-Eden, Der*	Berlin Komödienhaus	02/04/26
Bernhardt, D.E.	*Erdenbaum*	Stolp Stadttheater	01/29/26
Birbeau, Georges	*Figuranten*	Frankfurt /M. Neues Theater	10/31/25
Bogeler, Adolf	*weiße Weste, Die*	Hildesheim Stadttheater	10/14/25
Borchhardt, Rudolf	*Geliebte Kleinigkeit*	Düsseldorf Schau-spielhaus	12/13/25
Charlier, Gerd, and Charles Appelles	*Gaukelspiel der Liebe*	Harburg /O. Stadttheater	03/14/26
Cornelius, Franz	*Ring des Polykrates, Der*	Schwerin Landestheater	05/04/26
Coward, Noel	*Week-End*	Berlin Kammerspiele des Deutschen Theaters	04/24/26
Cremers, Paul Josef	*Muspilli, oder der Prinz von Oahu*	Lübeck Stadttheater	12/08/25
Dragely, Gabor, and Emmerich Liplai	*rote Mann, Der*	Hamburg Thalia Theater	03/02/26

Excking, Ottomar	*Glückswagen, Der*	Dresden Sächsische Landesbühne	01/09/26
Friedrich, Karl	*Verlorenen, Die*	Dresden Sächsische freie Wanderbühne	10/29/25
Fulda, Ludwig	*Durchgängerin, Die*	Berlin Residenztheater	12/18/25
Gheon, Henri	*Spiel vom Gehenkten, Das, der am Leben blieb*	Frankfurt /M. Künstler-theater	11/23/25
Glass, Montague, and Jules Eckert	*Pottasch und Perl-mutter*	Berlin Lustspielhaus	10/31/25
Günther, Johannes von, and Paul Baudisch	*Reinicke*	Munich Residenztheater	01/27/26
Harwich, Otto	*Herr mit den drei Vätern, Der*	Bremen Schauspielhaus	05/20/26
Hesse, Otto Ernst	*Liebeslehre, Die*	Schwerin Landestheater	10/13/25
Hesse, Otto Ernst	*Klinkutsch*	Hamburg Kleines Lust-spielhaus	12/01/25
Himmighofen, Friedrich, and Rolf Schmittheimer	*doppelte Bräutigam, Der*	Lübeck Stadttheater	05/25/26
Horst, Julius	*Radiotenor, Der*	Brunn Deutsches Schau-spielhaus	12/31/25
Impekoven, Toni, and Carl Mathern	*doppelte Moritz, Der*	Hamburg Kammerspiele	06/16/26
Jerome, Jerome K.	*Mein schönes Fräulein, darf ich wagen*	Düsseldorf Schau-spielhaus	10/06/25
Johst, Hanns	*Herr Monsieur, Der*	Krefeld Stadttheater	07/05/26
Kaiser, Georg	*mutige Seefahrer, Der*	Dresden Staatliches Schauspielhaus	11/12/25
Kaiser, Georg	*Margarine*	Berlin Komödienhaus	09/04/25
Kanzler, Friedrich	*Brief, Der*	Hamburg Kammerspiele	10/03/25
Kasack, Hermann	*Schwester, Die*	Heilbronn Stadttheater	01/24/26
Kästner, Leo, and Alfred Möller	*Dame, welche?, Die*	Hamburg Kleines Lust-spielhaus	02/21/26
Kaufmann, Willy	*Kavaliere der Herzog-in, Die*	Hannover Deutsches Theater	09/19/25
Kerl, F. A.	*Galgenfrist, Die*	Hildesheim Stadttheater	11/19/25

Kraatz, Curt, and Max Neal	*O diese Bubiköpfe*	Bad Nauheim Kurtheater	08/25/26
Krickeberg, Karl	*All verschieden*	Rostock Stadttheater	10/24/25
Lenz, Leo	*Totenkopfhusaren*	Hamburg Deutsches Schauspielhaus	12/26/25
Lonsdale, Frederic	*Mrs. Cheyneys Ende*	Berlin Theater in der Königgrätzerstrasse	03/12/26
Luria, Lajos	*Glatze und der Bubikopf, Die*	Flensburg Stadttheater	04/18/26
Marcrini, Carl	*Recht der zweiten Nacht*	Leipzig Kleines Theater	06/19/26
Maugham, W. Somerset	*oberen Zehntausend, Die*	Hamburg Thalia Theater	01/19/26
Monjardin, Alain	*Liebe im Zickzack*	Hamborn Stadttheater	02/24/26
Müller-Hoyer, Karl	*Gemeinde Schmuggeldorf*	Dresden Albert Theater	05/07/26
Nehlert, Benno	*Schwalben*	Halle Stadttheater	01/28/26
Neumann, Siegmund, and Erich Kuhn	*Gruschke*	Frankfurt /O. Stadttheater	10/21/25
Palitsch, Otto Alfred	*Kurve Links*	Cologne Kammerspiele	10/06/25
Pesset, Wolfgang	*Lassalle*	Bremen Schauspielhaus	11/25/25
Picard, Andre	*Herr von Saint-Obin*	Berlin Komödienhaus	12/27/26
Pirandello, Luigi	*Jeder nach seiner Art*	Darmstadt Hessisches Landestheater	10/19/25
Pirandello, Luigi	*Spiel der Parteien, Das*	Mannheim Nationaltheater	09/19/25
Pohlmann, Jarry	*Teufel durch Beelzebub, Den*	Gießen Stadttheater	11/27/25
Rehfisch, Hans-José	*Duell am Lido*	Berlin Staatliches Schauspielhaus	02/20/26
Rehfisch, Hans-José	*Nicjel und die 36 Gerechten*	Magdeburg Wilhelm Theater	10/18/25
Ritzel, Jörg	*Attentat, Das*	Coblenz Stadttheater	01/27/26
Rokow, Hans	*Ich suche meinen Mann*	Hamburg Kleines Lustspielhaus	02/26/26

Rollinghoff, C. A.	*Fräulein Eulenspiegel*	Berlin Intimes Theater	03/23/26
Schäffer, Albrecht	*Gefallige, Der*	Chemnitz Schauspielhaus	03/11/26
Schanzer, Rudolf and Ernst Walisch	*Rebhuhn*	Berlin Theater am Kurfürstendamm	05/01/26
Scheffler, Herbert	*Unsterblichkeit*	Bremen Schauspielhaus	05/20/26
Schendell, Werner	*Wehrgreis, Der*	Breslau Thalia Theater	11/03/25
Schlesinger, Hans	*Lelian*	Teplitz-Schönau Stadttheater	06/10/26
Schmalfeldt, Willy, and Christel Hilker	*Flucht ins Glück, Die*	Bad Salzschlirf Kurtheater	07/15/26
Schneider, Rudolf	*Bluff*	Stuttgart Landestheater	10/11/25
Schwarz, Otto, and Carl Mathern	*goldene Kalb, Das*	Frankfurt /M. Neues Theater	06/21/26
Selten, Fritz	*Foppke, der Egoist*	Berlin Residenztheater	02/25/26
Shaw, George Bernard	*Zurück zu Methusalem*	Berlin Tribüne Theater	09/11/25
Stavenhagen, Fritz	*deutsche Michel, Der*	Berlin Volksbühne	06/16/26
Stein, Leo Walter	*Held des Tages, Der*	Dresden Neues Theater	07/01/26
Stranik, Erwin	*Flucht, Die*	Klagenfurt Stadttheater	12/29/25
Sturm, Hans	*Irrgarten der Liebe*	Leipzig Schauspielhaus	11/08/25
Vogt-Wenzel, Thea	*Dr. Neuberg's Eheirrung*	Eger Stadttheater	01/13/26
Witt-Ebernitz, Hans	*Garderobe Nr. 7*	Frankfurt /O. Stadtheater	09/26/25
Witte, Julius, and Heinz Friedrich	*Gelegenheits-kavalier*	Zwickau Stadttheater	06/08/26
Zuckmayer, Carl	*fröhliche Weinberg, Der*	Berlin Theater am Schiffbauerdamm	12/22/25

NOTES

1. "Thielscher im Lustspielhaus," review of *Der wahre Jakob* in *Berliner Morgenpost*, 21 December 1924, n. p.

2. The most curious demonstration against the play took place in the Rhineland city of Mainz, where Zuckmayer grew up and upon whose citizens he based several characters. There demonstrators carried signs and protested loudly during the day but were found in the theatre at night, watching themselves portrayed on the stage.

3. The painter and scene designer Georg Grosz, himself convicted of blasphemy earlier in the decade for a drawing of the crucified Christ wearing a gas mask, presented Zuckmayer with a certificate of membership to the "League of Faithful Blasphemers" at the close of this season.

4. There was no sense of moral outrage in Berlin, where Zuckmayer's comedy premiered at the Theater am Schiffbauerdamm, only an extraordinary demand for tickets. The play continued to run in that theatre for the next two and one-half years.

5. Thirty per cent of all German Jews lived in Berlin during the Weimar Republic, and indeed many theatre critics, directors, actors, and playwrights were Jewish. Among directors, Leopold Jessner and Max Reinhardt were most prominent. Jewish playwrights who contributed outstanding comedies included Franz Arnold, Ernst Bach, Max Reimann, Rudolph Presber, Bruno Frank, Rudolf Bernauer, Max Mohr, along with dozens of others.

6. Günther Rühle, *Theater für die Republik* (Frankfurt: Fischer, 1967) 667.

10

The 1926–1927 Season

The German economy regained a measure of health during this season—a trend begun the previous year with help from the Dawes Plan.[1] Business activity increased, unemployment figures dropped, industrial output soared,[2] and more productions were staged in German theatres than at any other time since the war. The play receiving more productions than any other (nearly 1,100) was *Stöpsel* (The Runt) by Franz Arnold and Ernst Bach, which opened the previous season at Berlin's Neues Theater am Zoo under Arnold's direction. After a four-week run there, it opened under Bach's direction at the Munich Volkstheater. It ran in those two houses for the remainder of the 1925–1926 season, creating demand for bookings from theatres throughout the Reich, whose repertoires it then proceeded to dominate during this season.

Carl Zuckmayer's lusty comedy about love in the vineyards of the Rhineland maintained its popularity, although it did not challenge *Stöpsel* for heading the list of most frequently performed comedies of the season.[3] Zuckmayer was followed by the Englishman Frederic Lonsdale, whose "criminal-comedy" *The Last of Mrs. Cheyney,* titled *Mrs. Cheyneys Ende* in German, concerned an Australian "widow" thieving her way through British high society, stealing jewels and breaking the heart of every possible eligible, upper-crust British bachelor. It had opened in London's West End in 1924 and on November 10, 1925, in New York City to popular acclaim in both cities; it was subsequently made into a film and has enjoyed numerous revivals.[4] The German premiere, under the direction of Viktor Barnowsky, took place the previous season. Its success prompted over fifty provincial stages this season to mount productions. The appeal of *Mrs. Cheyneys Ende* among Berlin audiences resulted in large measure from the presence of Elisabeth Bergener in the title role, though its dialogue suffered from "sub-Wildean epigrams" (according to one German critic). German audiences in general found its plot and characters delightfully "English and exotic."[5]

Its treatment of criminality and commoners posing as aristocrats was similar to the Arnold and Bach farce, whose first act takes place in the lobby of a luxury hotel on the Lido in Venice. There all manner of newly rich German industrialists encounter destitute Italian aristocrats, and complications arise to dictate the plot's development in the remaining two acts. The first act is actually a one-act play, complete in itself and forming a prelude to coming events. The principal action concerns the attempt by the corpulent Otto Piper (played by—who else?—Guido Thielscher) to have a rendezvous with a young woman while he is in Venice on business. The lobby is an ideal meeting-place for all sorts of characters, and Piper arranges to meet "Ossi" later that evening. The hotel manager assists Piper's efforts by ordering the hotel string trio to provide background music for their encounter in a private dining room. The violinist of this group is Alphonse Vallé, an impecunious Italian count. The affair, however, miscarries when Ossi's husband discovers his wife kissing "Stöpsel" (the name Otto Piper prefers) before they get to the place of assignation.

Acts II and III take place in the ostentatious "Schloß Rosenhöh" (Rose Heights Palace) in Berlin, where Piper, his equally ostentatious wife Adele, and their daughter Erika barely endure the rigors of life in the palace's meagre thirty-eight rooms. The complication here is Adele's intention to wed Erika to a nobleman. She has thus enlisted the help of the matchmaker Baroness Winkelsbühl, whom Otto recognizes from an encounter years ago in a dance parlor when she was Mitzi Klinkert—a fact he naturally wants to keep secret from his wife. The "Baroness" has done her job, however; she introduces Erika to Count Toscani, who happens also to be Alphonse Vallé, violinist at the Lido hotel. Vallé recounts the hilarious story he heard in Venice about a rotund little businessman who called himself Stöpsel; Vallé says a pair of confidence tricksters extorted 400,000 lire from the little man by threatening him with court action for ruining their "marriage."

At this point, Arnold and Bach ingeniously arrange entrances by characters from Act I to join Vallé at the palace. Piper furiously tries to keep knowledge of his identity as Stöpsel from his wife, while trying simultaneously to dissuade her from marrying their daughter off to a man he assumes is simply another Italian con artist. He becomes convinced that he is surrounded by criminals, and he calls the police. When they arrive, they greet him with the name "Stöpsel." Piper silently recognizes that discretion is indeed the better part of valor, and he elects to grant the marriage of his daughter to the impoverished count.

Arnold and Bach's capitalization on the humorous potential of the wealthy mercantile class in league with criminals was reflected in ominous political trends during this season. Many German industrialists feared a return to the chaos of Ebert's presidency. They thus sought to support political parties with agendas fostering tighter domestic control. When publisher Hugo Bruckmann and industrialist Emil Kirdorff met with Adolf Hitler in a Munich villa in 1926, they arranged financial support for Hitler's National Socialist party. That included a subvention for Hitler's third book (*The Road to Recovery*) and underwriting publication of the Nazi daily *Der Angriff* (The Attack) in Berlin. Their meeting unknowingly mirrored "Stöpsel's" dealings with charlatans.[6]

COMEDY PREMIERES OF 1926–1927

PLAYWRIGHT(S)	PLAY TITLE	CITY and THEATRE	DATE
Achard, Marcel	*Wollen Sie mit mir spielen?*	Düsseldorf Schauspielhaus	12/31/26
Adler, Hans	*Liebst du mich?*	Stettin Bellevue Theater	02/16/27
Angermayer, Fred A.	*Kirschwasser*	Kiel Schauspielhaus	11/02/26
Arnold, Franz, and Ernst Bach	*Hurrah—ein Junge!*	Berlin Lustspielhaus	12/22/26
Barry, Philip	*Du und ich*	Brunn Schauspielhaus	10/24/26
Bergmann, Hjalmar	*Herr Sleemann kommt*	Bad Godesberg Schauspielbühne	03/09/27
Bernard, Tristram	*Perle, Die*	Berlin Theater der Komödie	01/01/27
Berr, Georges, and Louis Berneuil	*Dr. Bolbec und seine Gatte*	Berlin Renaissance Theater	08/04/27
Berstl, Julius	*Dover-Calais*	Danzig Stadttheater	12/23/26
Bolton, Guy, and George Middleton	*Adam und Eva*	Nuremberg Altes Stadttheater	11/17/26
Borrmann, Martin, and Gerhard Pohlmann	*Chaos bei Tinkauzer*	Königsberg Ostpreussisches Landestheater	11/13/26
Brecht, Bertolt	*Mann ist Mann*	Darmstadt Landestheater and Düsseldorf Städtisches Theater	09/25/26
Brentano, Bernard	*Geld*	Darmstadt Landestheater	01/15/27
Brod, Max, and G. R. von Nack	*Opunzie, Die*	Düsseldorf Städtisches Theater	02/16/27
Deval, Jacques	*Frau an der Kette, Die*	Berlin Theater an der Kurfürstendamm	11/20/26
Eckerle, Fritz	*heiße Zone, Die*	Kaiserslautern Landestheater	04/20/27
Engel, Alexander	*Strandgut im Kanal*	Hamburg Thalia Theater	03/26/27

Friedmann, Arnim, and Hans Kottow	*Amor in Nikolsburg*	Brunn Schauspielhaus	10/28/26
Friedrich-Freksa, Kurt	*Zeit auf Flaschen*	Frankfurt /M. Schauspielhaus	10/02/26
Hasenclever, Walter	*Ein besserer Herr*	Frankfurt /M. Schauspielhaus	01/12/27
Hauptmann, Carl	*Fasching*	Bad Godesberg Schauspielbühne	03/01/27
Havemann, Julis	*Schelmuffsky*	Lübeck Stadttheater	10/23/26
Hesse, Otto Ernst	*Komödianten*	Brandenburg Stadttheater	11/26/26
Hillers, Hans Wolfgang	*Jülchen und Schinderhannes*	Krefeld Stadttheater	11/10/26
Jacoby, Carl W.	*Kuken*	Frankfurt /O. Stadttheater	10/16/26
Jalant, Robert	*offene Tür, Die*	Erfurt Stadttheater	11/19/26
Kaiser, Georg	*Papiermühle, Die*	Aachen Stadttheater	01/26/27
Kornfeld, Paul	*Kilian, oder Die gelbe Rose*	Frankfurt /M. Schauspielhaus	11/06/26
Langhoff, Wolfgang	*Knock-out*	Wiesbaden Staatstheater	02/16/27
Lania, Leo	*Friedenskonferenz*	Krefeld Stadttheater	02/10/27
Lohmann, Louis	*tolle Hund, Der*	Göttingen Stadttheater	03/01/27
Lotichius, Erich	*Gesandte grosser Majestät*	Frankfurt /M. Schauspielhaus	06/29/27
Lutge, Karl	*Auktion der Tugend*	Halberstadt Stadttheater	02/26/27
Mann, Heinrich	*gastliche Haus, Das*	Munich Kammerspiele	01/21/27
Maugham, W. Somerset	*Frau Caesar*	Hamburg Thalia Theater	04/09/27
Mirande, Yves and Gustave Quinon	*Abgemacht*	Berlin Lessing Theater	06/17/27
Mirande, Yves, and Monczy Eon	*Bitte, were war zuerst da?*	Berlin Deutsches Künstlertheater	06/16/27
Noether, Erich	*Quintett*	Mannheim National Theater	06/08/26

Poek, Wilhelm	*Hexennacht*	Flensburg Stadt-theater	04/05/27
Pool, Jaap van den	*Spitzbub*	Oppeln Stadttheater	04/01/27
Porto-Riche, Georges	*Germaine*	Berlin Deutsches Theater	01/31/27
Rakous, Vojtec	*Modche und Resi*	Brunn Schauspielhaus	04/09/27
Rennspieß, Hilmar, and Richard Rolland	*bedrohte Unschuld, Die*	Berlin Theater in der Kommandantenstraße	04/17/27
Roßle, Wilhelm	*Erbiete mich als Kandidat*	Rudolfstadt Landes-theater	03/08/27
Sachs, Lothar	*Schach dem Mann*	Hamburg Thalia Theater	01/25/26
Schaeffer, Albrecht	*verlorene Sohn, Der*	Altona Stadttheater	10/11/26
Schiff, Bert	*Testament Das*	Gera Reussisches Theater	10/20/26
Schirmer, Paul and Edward Werner	*Eine heikle Kur*	Hamburg Kleines Lustspielhaus	03/08/27
Sling, Peter	*dreimal tote Peter, Der*	Munich Kammer-spiele	02/25/27
Slobada, Carl	*Rochus ist verloren*	Hamburg Thalia Theater	10/20/27
Sternheim, Carl	*Schule von Uznach*	Mannheim National Theater	09/21/26
Tiemann, Walter	*Geist in der Flasche, Der*	Leipzig Schau-spielhaus	10/15/26
Weither, E. A. von	*Piccol*	Freienwalde Kur-theater	09/09/26
Winterstein, Franz	*Kanal, Der*	Brunn Schauspielhaus	02/13/27
Wolf, Friedrich	*Mann im Dunkel, Der*	Essen Stadttheater	04/01/27
Zoder, Paul	*wiederaufgefundene Schneider, Der*	Harburg Stadttheater	09/26/26
Zoff, Otto	*zwei Abendteuerer, Die*	Frankfurt /M. Schauspielhaus	10/02/26

NOTES

1. The Dawes Plan was named for an American banker, Charles G. Dawes, who helped devise it. Dawes was later awarded the Nobel Peace Prize for his efforts and was elected vice-president of the United States in 1928. The "plan" which bore his name provided temporary relief for the German economy from ruinous reparation payments, but ultimately it proved unworkable.

2. German production of iron and steel was second only to that of the United States during this season, although American output far outpaced all other industrial economies combined. Germany accounted for 15 percent of world production, while the United States produced 53 percent of world totals.

3. Hans-José Rehfisch's *Nickel und die 36 Gerechten* (Nickel and the Thirty-Six Righteous Men) had nearly 300 performances this season, but it was actually a disappointment; Rehfisch had hoped to capitalize upon the success of his 1924–1925 *Wer weint um Juckenack?* and had allowed *Nickel* to open in several theatres at the same time during this season. Other theatres showed interest, but none of the productions ran for extensive periods of time on provincial stages.

4. The most notable of these was a 1980 production which opened in Chichester before moving to the West End, starring Joan Collins as Mrs. Cheyney, under the direction of Nigel Patrick. At its Broadway premiere in 1925, Ina Claire played the title role in a production that included Helen Hayes and Felix Aylmer.

5. Hans W. Fischer, review of *Mrs. Cheyneys Ende*, in *Die Welt am Montag*, 17 March 1926, n. p.

6. After arranging financial support for *Der Angriff*, Hitler named Joseph Goebbels editor of the publication; the first sentence Goebbels published was, "Germany is an exploitation colony of international Jewish finance capital."

11

The 1927–1928 Season

The beginning of this theatre season coincided with a belligerent speech President Hindenburg delivered in September, aimed at the victorious Allies. The speech was to have commemorated his victory over the Russians at Tannenberg, but in it he declared that Germany categorically rejected responsibility for starting World War I. That conflict, he said, was an unfortunate "means of self-determination [for Germany] in a world surrounded by enemies." It was Hindenburg's quixotic and undiplomatic way of pleading for reconciliation with the Allies. Hindenburg wanted the Allies to regard Germany as an equal partner; to that end, the Reich had concluded treaties with the Soviet Union and with Yugoslavia in the search for a lasting peace in Europe. His presumptions fell on deaf Allied ears, especially after his January speech rejecting the democratic aspirations of the German people. To Hindenburg, the republic was an unfortunate result of military defeat, and he stated his unequivocal disinclination to celebrate the upcoming tenth anniversary of the Weimar Republic's founding. Hindenburg was in fact more interested in preserving his own legacy as a German hero, and he unashamedly exploited the arts to do so. His Hindenburg Foundation sponsored showings of *Der Weltkrieg* (The World War) during this season, a film in two parts based on Reich archival footage. The first part premiered in October and attracted huge audiences wherever it and its sequel were shown. Profits from ticket sales went back to the foundation.

Attempts at "reconciliation" and the ironic consequences of assumed "heroism" were themes Franz Arnold and Ernst Bach parodied in their *Hurra—ein Junge!* (Hooray—it's a Boy!), which opened last season and became the most frequently performed comedy of this season. It followed many of the traditional Arnold and Bach precedents, aided again by the talents of their standard-bearer, Guido Thielscher. The comedy's initial focus was the respectable Professor Weber who, in his student days, had performed a "heroic" deed for his landlady when she became terminally ill. Her dying wish was that her illegitimate son, born twenty years earlier, have a real father. Weber heedlessly agreed to marry the woman, and her son, whom Weber had never met, became Weber's adoptive offspring. The landlady died in peace.

Professor Weber remarried and established a solid middle-class life; into it, however, stumbles a man named Franz Pappenstiel (played by Thielscher), who is the "son" of Weber's first "marriage." The son's years far exceed the father's, but no matter—he seeks knowledge of his papa and admission to the family. There ensue several situations crafted for Thielscher's talents, including a wrestling match with pyjamas laced with itching powder, Thielscher dressed as a woman, Thielscher dressed in a schoolboy uniform, and so on. Professor Weber naturally wishes to conceal Pappenstiel's origins from his wife Henny, but his fabrications pile one on top of the other until their marriage appears to be on the verge of collapse. Complicating the matter is the appearance of Pappenstiel's biological father. In the end, however, there is reconciliation. Pappenstiel agrees to move on, and the Weber marriage survives.

The Arnold and Bach perennial shared prominence as the season's top comedy with *Ein besserer Herr* (A Better Sort of Gentleman) by Walter Hasenclever, which had premiered on January 12, 1927, in Frankfurt under the direction of Richard Weichert. Weichert and Hasenclever were associated with Expressionism and had enjoyed a productive artistic relationship; the director had staged Hasenclever's *Der Sohn* (The Son) in Mannheim during the war, the 1919 Expressionist treatment of *Antigone*, and *Jenseits* (Beyond the Horizon) of 1921, both in Frankfurt. The world premiere of their collaborative attempt at popular comedy in Frankfurt was unusual by several counts; most surprising was the wide acceptance the play found among audiences during this season and for several succeeding ones. It was a social satire, according to critic Alfred Kerr, in the tradition of Frank Wedekind, Georg Kaiser, and Carl Sternheim.[1] Its target was the rapacious species of capitalism rampant in the Weimar Republic and personified in the character of Louis Compass. His disreputable counterpart was a gigolo named Hugo Möbius. Both characters reflected the shady side of economic recovery, practiced to the extreme in the years after the Great Inflation. Kerr's observations notwithstanding, its overly cerebral dialogue more closely resembled that of George Bernard Shaw, and its parodistic treatment of conjugal mores resembled that of Oscar Wilde.

It opens with two different plots; the first concerns the Compass family, whose father Louis determines that his nineteen-year-old daughter Lia must marry. The most businesslike way to find her a husband is through classified advertising in the newspaper—then a novelty. Möbius, in parallel scenes, is the plaything of Frau Schnütchen, a woman in her late forties (or maybe her fifties) who pampers Möbius, gives him money, and imagines that she is his only love interest. Möbius, however, keeps several ladies happy, all of whom provide him with a generous, and tax-free, living.

The plot thickens when Möbius reads the Compass advertisement; Möbius arranges to meet Lia and pose as a big game hunter just returned from Zanzibar.

She falls immediately in love with him, and he (to his surprise) with her. Frau Compass hires a private detective to check up on Möbius, and when she learns of his true vocation, both she and her husband try to liquidate him. Their attempts only strengthen Lia's resolve to marry Möbius. When Herr Compass tries to buy Möbius off, Möbius rejects all his offers. The crisis reaches a resolution in the final scene, when Möbius and his lawyer deftly convince several elderly women not to press charges against their beloved Hugo. Herr Compass realizes that Hugo has a keen sense for business (something his own son has never exhibited) and offers him a job as his company's representative in Zanzibar. Hugo accepts, and Lia is happy.

This play moves along quickly, although it is not the facile work of craftsmanship one finds in Arnold and Bach. It owes more, as noted above, to Shaw, whose work was becoming increasingly popular in the Weimar Republic. Hasenclever's treatment of sex as a commodity paralleled Shaw's in *Mrs. Warren's Profession*; its outright parodistic tendencies were similar to those of Sternheim. There are several references to topical political concerns, the most obvious of which is "racial purity" in marriage. The comedy concludes with Hugo calling out "Sieg heil!" in happiness.

COMEDY PREMIERES OF 1927–1928

PLAYWRIGHT(S)	PLAY TITLE	CITY and THEATRE	DATE
Armont, Paul	*Eine Kleine ohne Bedeutung*	Berlin Kleines Theater	12/25/27
Arnold, Franz, and Ernst Bach	*Unter Geschäftsaus-sicht*	Berlin Lustspielhaus	12/20/27
Bach, Hugo	*Erbschaft, Die*	Plauen Stadttheater	08/15/28
Becker, Matthias	*Prinzessin aus Guyana, Die*	Altona Stadttheater	06/04/28
Becker-Trier, Heinz	*Turnlehrer Heinrich Ziegenspeck*	Trier Stadttheater	12/03/27
Britting, Georg	*Paula und Bianka*	Dresden Staatliches Schauspielhaus	05/15/28
Chabrol, Marcel	*Liebhaber seiner Frau*	Magdeburg Wil-helmstheater	03/03/28
Coward, Noel	*Ehe von Welt, Die*	Berlin Die Komödie	11/25/27
Daudet, Alphonse	*zwei Väter der Familie, Die*	Halberstadt Stadttheater	02/09/28
Dekobra, Maurice	*Perlen von Chikago, Die*	Krefeld Stadttheater	11/17/27

Doring, Otto	*Erbe gesucht*	Bautzen Stadttheater	01/28/28
Dunning, Phillip and George Abbott	*Broadway*	Berlin Komödienhaus	03/09/28
Duschinsky, Richard	*Tanzer im Fasching*	Bad Nauheim Kur-theater	06/20/28
Dymow, Ossip	*Bronx Express*	Berlin Deutsches Theater	12/02/27
Eger, Rudolf	*Woronoff*	Frankfurt /O. Stadttheater	02/18/28
Ernst, Paul	*Heilige Krispin, Der*	Bonn Stadttheater	11/25/27
Fenk, Willi	*Fleisch*	Milling Landes-theater	04/19/28
Fleisser, Marieluise	*Pioniere in Ingolstadt*	Dresden Die Ko-mödie	03/26/28
Fodor, Ladislas	*Arm wie ein Kirchenmaus*	Breslau Lobe The-ater	04/28/28
Friedmann-Friedrich, Fritz	*Herr von . . . , Der*	Berlin Berliner Theater	12/23/27
Gabelenitz, Georg von	*Schwedenkönig, Der*	Dresden Sächsische Landesbühne	10/04/27
Galsworthy, John	*Familienvater, Der*	Bochum Stadt-theater	05/18/28
Heynicke, Kurt	*Wer gewinnt Lisette?*	Darmstadt Landes-theater	05/06/28
Hillers, Wolfgang Hans	*tolle Baron, Der*	Ulm Stadttheater	12/01/27
Hirschfeld, Ludwig	*Frau, die jeder sucht, Die*	Munich Residenz-theater	06/28/28
Hoffmeier, Ludwig	*Um ihn*	Kassel Staatstheater	04/12/28
Hopkins, Arthur	*Artisten*	Berlin Deutsches Theater	06/09/28
Hunefeld, E. G. von	*Karnevalkonzert, Das*	Bremen Stadttheater	02/14/28
Ilges, F. Walter	*Gräfin Dubarry*	Bochum Stadt-theater	02/17/28
Joachimsohn, Felix	*Fünf von der Jazzband*	Berlin Staatliches Schauspielhaus	09/22/27
Johst, Hanns	*Ausländer, Der*	Hamburg Thalia Theater	10/14/27

Kaiser, Georg	*Präsident, Der*	Frankfurt /M. Schauspielhaus	01/28/28
Kamare, Stefan von	*Leinen aus Irland*	Munich Residenz-theater	02/05/28
Kesten, Hermann	*Maud liebt beiden*	Kassel Kleines Theater	04/03/28
Kihn, Hans Alfred	*Eselsklippen*	Dresden Die Komödie	12/05/27
Kihn, Hans Alfred	*Jenny steigt empor*	Leipzig Altes Theater	09/22/27
Kivi, Alexis	*Heideschuster, Die*	Coburg Landes-theater	10/27/27
Knoeller, Fritz	*So und so geht der Wind*	Munich Kammer-spiele	03/06/28
Knopf, Julius	*Haar in der Ehe, Das*	Frankfurt /O. Stadttheater	01/21/28
Kordt, Walter	*Wider Willen*	Bad Godesberg Stadttheater	02/10/28
Langer, Frantisek	*Grand Hotel Nevada*	Kiel Stadttheater	04/14/28
Lauckner, Rolf	*Entkleidung des Antonio Carossa, Die*	Chemnitz Schauspielhaus	12/03/27
Lekisch, Hermann, and Max Malen	*Daniel in der Löwengrube*	Mainz Stadttheater	11/30/27
Lekisch, Hermann, and Hans Bernhoft	*Hallo, wir fliegen*	Salzschlirf Kur-theater	06/29/28
Lernet-Holenia, Alexander	*Erotik*	Breslau Lobe Theater, Frankfurt /M. Schauspielhaus	12/23/27
Lilienfein, Heinrich	*Freiheit wider Willen*	Koblenz Stadt-theater	11/15/27
Lonsdale, Frederic	*Flucht aus Aegypten, Die*	Bad Godesberg Schauspielhaus	01/11/28
Lonsdale, Frederic	*Zur gefallenen Ansicht*	Nuremberg Altes Theater	02/04/28
Lothar, Rudolf	*gute Europäer, Der*	Frankfurt /O. Stadttheater	11/12/28
Marchand, Collette, and Louis Marchand	*Cheri*	Berlin Theater am Kurfürstendamm	12/06/27

Marchand, Leopold	*Wir sind keine Kinder mehr*	Hamburg Thalia Theater	10/20/27
Marx, E. F.	*tote Gast, Der*	Breslau Schlesische Bühne	02/06/28
Maugham, W. Somerset	*Finden Sie, daß Constance sich richtig verhält?*	Berlin Deutsches Theater	01/27/28
Morgan, Paul, and Kurt Robitschek	*Hallo Überfall*	Berlin Theater der Komiker	11/30/27
Netto, Hadrian Maria	*Schlachtenalarm*	Breslau Lobe Theater	10/22/27
Netto, Hadrian Maria	*Triumph der Jugend*	Weimar National Theater	04/19/28
Nolte, Otto de	*Erbschleicherin, Die*	Spandau Volkstheater	02/13/28
Pagnol, Marcel	*Schieber des Ruhms*	Düsseldorf Schauspielhaus	09/12/27
Ploetz, Ludwig von	*Haus in der Sonne, Das*	Bremerhaven Stadttheater	10/27/28
Renker, Gustav	*Krauses Ozeanflug*	Bad Mergentheim Kurtheater	08/28/28
Rindom, Swend	*Premiere, Die*	Hamburg Deutsches Schauspielhaus	11/12/27
Robitschek, Kurt	*Fall Kuhlmayer, Der*	Berlin Theater der Komiker	04/01/28
Rothe, Hanns	*brennende Stall, Der*	Leipzig Altes Theater	01/28/28
Savoir, Alfred	*Statist vom Metropol-Theater, Der*	Hamburg Thalia Theater	09/30/27
Schiffer, Marcellus	*Ein Stück Malheur*	Berlin Komödienhaus	06/19/28
Seiler, Ernst	*Zungelein an der Wage, Das*	Gotha Landestheater	05/08/28
Sternheim, Felix	*Kopfsprung, Der*	Salzburg Stadttheater	08/20/28
Sturm, Hans	*Spiel mit dem Feuer*	Bremen Schauspielhaus	09/30/27
Toller, Ernst	*Rache des verhöhnten Liebhabers, Die*	Braunschweig Landestheater	05/19/28

Verneuil, Louis	*Beverly weiß alles*	Berlin Theater in der Lutzowstraße	08/14/28
Walter, Robert	*grosse Hebammekunst, Die*	Cologne Schau-spielhaus	10/08/27
Weil, Robert	*Paradies der Ehe, Das*	Berlin Rose Theater	05/26/28
Wiegand, Carl Friedrich	*Simulanten, Die*	Baden-Baden Städtisches Schauspielhaus	03/26/28
Winter, Theodor	*Ausgerechnet Pupke*	Liegnitz Stadttheater	02/17/28
Winterstein, Franz	*Ein Milliardär schreit um Hilfe*	Frankfurt /O. Stadttheater	03/24/28

NOTE

1. Günther Rühle, *Theater für die Republik* (Frankfurt: Fischer, 1967) 889.

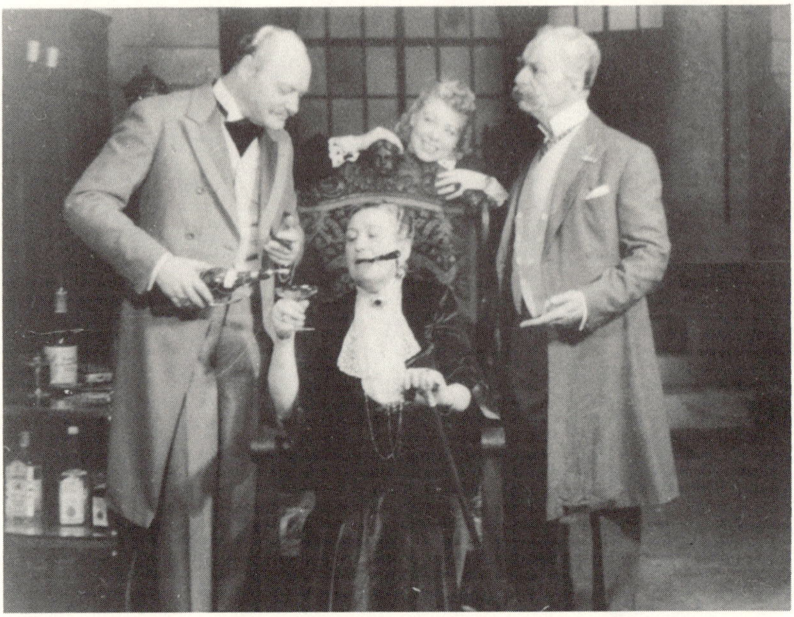

Mathilde Einzig (center) in Impekoven and Mathern's *Die drei Zwillinge* [The Three Twins], 1919. (Courtesy of the Theatre Museum of the University of Cologne)

Antonie Klischat and Albert Fischel in Max Mohr's *Improvisationen im Juni* [Improvisations in June], 1922. (Courtesy of the Theatre Museum of the University of Cologne)

Georg Kaiser's *Nebeneinander* [Side by Side], setting designed by Georg Grosz, for the 1923 world premiere production at the Frankfurt Schaspielhaus. (Courtesy of the Theatre Museum of the University of Cologne)

Constanze Metz and Franz Schneider in Carl Zuckmayer's *Der fröhliche Weinberg* [The Merry Vineyard], 1925. (Courtesy of the Theatre Museum of the University of Cologne)

The incomparable Guido Thielscher (center) in Arnold and Bach's *Hurra—ein Junge!* [Hurrah—It's a Boy!], 1926. (Courtesy of the Theatre Museum of the University of Cologne)

Marianne Berger and Heinz Rühmann in Avery Hopwood's *Fair and Warmer*, 1927. (Courtesy of the Theatre Museum of the University of Cologne)

Arnold and Bach's *Hulla di Bulla*, 1929. (Courtesy of the Theatre Museum of the University of Cologne)

Rosa Valetti (left) and Käthe Haack in Bruno Frank's *Sturm im Wasserglas* [Tempest in a Teacup], 1929. (Courtesy of the Theatre Museum of the University of Cologne)

Rosa Valetti with "Toni" in Bruno Frank's *Sturm im Wasserglas* [Tempest in a Teacup], 1929. (Courtesy of the Theatre Museum of the University of Cologne)

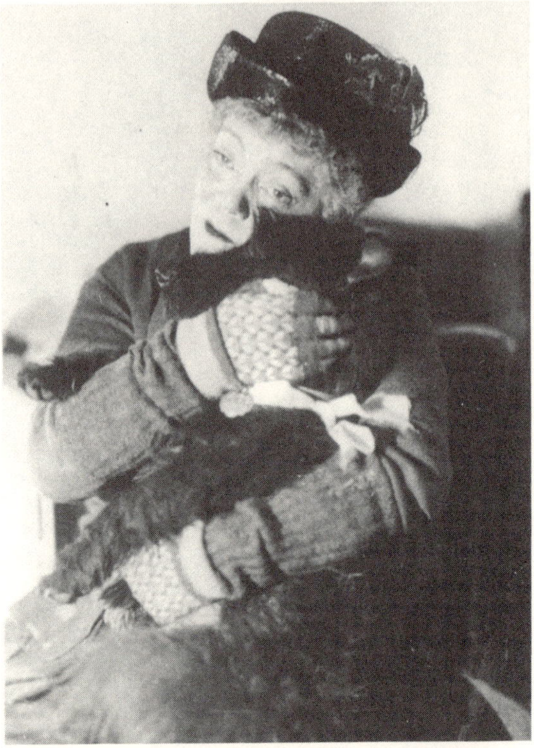

Charlotte Anders (center) in Bernauer and Östreicher's *Konto X* [Account X], 1930. (Courtesy of the Theatre Museum of the University of Cologne)

12

The 1928–1929 Season

Several noteworthy trends in the German theatre accelerated during this season. Two of them conjoined in the widespread popularity of W. Somerset Maugham's comedy *The Constant Wife*, which bore the awkward German title *Finden Sie, daß Constance sich richtig verhält?* (Do You Think Constance Conducted Herself Properly?). Maugham's treatment of Constance, the wife who remained "constant" in the face of her husband's infidelity, signaled the emergence of a female type who was more independent than her predecessors. The work several female comic playwrights premiered during the Weimar Republic. Most notable among them was Marieluise Fleisser, whose *Pioniere in Ingolstadt* (Pioneers in Ingolstadt) had premiered the previous season,[1] although any list of German female comic playwrights should include Hartwig Bonner, Gabriele Eckehard, Wilma von Loesch, Hanna Rademacher, and the novelist Christa Winsloe. Some historians have suggested that the career of Rosa Luxemburg initiated the rise of the "independent woman" in the German consciousness. Certainly the emergence of comic playwrights indicates a trend, although only translators, such as Mimi Zoff, Bertha Pogson, and Berta Szeps-Zuckerkandl, realized any monetary gain for their work on the stage.

The importance of translation should be recognized as well, since by this season several foreign-language comic playwrights, in addition to Maugham, were enjoying numerous productions of their plays in Germany. George Bernard Shaw was among the most significant of these, thanks to the excellent translations of Siegfried Trebitsch (1868–1956). In 1902 Shaw granted Trebitsch exclusive rights to negotiate with any German producer on his behalf—although there was never a written contract between them. Shaw's plays grew in popularity before the war, especially *The Devil's Disciple* (which Trebitsch titled *Ein Teufelskerl*, meaning "a devilish fellow"); Shaw's first play in German, it premiered in 1903. There followed a string of popular successes, and by 1926, when Shaw received the

Nobel Prize for Literature, he was regarded as a classic in the provinces as much as in Berlin, although the number of Shaw performances in any one season had rarely exceeded one hundred. Critic Alfred Kerr nevertheless stated that Shaw compared favorably with Shakespeare as a "German classic."[2] American playwrights did well in the Weimar Republic, too; Avery Hopwood's success was the most obvious and was never duplicated by another American. Subsequent to his *Fair and Warmer* of the 1922–1923 season were such American comedies as *Boomerang* by Winchell Smith and Victor Mapes (1925), *Adam und Eve* by Guy Bolton and George Middleton (1926), *Broadway* by Phillip Dunning and George Abbott, *Burlesque* by Arthur Hopkins, *The Front Page* by Ben Hecht and Charles MacArthur, and *The Royal Family* by George S. Kaufman and Edna Ferber, all in 1928, and all of which did moderately well at the box office.

The 1928–1929 season also marked the popularity, for the first time, of comedies by Central European playwrights. The Hungarian Ladislas Fodor's *Arm wie ein Kirchenmaus* (Poor as a Church Mouse) was a romantic comedy in the style of his compatriot Miklos Laszlo's *Parfumerie* and resembled in some ways the comedies of Ferenc Molnar.[3] It also resembled Franz Arnold and Ernst Bach's *Unter Geschäftsaussicht* (Business is Business, premiered in December of the preceding season) in its treatment of the business world. Fodor's was the more sentimental view, chronicling the ascent of a modest stenographer named Susie Sachs to the executive ranks of a large Viennese financial concern. Susie succeeds despite, or perhaps because of, her demure temperament (hence the title). By the comedy's conclusion, her successes include several takeovers, including the affections of the company's president.

Arnold and Bach's comedy enjoyed three times as many performances (over 600) as the Fodor play; in fact, it appeared on German stages twice as many times as its nearest competitor (Maugham's *The Constant Wife*). Its action featured the dancer Pussy Angora and the adventures of Eduard Haselhuhn, an accountant from a provincial town sent to Berlin to straighten out the finances of an insolvent enterprise. His presence in Berlin is, of course, merely the pretext for the farcical misadventures the playwrights have contrived; those contrivances involve stenographers who fall in love with him, a party at which he loses his trousers, and being arrested for disturbing the peace. Arnold and Bach had, in other words, created another brilliant vehicle for Guido Thielscher; in the world premiere performance of *Unter Geschäftsaussicht* (Business is Business), Thielscher celebrated his fiftieth season as a professional actor, winning acclaim of audiences and critics alike.

Among the most remarkable comedies of this season was Curt Goetz's *Hokuspokus*, which rivaled Fodor's in popularity (it ran over 350 times in Berlin alone during the remainder of the Weimar Republic). Goetz ridiculed the whole idea of success in the theatre. Its opening scene is a none-too-subtle parody of the opening scene in Johann Wolfgang Goethe's *Faust I*, in which a theatre director discusses with an actor, a critic, a dramaturg, and his accountant the fact that he is bankrupt. A discussion follows of what is needed in the modern repertoire, as light slowly fades down on their scene and up to one on the opposite side of the stage. There, in a lavishly decorated office, a Justice Ministry official discusses a murder trial that might involve government officials. Subsequent scenes involve seasick ship captains, the suspicious drowning of an unwanted, troublesome husband, and a possible affair between the drowned man's wife and the minister of justice—all of which leads to a highly theatrical courtroom scene.

In some ways, *Hokuspokus* resembled *Six Characters in Search of an Author* by Luigi Pirandello, whose plays (like many of the American comedies) had been produced frequently throughout the life of the Weimar Republic. Goetz's comedy, like Pirandello's, used techniques found in popular plays to make a thematic point. Goetz's concerns were "what the German theatre has come to" (as discussed in the play's first scene), what kind of fare theatre audiences were demanding, and the kind of plays producers had to present if they were to avoid bankruptcy. In effect, the play ridiculed its own audiences—which paid off handsomely for Goetz, because the play was presented hundreds of times during the late 1920s and early 1930s.

COMEDY PREMIERES OF 1928–1929

PLAYWRIGHT(S)	PLAY TITLE	CITY and THEATRE	DATE
Auernheimer, Raoul	*Feuerglocke, Die*	Munich Bayerisches Staatstheater	05/07/29
Auriel, Denis	*Herr und Frau Soundso*	Berlin Die Tribüne	02/05/29
Arnold, Franz, and Ernst Bach	*Weekend im Paradies*	Berlin Lustspielhaus	12/22/28
Ballewski, Otto	*Sonnenbad, Das*	Berlin Walhalla Theater	06/02/28
Becker, Herbert	*Regeneration*	Erfurt Stadttheater	10/27/28
Bernhard, Andre	*Zimmer zu vermieten*	Berlin Trianon Theater	05/21/29
Bibesco, Antoine	*Welche war's?*	Berlin Theater in der Behrenstraße	06/05/29
Birabeau, Andre	*Eine kleine Sunde*	Breslau Lobe Theater	10/06/28
Blumberg, Hans	*Blaue vom Himmel, Das*	Halberstadt Stadttheater	11/27/28
Blume, Bernhard	*Feurio*	Stuttgart Landestheater	10/27/28
Bourdet, Edouard	*Soeben geschrieben*	Berlin Kammerspiele	01/17/29
Buchhorn, Josef	*Was ist mit Kate?*	Cottbus Stadttheater	04/19/29

Burkhardt, Hermann, and Harry Waldau	*Im siebenten Himmel*	Berlin Schloßpark Theater	07/01/29
Cornelius, Franz, and Martin Klinger	*Jungesellensteuer*	Berlin Central Theater	09/15/28
Cynge, Fleming, and Sven Rindom	*rote Mantel, Der*	Hamburg Thalia Theater	03/27/29
Dell, Floyd, and Thomas Mitchell	*Freudiges Ereignis*	Berlin Komödie	08/01/29
Duschinsky, Richard	*November in Österreich*	Berlin Renaissance Theater	12/10/28
Ehm, Ferdinand	*Mann im gefährlichen Alter, Der*	Komotau Stadttheater	12/04/28
Englander, Fritz	*Nacht der drei Frauen, Die*	Berlin Residenztheater	11/13/28
Essig, Hermann	*Weiber von Weinberg, Die*	Oldenburg Landestheater	05/25/29
Eulenberg, Herbert	*himmlische Handelsmann, Der*	Krefeld Stadttheater	01/07/29
Eulenberg, Herbert	*Scheidungsfieber*	Kassel Kleines Theater	04/27/29
Frank, Paul	*Grand Hotel*	Berlin Lustspielhaus	08/31/29
Fürst, Ernst	*Maria Trubach*	Nordhausen Stadttheater	11/06/28
Galsworthy, John	*Lebenskunstler*	Stettin Stadttheater	03/12/29
Geraldy, Paul, and Robert Spitzer	*Unwiderstehliche, Der*	Berlin Kammerspiele	08/31/29
Gerber, Eugen	*Kolonialwaren und Liebe*	Krefeld Stadttheater	11/22/28
Gilbert, Robert	*Prosit Gypsy*	Berlin Deutsches Künstlertheater	04/19/29
Gray, David, and Mary Hopwood	*Heutzutage*	Hamburg Deutsches Schauspielhaus	11/08/28
Günther, Johannes von	*große Wurf, Der*	Mainz Stadttheater	10/17/28
Guitry, Sacha	*Wir wollen träumen*	Hamburg Kammerspiele	02/23/29
Hasenclever, Walter	*Ehen werden im Himmel geschlossen*	Berlin Kammerspiele	10/12/28

Hecht, Ben, and Charles MacArthur	*Reporter*	Berlin Berliner Theater	06/11/29
Herbst, Maxim	*Seher Charitas, Der*	Landshut Stadttheater	03/21/29
Herfurth, Emil	*Halt, nicht weiter spielen!*	Greifswald Stadttheater	03/09/29
Huber, Robert	*Fliegen am Markt*	Koblenz Stadttheater	03/04/29
Johst, Hanns	*Komödie am Klavier*	Düsseldorf Städtisches Theater	10/24/28
Jotuni, Maria	*Mannes Rippe, Des*	Lübeck Stadttheater	04/08/29
Kästner, Leopold, and Harry Luck	*Beide waren verreist*	Hamburg Thalia Theater	04/24/29
Kaufman, George S., and Edna Ferber	*Eine königliche Familie*	Dresden Staatliches Schauspielhaus	12/20/28
Kelemann, Viktor	*Märchen von der Fledermaus, Das*	Dresden Sächsische Landesbühne	02/20/29
Landsberger, Arthur	*Mein Mann fliegt nach Paris*	Berlin Trianon Theater	11/29/28
Langer, Felix	*Kummerer, Der*	Erfurt Stadttheater	05/07/29
Lengyel, Melchior	*Tihamer*	Berlin Theater im Palmenhaus	11/24/28
Lenz, Leo	*Trio*	Frankfurt /O. Stadttheater	10/13/28
Lernet-Holenia, Alexander	*Parforce*	Düsseldorf Schauspielhaus	12/31/28
Lernet-Holenia, Alexander	*Tumult*	Munich Residenztheater	05/06/29
Lichtenberg, Wilhelm	*Roman nachher, Der*	Frankfurt /O. Stadttheater	11/24/28
Lonsdale, Frederick	*Sind wir das nicht alle?*	Hamburg Deutsches Schauspielhaus	09/29/28
Lunde, Arvid	*Soll man eine berühmte Frau heiraten?*	Freiburg /Br. Stadttheater	10/02/28
Malleson, Miles, and Michel Neville	*Liebe auf dem zweiten Blick*	Gießen Stadttheater	07/02/29
Mann, Heinrich	*Bibi, Jugend*	Berlin Theater in dem Palmenhaus	10/22/28
Martens, Albert	*Bully-Film A.G., Die*	Bad Oeynhausen Kurtheater	09/14/28

Maugham, W. Somerset	*zehnte Mann, Der*	Magdeburg Städtisches Theater	06/17/29
Meisel, Hans	*Geschäft*	Dresden Staatliches Schauspielhaus	11/11/28
Meisel, Hans	*Störungen*	Berlin Staatliches Schauspielhaus	06/04/29
Michaelis, Sophus	*Paul und Virginie*	Kiel Stadttheater	06/20/29
Möbius, Martin R., and Werner Heinrich	*Heimliche Hochzeit*	Dresden Die Komödie	01/19/29
Nabl, Franz	*Schichtwechsel*	Annaberg Stadttheater	02/01/29
Nerz, Ludwig, and Maria Luise Mayer	*Meine liebe, dumme Mama*	St. Polten Stadttheater	00/00/28
Neydissor, Clemens	*Gelegenheit macht Liebe*	Frankfurt /M. Schauspielhaus	
Österreicher, Rudolf	*Sachertorte, Die*	Baden-Baden Städtisches Schauspielhaus	08/29/29
Pagnol, Marcel	*große ABC, Das*	Munich Volkstheater	09/14/28
Raphaelson, Samson	*Jazz-Sänger, Der*	Brunn Schauspielhaus	03/31/29
Rice, Elmer	*So sind wir*	Munich Prinzregenten Theater	11/24/28
Robitschek, Kurt, and Frank Günther	*Selige Theophil, Der*	Berlin Theater der Komiker	12/16/28
Rommel, Georg	*Karl der Große und die Anderen*	Schwerin Staatstheater	04/20/29
Scheffler, Herbert	*Schwefelbande, Die*	Gotha Landestheater	10/25/28
Schiff, Bert	*Elise Ademann*	Liepzig Altes Theater	09/01/28
Szenes, Bela	*Ich heirate nicht*	Hamburg Thalia Theater	05/07/29
Unger, Hellmuth	*Kolpack muß tanzen*	Berlin Neues Theater	10/31/28
Verneuil, Louis	*Herr Lamberthier*	Berlin Lessing Theater	09/29/28
Walter, Robert	*Generalstab von Venus, Der*	Cologne Städtische Bühne	02/24/29
Wellenkamp, Bruno	*Freundliche Revolution*	Nuremberg Intimes Theater	10/30/28
Wellenkamp, Bruno	*Frisör von Roßlagen, Der*	Berlin Schiller Theater	06/05/29

Woikow, J. M.	*Liebe auf dem Lande, Die*	Frankfurt /M. Schauspielhaus	09/19/28
Wunzer, Rudi and Peter Wagner	*verborgene Ähnlichkeit, Die*	Darmstadt Landestheater	04/24/29
Zobelitz, Hans Kaspar von	*Susa, das Kind*	Wiesbaden Staatstheater	05/02/29

NOTES

1. Fleisser was a "protegé" of Bertolt Brecht, who claimed responsibility for the final form of *Pioniere in Ingolstadt* and for arranging its premiere in Dresden on March 26 1928. A recent study of Brecht's relationships with women by John Fuegi claims that Elisabeth Hauptmann is the "real" librettist of *Die Dreigroschenoper* (The Three Penny Opera), which opened this season and became Brecht's most successful theatre work during the Weimar Republic.

2. Quoted in Samuel Weiss, ed., *Bernard Shaw's Letters to Siegfried Trebitsch* (Palo Alto: Stanford University Press, 1986) 200.

3. Both Laszlo and Molnar share the distinction of having written plays that were later the basis of popular musicals on Broadway, thus introducing the "Hungarian style" to American audiences. Laszlo's *Parfumerie* became *She Loves Me* in 1963, with music by Jerry Bock and lyrics by Sheldon Harnick. It ran for 302 performances in New York. Molnar's *Lilliom* became Rodgers and Hammerstein's *Carousel*, which opened in 1945 on Broadway and ran for 890 performances.

13

The 1929–1930 Season

This season marked the fifth year of Hindenburg's presidency, an administration rife with corruption, parliamentary subterfuge, and resort to authoritarian control. It was also a season distinguished by profound, though initially imperceptible, transformations in nearly all fields of public endeavor. It marked the practical end of the democracy in the Weimar Republic, as Chancellor Brüning was unable to forge a ruling coalition in the Reichstag. He began the regular implementation of Article Forty Eight of the Weimar constitution, the "Enabling Act" giving him rule by emergency decree.[1]

Complicating the political picture was the death of Gustav Stresemann in September. Stresemann had been a leading centrist politician whose ability to forge alliances with parties on the left and right had permitted normal legislative procedure to function. His absence, according to Count Harry Kessler, sent parties further to ideological extremes, "causing a rupture in the [governing] coalition, spurring demands for a dictatorship. . . . It's going to be a terrible year."[2]

Kessler, of course, had no idea how quickly events were to turn nor how terrible the year was to become. Four weeks after Stresemann's funeral, the American stock market collapsed, ending all prospects for a permanent economic recovery in Germany. Since 1925 the German economy had enjoyed artificial expansion thanks to the $50 billion loan accorded the Reich government to spur investment; American banks now began calling in the loans, resulting initially in a decline of German business activity, followed by shrinkage in investment, then by layoffs in all industries, then by bankruptcies, ending in wholesale economic and political disintegration.

The three most popular comedies on German stages during this season reflected audience intuition of political decline and distrust of the Establishment. Two of them were of foreign origin: *Topaze* (whose German title was *Das große ABC*, or The Big ABC) by Marcel Pagnol, and *The Apple Cart* (whose German title was *Der*

Kaiser von Amerika, or The Emperor of America) by George Bernard Shaw. *Topaze* was an indictment of education and the political system, although it did not target German schools or politics specifically. Its condemnation of corruption in education and government, however, was transparent.[3]

Pagnol's comedy about a schoolteacher who falls comic victim to postwar decadence and corruption had already run the previous season to full houses in Paris, where it had premiered. Ernst Bach gave *Topaze* its German premiere at his Volkstheater in Munich, and *Das große ABC* enjoyed dozens of subsequent productions in several German theatres. It dealt with the myriad foibles Topaze encounters on his way to becoming a millionaire grafter in the employ of a corrupt government official. He begins as a virtuous pedagogue in love with the headmaster's daughter. When the headmaster orders him to alter the grades of a rich student (in a scene that is a masterpiece of comic dialogue and timing), Topaze loses both his job and his would-be bride.

He is rescued by a woman who engages him to provide private tutoring to her "nephew." The woman turns out to be a courtesan in league with a corrupt alderman, compact of dishonesty and deception. Topaze accepts the position of "front man" heading a phony corporation selling mechanized street sweepers to the local government. The alderman awards the contract to Topaze and collects most of the profits himself. From that point, Topaze masters the fine points of municipal graft. Sewer workers, for example, release noxious fumes from underground valves near the entrances of posh restaurants; when restaurant owners complain, Topaze assigns sewer workers to "repair" the problem for an expensive fee. At each step of his descent into corruption, Topaze protests vigorously: "I have gotten rich by trading influence, corrupting officials, and betraying the trust of others! If society were well-regulated I would be in prison." Yet each downward step greets him with cheers of congratulation, and his riches pile up. Even the headmaster's young daughter (who rejected him when he was virtuous and upstanding) now wishes to marry him because he has become so successful.

Topaze is, as his name implies, a gem of innocence immersed in a cesspool of dissipation, even though his own decay is inevitable in such an environment. Pagnol brilliantly structures surprise reversals and opportune revelations around his farcical hero's degeneration. German audiences recognized in this French comedy several features they could identify in their own political situation. As does George Bernard Shaw's *The Apple Cart*, the play derides government, its officialdom, and its propensity for wickedness.[4] Shaw's comedy actually exceeded Pagnol's in the number of performances this season, largely because Shaw was already so well known.

Shaw set his political fantasia in the future; its dilemma consisted of an English king named Magnus abdicating his throne, thus upsetting the apple cart, and running for prime minister. He is the most capable man in the realm, and there is every likelihood of his victory. None of that happens in the plot, however; the play itself is taken up with Shavian discourse on democracy.

King Magnus and his cabinet ministers (who include two women, named

Amanda and Lysistrata), Queen Jemima, and the royal mistress Orinthia, are troubled by demands that England become a democracy. The new trade minister Bill Boanerges insists that democracy is what the workers want. "I tell them they have the vote, and theirs is the power and the glory. I say to them, 'You are supreme. Exercise your power.' They say, 'That's right. Tell us what to do.' And I tell them. I say, 'Exercise your vote intelligently by voting for me.' And they do. That's democracy, a splendid thing for putting the right men in the right place."

The plot gets complicated when the United States offers to rejoin the British Empire, with Magnus as its Emperor (hence the German title). The cabinet is completely nonplussed by the news; Magnus abdicates and plans to run for prime minister, for he fears that England will become "simply another star on the American flag and that London will be outvoted by Tennessee."

The play was based on Shaw's conviction that "our professed devotion to political principles is only a mask for our idolatry of eminent persons. *The Apple Cart* exposes the unreality of both democracy and royalty as our idealists conceive them."[5] It ran for over 200 performances at the Deutsches Theater alone (where it premiered, with Werner Krauß as King Magnus) and over 250 times on other German stages. In many ways, it resembled a German bourgeois comedy because Magnus was distinctly middle class, with bourgeois concerns masquerading as affairs of state. He was a mild-mannered, well-intentioned fellow beset by people who badgered him with their own petty preoccupations. In that regard, at least, Shaw's comedy resembled the most popular comedy of the 1929–1930 season, a political satire by Franz Arnold and Ernst Bach titled *Week-end im Paradies* (Week-end in Paradise).

Arnold and Bach's comedy had over 1,200 performances during the 1929–1930 season, making it the most popular comedy in any single Weimar season. Its central character, Leo Dittchen (played by Guido Thielscher[6] at the world premiere production in Berlin), was a diligent and faithful civil servant always overlooked for promotion. He lacks political connections, which are essential for advancement. He unexpectedly acquires them when he happens upon his superiors with their girlfriends at the Hotel zum Paradies in a Berlin suburb. "Paradise" turns into potential hell, so in exchange for his silence they provide Dittchen with the advancement his career has hitherto lacked. He becomes supervisor of his office the next day, followed quickly by his promotion to manager of an entire bureau, proceeding soon thereafter to chief of an entire division. He sits at the bureaucratic pinnacle, only to discover that his wife is involved with an elected government official and that he, too, is thus implicated.

The playwrights' satire was aimed particularly at the German *Beamter*, or civil servant, whose reputation for peremptoriness was well known.[7] An important subplot in *Week-end*, however, involves Adele Haubenschild, a legislator claiming to represent "over 200 womens' organizations." She decries the moral decline in the Weimar Republic and dedicates herself to "retrieving the level of public civility from the swamp." The chief problem, she says, is the "week-end movement" in Germany; thousands of illicit meetings between married men and unmarried women are taking place on week-ends all over the country. Such trends are imports from foreign countries; like "Negro dancing," she claims, they will lead the country into complete moral collapse. Adele's concerns echoed the demands of a politician elected as minister for internal affairs in Thuringia during this season. He was Wilhelm Frick, the first National Socialist cabinet member of a provincial government anywhere in Germany.

Soon after his election, he promulgated his "Proclamation against Negro Culture," issuing ordinances designed to limit "foreign racial influences" such as "the jazz band, hit music, Negro dances, Negro songs, Negro plays, and the glorification of Negro culture which strikes German sensibilities squarely in the face." Police authorities in Thuringia were advised to close down any cabarets and other entertainment establishments that did not comply with Frick's ordinances.

Weimar performers had encountered official restraints in the past, but if their work proved popular with audiences it was usually accorded permission for public presentation. German comedy, however, began during this season to experience an additional threat, that of economic competition from the sound film. Film versions of popular stage comedies had rarely experienced much success in Germany. Silent film comedy depended in large measure upon visual artistry, while stage comedy often exploited verbal drollery. The advent of sound synchronization allowed film to capture some of stage comedy's market. Film also paid actors much more than did theatre work. The first sound comedy film to capitalize on a popular stage comedy was *Hokuspokus*, based on the Curt Goetz play of 1926. It had been one of the most popular comedies of the previous season. The film version starred Lillian Harvey, Gustaf Gründgens, and Oskar Homolka.

Arnold and Bach had resisted the release of film rights to their comedies, since their success as stage works was so phenomenal and lucrative that film versions would, they reasoned, serve only to diminish their theatrical audience. Yet neither escaped this season unscathed. On November 1, 1929, Ernst Bach died at the age of fifty-four in Munich, shortly after his production of *Topaze* opened. The last work he created with Franz Arnold, *Hulla di Bulla*, premiered six weeks later.

COMEDY PREMIERES OF 1929–1930

PLAYWRIGHT(S)	PLAY TITLE	CITY and THEATRE	DATE
Adler, Hans	*Drei Herren im Frack*	Berlin Tribüne Theater	11/30/29
Adler, Hans, and Paul Frank	*Premiere*	Augsburg Stadttheater	02/26/30
Andersen, Ingeborg	*Blauen Amidam*	Kiel Schauspielhaus	01/16/30
Armont, Paul, and Marcel Gerbidon	*Madame hat Ausgang*	Berlin Kleines Theater	03/03/30

Arnold, Franz, and Ernst Bach	*Hulla di Bulla*	Berlin Komische Oper	12/21/29
Atherton, William	*Ist denn das so richtig?*	Brunn Schauspielhaus	09/28/29
Begovic, Milan	*amerikanische Yacht im Hafen von Spalato, Die*	Hamburg Deutsches Schauspielhaus	03/20/30
Bernauer, Rudolf, and Rudolf Österreicher	*Konto X*	Berlin Neues Theater	07/14/30
Berstl, Julius	*Scribbys Suppen sind die Besten*	Berlin Komödienhaus	09/15/29
Bertuch, Max	*Ist das nicht nett von Colette?*	Dresden Komödie	12/09/29
Besser, Joachim	*Eintracht m. b. H.*	Plauen Stadttheater	11/07/29
Bonner, Hartwig	*Was spät kommt, kommt doch*	Leipzig Schauspielhaus	01/18/30
Bronnen, Arnolt	*Reperationen*	Mannheim National Theater	01/30/30
Bruinier, Hans	*Europa auf dem Stier*	Bad Pyrmont Schauspielhaus	07/08/30
Brust, Alfred	*Nachthorn, Das*	Coburg Landestheater	12/16/29
Burke, Edwin	*Sache, die sich Liebe nennt, Die*	Hamburg Deutsches Schauspielhaus	10/26/29
Cornelius, Franz	*Kameradschaftsehe*	Schwerin Staatstheater	09/25/29
Coward, Noel	*Tratsch*	Berlin Theater am Schiffbauerdamm	05/14/30
Davis, Gustav	*Präsident Haversa*	Hamburg Thalia Theater	01/17/30
Eulenberg, Herbert	*Kuckuck und sein Kind*	Krefeld Stadttheater	01/23/30
Feuchtwanger, Lion	*Wird Hill amnestiert?*	Berlin Staatliches Schauspielhaus	04/24/30
Frank, Bruno	*Sturm im Wasserglas*	Dresden Staatliches Schauspielhaus	08/29/30
Frank, Paul, and Ludwig Hirschfeld	*Geschäft mit Amerika*	Stuttgart Schauspielhaus	02/08/30
Froschel, Georg	*Gerechtigkeit für Holubel*	Breslau Lobe Theater	10/06/29

Fulda, Ludwig	*Frau Fräulein*	Hamburg Thalia Theater	11/27/29
Gottwald, Fritz, and Joe Gribitz	*Wie wird man reich?*	Leipzig Altes Theater	06/04/30
Grube, Max	*Attentat, Das*	Görlitz Stadttheater	11/16/29
Halbert, Abram	*Dame Sabine, Die*	Bremen Stadttheater	10/16/29
Herzog, Alfred	*Krach um Lt. Blumenthal*	Leipzig Kleines Theater	05/10/30
Hofmeier, Ludwig	*Ehe nach dem Buch, Die*	Stuttgart Landestheater	06/06/30
Impekoven, Toni, and Carl Mathern	*neue Sachlichkeit, Die*	Frankfurt /M. Schauspielhaus	04/01/30
Joachimson, Felix	*Ein häßliches Mädchen*	Hamburg Deutsches Schauspielhaus	01/15/30
Kaiser, Max	*geborgte Familie, Die*	Koslin Pommersches Bundestheater	02/18/30
Kelemann, Viktor	*Skandal in Savoy*	Berlin Tribüne Theater	05/16/30
Kihn, Hans Alfred	*Rieckchens Heimkehr*	Leipzig Kleines Theater	11/02/29
Kihn, Hans Alfred	*Tinkelsee*	Dortmund Stadttheater	01/11/30
Lakatos, Ladislas	*Achtzehnjährige*	Hamburg Thalia Theater	01/11/30
Langer, Frantisek	*Bekehrung des Ferninand Pistoria, Die*	Breslau Thalia Theater	10/19/29
Larric, Jack	*Gloria*	Dresden Sächsische Bühne	09/05/29
Lenz, Leo	*Parfum meiner Frau, Das*	Görlitz Stadttheater	10/26/29
Lernet-Holenia, Alexander	*Attraktion, Die*	Kassel Staatstheater	05/28/30
Lichtenberg, Wilhelm	*Seine Majestät, das Publikum*	Gießen Stadttheater	08/28/30
Lichtenberg, Wilhelm	*Dame mit dem schlechten Ruf, Die*	St. Pölten Stadttheater	11/23/29
Lonsdale, Frederic	*Vogel, die am Morgen singen*	Berlin Theater in der Behrenstraße	05/02/30
Lotichius, Erich	*Spiel in Europa*	Elberfeld Stadttheater	09/17/29
Mann, Klaus	*Gegenüber von China*	Bochum Stadttheater	01/27/30

Meyer-Sanden, Willy	*Sprung in die Jugend*	Rheydt Schauspielhaus	02/09/30
Mohr, Max	*Welt der Enkel, Die*	Hamburg Deutsches Schauspielhaus	02/22/30
Möller, Alfred, and Hans Lorenz	*Herr mit den Fragenzeichen, Der*	Hamburg Thalia Theater	04/03/30
Müller, Hans	*Große Woche in Baden-Baden*	Bremen Schauspielhaus	12/25/29
Natanson, Jacques	*Vielgeliebte, Der*	Gera Reußisches Theater	04/29/30
Netto, Hadrian Maria	*Abenteuer in den Pyranaen*	Dresden Sächsisches Landestheater	12/03/29
Neumann, Alfred	*Frauenschuh*	Hamburg Thalia Theater	02/06/30
O'Bordigan, John	*Nacht zum Donnerstag, Die*	Dresden Albert Theater	09/27/29
Pagnol, Marcel	*Marius*	Breslau Lobe Theater	10/19/29
Pirandello, Luigi	*Heute Abend wird aus dem Stegreif gespielt*	Köningsberg Neues Schauspielhaus	01/25/30
Platz, Augustus	*Schumichen sucht Wohnung*	Leipzig Komödienhaus	03/15/30
Richter-Halle, Hermann	*Wetten, daß . . .?*	Berlin Lessing Theater	05/25/30
Rindom, Svend	*Ein Teufelsmädel*	Kiel Schauspielhaus	11/27/29
Rossler, Carl	*Ich habe keine Zeit*	Gießen Stadttheater	06/25/30
Rossler, Carl	*Schuh und Leder*	Liegnitz Stadttheater	02/06/30
Rutza, Ernst	*Werkspionage*	Nuremberg Altes Theater	05/10/30
Sachs, Lothar	*Frau im Netz*	Dortmund Stadttheater	06/03/30
Savoir, Alfred	*Er*	Berlin Tribüne Theater	03/12/30
Schmidt, Friedrich	*Mann ohne Liebe, Der*	Stolpe Stadttheater	01/17/30
Schmidt, Lothar	*Training*	Braunschweig Landestheater	04/12/30
Schweifert, Fritz	*Marguerite*	Berlin Theater in der Stresemannstraße	08/29/30
Shaw, George Ber-nard	*Kaiser von Amerika, Der*	Berlin Deutsches Theater	10/19/29

Stemmle, Robert Adolf	*30,002 will arbeiten*	Gotha Landestheater	01/31/30
Stoskopf, Gustave	*Skandal um Ropfers*	Leipzig Komödienhaus	04/17/30
Tolstoy, Alexei	*Komödie der Verjungung*	Frankfurt /M. Schauspielhaus	12/14/29
Ungar, Hermann	*Gartenlaube, Die*	Berlin Theater am Schiffbauerdamm	12/12/29
Unruh, Fritz von	*Phaea*	Berlin Deutsches Theater	05/13/30
Wasser, Emil	*Aussenseiter*	Zittau Stadttheater	03/15/30
Zeinicke, Edmund	*Otto in Noten*	Constance Stadttheater	09/22/29
Zickel, Richard	*Wohnungsnot*	Coburg Landestheater	10/14/29

NOTES

1. Article Forty Eight had been invoked only twice before: once in the wake of Erzberger's assassination and once during the inflationary period. It was used five times in 1930, and by 1932 it was invoked sixty times, as lawmaking activity in the Reichstag ground virtually to a halt.

2. Count Harry Kessler, *Tagebücher 1918–1937* (Frankfurt: Suhrkamp, 1982) 629.

3. There were obvious similarities between *Topaze* and the aforementioned *Flachsmann als Erzieher* (Flachsmann the Educator) of a previous generation. Even more significant were the parallels between *Topaze* and the most popular film of this season, *Der blaue Engel* (The Blue Angel). The film was based on Heinrich Mann's scathing indictment of corrupt authoritarianism in German schools, titled *Professor Unrat*; it starred Marlene Dietrich and Emil Jannings in a screenplay by Carl Zuckmayer.

4. Although *Das große ABC* enjoyed its greatest popularity during the Weimar years, German audiences remained sensitive to the play and its criticism of government for years afterward. Its first post–World War II production, which took place in Munich in 1952, met with outcries from citizens who claimed the play attacked democracy. The Bavarian government voted to close the production, and it has only rarely been produced there since.

5. George Bernard Shaw, Preface to *The Apple Cart* (New York: Brentano, 1931), vi.

6. Guido Thielscher celebrated his seventieth birthday in September of this season.

7. The outstanding comic prototype for the *Beamter* in German drama is Wehrhahn, the local magistrate in Gerhart Hauptmann's *Der Biberpelz* (The Beaver Coat).

14

The 1930–1931 Season

The economic decline in Germany precipitated by the previous year's collapse of the American stock market continued to have profound consequences for the German theatre during this season. Dozens of private theatres declared bankruptcy, and several municipal theatres closed temporarily or were taken over by entertainment conglomerates. The German theatre also continued to suffer declines in attendance due to the popularity (and lower ticket prices) of the sound film. This season saw the premieres of several musical films which attracted millions of patrons; the most popular among them was *Drei von der Tankstelle* (Three Guys from the Gas Station), with Lillian Harvey, Willi Fritsch, and Heinz Rühmann.[1]

Political upheaval followed the wake of economic uncertainty.[2] In October, voters gave National Socialists unprecedented victories in Reichstag elections, while local legislatures experienced an even greater number of Nazis in their midst.[3] The result was a civil unrest similar to that experienced a decade earlier, when the Reich government dispatched troops to restore order. The Reich government now found itself weakened and unable to extinguish the frequent flareups between antagonistic militias of extremist parties. There were dozens of gunfights between Nazi and Communist sympathizers in several cities, few of which the government was able to curtail. The most notorious of these violent encounters occurred when Horst Wessel, active in the Nazi Storm Troopers (and putative composer of the Nazi anthem, "Hold High the Flag"), was shot to death in his Berlin apartment; his attackers were militia members of the Communist party. A Berlin court found them guilty and sentenced them to six years of hard labor soon after the national elections.

German courts arbitrated cultural affairs, too. They awarded Bertolt Brecht a modest settlement in his suit against Warner Brothers over the filming of his *Die Dreigroschenoper* (The Three Penny Opera); courts then heard cases filed to ban the film from public exhibition. Courts upheld the ban against the American film version of Erich Maria Remarque's popular novel *Im Westen nichts Neues* (All Quiet on the Western Front); protestors claimed the film was "an insult to German prestige," and Nazi sympathizers had repeatedly interrupted showings in Berlin.[4] A Thuringian court lifted the ban against the proabortion play *Frauen in Not* (Women in Need), while Max Reinhardt was pressured under threat of legal constraint to cancel his planned production of the Brecht-Weill opera *Mahagonny* at his Deutsches Theater in Berlin.[5]

The most popular comedy of this season, Bruno Frank's *Sturm im Wasserglas* (Storm in a Water Glass, but "Tempest in a Teacup" is more apt in English), was a treatment of political upheaval and judicial confrontation. It swept through dozens of theatres to amass nearly 1,000 performances after its August premiere in Dresden. Its relatively late premiere made the triumph of *Sturm im Wasserglas* distinctive; most successful comedies in the Weimar Republic had premiered at least one season previous. This comedy proved to be so irresistibly funny, heartwarming, and simultaneously politically germane that theatres clamored for rights to it, setting aside their scheduled repertoires in hopes of exploiting its popularity.[6] It is best defined as a romantic comedy about civic corruption, the press, lost dogs, and the possibility of love—all of which nearly guaranteed interest among German audiences. Frank's superb use of familiar comic devices and romantic intrigue, however, positioned it for lasting, and lucrative, approbation.

Its central characters were attractive members of the "upper crust" in republican Germany who meet an unexpected but well-deserved downfall. It begins in the luxurious drawing room of Viktoria Thoss, who awaits her husband's return from a legislative conference, as a newspaper reporter arrives to interview him. Their conversation is interrupted by the poorly dressed, uneducated Frau Vogel, who excitedly pleads for her "Toni," recently taken into custody. She agrees to depart when Viktoria agrees to advise her husband, the city's vice-mayor, about "Toni." When he arrives, he is preoccupied with the stormy city council meeting he has just left, where a debate erupted about the salary of the council's doorman and the recent case of a dog impounded for the owner's failure to get a proper license. Just then Frau Vogel reappears to claim that the dog is her "Toni" and that Thoss must help her. Thoss dismisses her claim and has her thrown out of his house.

Thoss's peremptoriness sets off a chain of events that lead to his downfall. The newspaper reporter, who witnessed Frau Vogel's plea, writes a lead story the next day from the dog's viewpoint, and citizens rise up to call for Thoss's impeachment. Further investigations reveal that Thoss is romantically involved with the wife of the reporter's employer, the newspaper publisher. The transparent subject matter throughout the play is idealism versus political reality. The older men are jaded, while the young newspaper reporter appears fresh and idealistic. The publisher's wife (and Thoss's paramour) is decadent, while Viktoria is naïve. Frau Vogel and her dog, like the German people in general, are genuine and unaffected.

The play's conclusion takes place at the city courthouse, where the publisher is divorcing his unfaithful wife. The reporter appears, having been arrested for stealing Toni from the dog pound. He sings, "I'm looking for a dog/Who'll neither scratch nor bite/But chews up broken glass/And shits out diamonds bright!" Thoss has departed for Berlin to accept the job of running a big company, and Frau Vogel meantime got 20,000 marks in donations for Toni. The reporter informs the judge that he stole Toni, but only to keep the dog from being euthanized. A veterinarian testifies that Toni is a mutt with no claim to a pedigree (satirizing the Nazi racial theories) and guesses his worth to be about eight marks. Viktoria appears to testify on the reporter's behalf, telling the court that despite the dog's lack of breeding, he has worth beyond monetary value because he is "pure in heart." The implication is that Viktoria can now recognize such things, for she has left her husband and has fallen in love with the reporter.

The last effort by Franz Arnold and Ernst Bach, *Hulla di Bulla,* was one of their best, arranging three distinct targets for their final comic exercise. It parodied the aristocracy as had so many other Weimar comedies (including their own *Stöpsel*). It ridiculed republican politicians but in a kinder, gentler way than did its chief competitor of this season, Frank's *Sturm im Wasserglas*. Finally, it mocked the German film industry for its pretentiousness. Subplots romanticized charlatans and swindlers, as earlier successes on the Weimar stage had done; the difference here was how the playwrights kept so many different plot strands going simultaneously to the play's conclusion.

The initial complication is one of mistaken identity. Guido Thielscher, in his ultimate Arnold and Bach premiere, played a film extra named Papendieck who is working one day at Berlin's ornate City Palace, former home of the deposed Kaiser Wilhelm II, whose family is eager to rent the palace as a way of earning extra money. Shooting for a revolutionary epic has just begun when word comes that the film company must vacate the premises for the arrival of His Royal Highness the King of Hamudistan, Abdulla di Bulla. The republican government, eager to loan the King money and secure oil leases in his country, has arranged to give him a German-style "royal treatment" in the kaiser's former apartments.

Word of the film company's abrupt departure does not reach Papendieck in time, however, and he assumes that King Abdulla and his retinue are leading actors in the film for which he has been hired for one day's shooting. Several comic scenes swiftly unfold, including one of matchless hilarity in which King Abdulla's lieutenants plot his overthrow in favor of his cousin, the eponymous Hulla di Bulla. Convinced that the "actor" playing King Abdulla needs to play his part more convincingly, Papendieck reveals the plot to him. The perpetrators are arrested and Papendieck is awarded the title Duke of Hamudistan.

Next day comes word that Hulla di Bulla has indeed effected a coup d'état and that King Abdulla is in fact an ex-king. That means Papendieck is an ex-duke as well, but all ends happily as Abdulla di Bulla departs for London (where he has secretly deposited millions in gold bullion), republican politicians are mollified, Papendieck departs for his next assignment as a film extra, and a Pseudolus-like confidence trickster agrees to marry his Hamudistan-speaking girlfriend.

In many ways, *Hulla di Bulla* was a summation of the Arnold and Bach *oeuvre,* improving nearly every comic device, linguistic gag, and character foible heretofore employed in their previous efforts. The background of film production provided limitless possibilities for mistaken identities, with Thielscher appearing in various Oriental costumes. The use of the bogus Hamudistan language granted several instances of misunderstanding, misconceptions, and humorous disagreements. The more fully developed characters bestowed the entire dramatic action with more than just setups for Papendieck's comic disingenuousness. The play was in fact a comic portrait of republican life, with a full complement of republican contentiousness, a romantic fascination with political violence, and a penchant for financial corruption.

Surprisingly popular this season was a comedy which, like *Sturm im Wasserglas*, had also premiered late. Carl Zuckmayer's *Der Hauptmann von Köpenick* (The Captain of Köpenick) premiered so late in the season (on March 3) however, that it could not capture enough ticket sales to give Bruno Frank or Arnold and Bach serious competition. It managed 250 performances by July 31, but about a third of them took place at Max Reinhardt's Deutsches Theater, where the comedy premiered with Werner Krauß in the title role. The following season, Zuckmayer's treatment of a paradigmatic episode in German history equaled the successes of Arnold and Bach and surpassed anything ever written by an individual Weimar playwright.

COMEDY PREMIERES OF 1930–1931

PLAYWRIGHT(S)	PLAY TITLE	CITY and THEATRE	DATE
Ackermann, Werner	*Fünf Akte Lotterie*	Frankfurt /M. Künstlertheater	01/07/31
Adam, Robert	*Margot und das Jugendgericht*	Frankfurt /M. Schauspielhaus	05/27/31
Arnold, Franz	*öffentliche Ärgernis, Das*	Berlin Neues Theater am Zoo	12/21/30
Bernard, Tristan	*Jules, Julien, und Juliette*	Berlin Kammerspiele des Deutschen Theaters	12/23/30
Beste, Konrad	*Schleiflack*	Braunschweig Landestheater	11/14/30
Blum, Robert	*Schoffer Antoinette*	Berlin Theater in der Behringerstraße	05/04/31
Blume, Bernhard	*Gelegenheit macht Liebe*	Frankfurt /M. Schauspielhaus	02/14/31
Bodet, Robert	*Vorsicht, Kurve*	Bremen Stadttheater	09/16/30
Bois, Curt, and Max Hansen	*Dienst am Kunden*	Berlin Komödie	04/30/31

Bourdet, Edouard	*schwache Geschlecht, Das*	Berlin Theater am Kurfürstendamm	01/27/31
Brust, Alfred	*Schmoff*	Gera Reußisches Theater	12/12/30
Cammerlohr, Franz	*Tempo über Hundert*	Dresden Staatliches Schauspielhaus	09/25/30
Conried, Max	*große Objekt, Der*	Dresden Staatliches Schauspielhaus	06/19/31
Conried, Max	*Jugend zu zweit*	Hamburg Thalia Theater	09/23/30
Deval, Jacques	*Etienne*	Berlin Tribüne Theater	10/18/30
Ebermayer, Erich	*Dreieck des Glücks*	Halberstadt Stadttheater	12/05/30
Ferrago, Alexander	*Gruß aus Salzburg*	Munster Kammerspiele	12/25/30
Frank, Bernhard	*Hufnagel*	Düsseldorf Schau-spielhaus	09/27/30
Giradoux, Jean	*Amphytrion 38*	Berlin Theater in der Stresemannstraße	01/15/31
Goetz, Wolfgang	*Cavaliere*	Hamburg Deutsches Schauspielhaus	12/26/30
Goldbaum, Walter	*Kongreß von Lugano, Der*	Berlin Schloßpark Theater	09/18/30
Goretsch, Robert	*Journalist über Bord*	Dresden Schauspielhaus	10/30/30
Grube, Herbert	*goldene Schlüssel, Der*	Wuppertal Städtische Bühne	11/16/30
Hasenclever, Walter	*Kommt ein Engel geflogen*	Berlin Komödie	03/21/31
Hell, Peter	*Alles für Marion*	Berlin Theater in der Behrenstraße	12/23/30
Heller, Ferdinand, and Adolf Schutz	*Banditen im Frack*	Teplitz-Schönau Neues Stadttheater	01/29/31
Horváth, Ödön von	*Italienische Nacht*	Berlin Theater am Schiff-bauerdamm	03/20/31
Johnson, Larry	*Ein kluges Kind*	Munich Kammerspiele	10/23/30
Kaibel, Franz	*Indizienbeweis*	Wuppertal Städtische Bühne	09/18/30
Katayev, Valentin	*Quadratur des Krises, Die*	Leipzig Schauspielhaus	10/11/30
Kessler, Richard	*Manikure*	Flensburg Stadttheater	11/05/30

Kraatz, Curt and Max Neal	*Hurra, wir treiben Sport*	Bromberg Deutsche Bühne	10/10/30
Kurtz, Rudolf	*Hut ab vor Onkel Eddie*	Stettin Stadttheater	11/01/30
Langer, Felix	*Was tun Sie, wenn . . ?*	Stettin Stadttheater	09/12/30
Lenz, Leo	*Ständchen bei Nacht, Das*	Görlitz Stadttheater	10/18/30
Lenz, Leo	*stille Kompagnon, Der*	Frankfurt /O. Stadttheater	02/10/31
Maugham, W. Somerset	*Brotverdiener, Der*	Berlin Renaissance Theater	12/20/30
Merck, Hanns, and Rudolf Eger	*Gastspiel am See*	Nuremberg Intimes Theater	12/25/30
Molnar, Ferenc	*Fee, Die*	Berlin Komödie	12/19/30
Mühlfeld, Megerle von	*Fensterpützchen*	Berlin Kleines Theater	04/25/31
Nachmann, Julius	*Aristide Fernino*	Eger Stadttheater	01/07/31
Nikolaus, Paul, and Egon Jacobson	*blaue Maritzius, Die*	Augsburg Stadttheater	03/17/31
Ortner, Hermann Heinz	*Literature G.m.b.H.*	Rudolsstadt Landestheater	03/13/31
Pirandello, Luigi	*Hänschen--hute Dich*	Chemnitz Schauspielhaus	06/06/31
Polgar, Alfred	*Defraudanten, Die*	Berlin Volksbühne	12/12/30
Reimann, Hans, and Walter Rene	*Dreizehnte April, Der*	Saarbrücken Apollo Theater	05/16/31
Rickelt, Gustav	*Reparationsagent, Der*	Guben Stadttheater	10/11/31
Rohde, Carl G.	*Schlager der Saison, Der*	Stendal Landestheater	01/06/31
Sachs, Lothar	*Heiraten—aus-geschlossen*	Leipzig Schauspielhaus	02/08/31
Samson, Ralph	*Drum prufe, wer sich ewig bindet*	Leipzig Schauspielhaus	03/21/31
Savoir, Alfred	*Dompteur, Der*	Berlin Theater am Schiff-bauerdamm	03/06/31
Schurek, Paul	*Wozu der Lärm?*	Flensburg Stadttheater	02/25/31
Sterk, Wilhelm	*Liebe unmodern*	Berlin Kleines Theater	01/24/31

Straßmann, Franz	*Küße im Schlafrock*	Altona Schiller Theater	08/13/31
Szell, Josef	*fünfundzwan-zigste Frau, Die*	Darmstadt Landestheater	01/13/31
Vaszary, Josef Janos	*Ich vertraue Dir meine Frau an*	Hamburg Thalia Theater	05/23/31
Verneuil, Louis	*Ein Held gesucht*	Frankfurt /M. Neues Theater	12/25/30
Verneuil, Louis, and Georges Berr	*Miss Deutschland*	Nuremberg Intimes Theater	02/28/31
Vitez, Nikolaus	*Benutzen Sie die Gelegenheit*	Coburg Landestheater	10/28/30
Wendler, Otto Bernhard	*Liebe, Mord, und Alkohol*	Berlin Tribüne Theater	02/21/31
Wesse, Curt	*Schiffbruch Ahoy!*	Wiesbaden Staatstheater	01/11/31
Wiesalla, Josef	*Hochspannung*	Leipzig Kleines Theater	08/22/31
Zeitz, A. H.	*Eine Frau macht Politik*	Halle Stadttheater	09/23/30
Zoff, Otto	*weissen Handschuhe, Die*	Stuttgart Schauspielhaus	03/21/31
Zuckmayer, Carl	*Hauptmann von Köpenick, Der*	Berlin Deutsches Theater	03/05/31

NOTES

1. Heinz Rühmann (1902–1994) had a long and illustrious career in both theatre and film. His breakthrough came in a Munich production of Avery Hopwood's *Fair and Warmer* during the 1926–1927 season. Critics of that production unanimously agreed he had, at age twenty-five, joined the ranks of established German comic actors Max Pallenberg, Max Adalbert, and Hans Waßmann. Adalbert (1874–1933) starred in the second-most popular film of this season, a military farce titled *Drei Tage Mittelarrest* (Three Days Confined to Barracks), directed by Carl Boese.

2. Unemployment soared during this season. At the time of the October elections, 3 million were out of work, and 4 million were unemployed by the end of the year. Even during the worst parts of the inflationary period in 1923, unemployment figures stayed below 2.7 million. Complicating the picture was the fact that many of those still working had taken severe pay cuts.

3. The city of Oldenburg had a majority of Nazis on their city council after the October elections; the Nazis also made gains in Danzig, Mecklenburg, and Bremen.

4. Joseph Goebbels, director of Nazi chicanery in Berlin, later boasted that turning dozens of white mice loose at the theatre where *All Quiet on the Western Front* premiered was one of his proudest achievements.

5. Brecht and Weill's *The Threepenny Opera* continued to run in Berlin and in other German theatres, Brecht's legal and artistic problems notwithstanding. Their attempt to duplicate the popular success of *Threepenny Opera* at Berlin's Theater am Schiffbauerdamm, *Happy End*, met with failure. So did the Berlin production of Brecht's "comedy" *Mann ist*

Mann at the Staatliches Schauspielhaus. Critic Alfred Kerr described it as a "farce of mistaken identity" and denounced it as "nonsense from a small talent . . . [which] is simply intellectually retarded and childishly pitiful." Quoted in Günther Rühle, *Theater für die Republik* (Frankfurt: Fischer, 1967), 732.

6. Nearly all theatres in the Weimar Republic, public and private, operated as true "repertoire" establishments, running different productions simultaneously. When a play like Frank's, Arnold and Bach's, or those of other popular playwrights offered opportunities for unexpected box office revenues, theatres altered their calendars to permit more performances toward the end of a season. Very few, however, ran one production exclusively.

15

The 1931–1932 Season

The last full theatre season of the Weimar Republic suffered from the ills that afflicted German society as a whole. Dozens of private theatres suspended operation or went out of business entirely, while provincial and municipal subsidies to theatres decreased or were suspended altogether. Some formerly subsidized houses attempted to survive by forming cooperative ventures, sharing payroll, scenic, and administrative costs.[1]

Banks, savings institutions, depositors, and investors fared the worst. Numerous regional banks declared insolvency and halted withdrawals. When the banks did open, most depositors removed their savings, further decreasing any funds available for mortgages or capital investment. As a result, industrial output dwindled. German automobile production, for example, dropped by twenty-seven percent in the first six months of 1931.[2] Trading activity on most exchanges stopped for much of the year. The Reich government managed to negotiate a loan from American banks for $100 million, thanks to President Herbert Hoover's efforts to convince former World War I allies that a moratorium on German war reparations was necessary to reestablish stability.[3]

Economic adversity was the subject of a popular romantic comedy of this season, *Konto X* (Account X) by Rudolf Bernauer and Rudolf Österreicher. "The two Rudis," as they were known in the popular press, had attempted for the past several seasons to displace Franz Arnold and Ernst Bach as the leading duo of comic playwrights on the German stage. This season, with Franz Arnold attempting to carry on alone after the death of his longtime partner, Bernauer and Österreicher finally realized their ambitions.[4] They subtitled it "a play about love and other unmodern things," but its main title derived from an account set up to maintain the family of Countess von Waldhosen. The countess, her daughter Ulli, and her son Kurt, receive RM 3,000 every month, assuming its source is their ancient family's estate. But this ancient family has no estate. The money comes from Dr. Siegfried

Schiller, who is secretly in love with Ulli von Waldhosen and is Jewish in the bargain. An additional complication is Ulli's brother Kurt, who has run up huge gambling debts. Resolving the play's numerous dilemmas is the doughty accountant Reissnagel. Had the play had been written by Arnold and Bach, Reissnagel would have been Guido Thielscher's role. He is a lovable, if irascible, figure bouncing from one situation to the next, "negotiating every curve with aplomb, facilitating every discovery, rendering the play's affable conclusion,"[5] which ultimately includes the engagement of a "mixed marriage" between the blue-blooded Ulli and her Jewish protector. The Nazi press, which by this season had an increasingly wide readership, predictably denounced the play's conclusion.

Nazi response to the most popular comedy of the season, Carl Zuckmayer's *Der Hauptmann von Köpenick* (The Captain of Köpenick), was vitriolic. The subject matter of this comedy was altogether familiar to most Germans, since it was based on an incident that had taken place in 1906. It was the subject of several nonfiction books and articles in the popular press, of popular songs, of a best-selling novel by Wilhelm Schäfer in 1930, and even of two previous dramatic treatments. Zuckmayer's treatment exceeded all others in popularity, a remarkable achievement considering the fact that a film based on Zuckmayer's play ran to full houses during this season as well. This comedy of Wilhelminian manners had nevertheless nearly 1,000 performances during this season, even though the Nazi press attacked it, nationalist deputies in the Reichstag denounced it, and Joseph Goebbels assured Zuckmayer that he, too, like the play's "hero" Wilhelm Voigt would languish for years in Berlin's Moabit Prison once the Nazis took power.

Wilhelm Voigt (1850–1922) was a cobbler who missed the train of economic progress during the *Gründerjahre*, those decades of the late nineteenth century when the German economy expanded exponentially. He was able to augment his meagre earnings in the shoemaking trade with minor burglaries, and police records indicate that he spent substantial portions of his life in local jails. His luck changed when he received a lengthy sentence to Moabit Prison, where he came under the tutelage of an eccentric prison warden whose passion was Prussian military history. His Sunday pastime was to arrange groups of prisoners in miniature military formations and call out their movements as if they were General Yorck's divisions at Jena,[6] General Gneisenau's at Kolberg, or Moltke's in the Franco-Prussian War. Voigt gained a thorough knowledge of military jargon from the warden, and upon his release from Moabit he bought a Prussian captain's uniform. One afternoon in 1906 he commandeered a platoon in Berlin and ordered them to accompany him via trolley car to Köpenick (a Berlin suburb), where he demanded from the mayor a work permit and the municipal strongbox. The mayor and other Köpenick officials immediately complied with "the Captain's" requests, because Voigt blustered with an authentic air of military bombast. Good Germans obey orders, after all, and Voigt made a clean getaway.

The mysterious "Captain" Voigt turned himself in soon after the Köpenick escapade, but by that time he had become a minor celebrity. Kaiser Wilhelm II gave Voigt an audience and a lifetime pension, noting with unconscious irony that

Voigt, more than any real soldier, had demonstrated the reverence Germans felt for a uniform.[7] Zuckmayer's innovation was to use the uniform itself as a central character in the play; it appeared in every scene, passing from its creator (a Jewish tailor in Potsdam) through the hands of several owners and ingeniously intermingling with the cobbler's various misadventures. When Voigt and the uniform are finally joined with each other in a decrepit thrift store, the play took a turn toward comic inevitability. It gave Germans a well-deserved chance to laugh at themselves and their pretensions to "greatness" as a military power. Zuckmayer's bogus captain thumbed his nose at nearly everything Hindenburg and German nationalists represented, while illuminating the stupidity, more obvious during this season than it had been in 1906, of fawning obsequiousness in the face of authority.[8]

Meanwhile the National Socialist German Workers' party, whose members were fixated both on uniforms and on authority figures, continued to win local and provincial elections. They took over the legislatures of Saxony-Anhalt, Mecklenburg-Schwerin, and the Oldenburg legislatures; a Nazi was elected president of the Prussian legislature. They worked hardest of all to make their leader a German citizen so he could run for Reich president. In a series of complicated legislative maneuvers, the provincial government of Braunschweig appointed "the author Adolf Hitler" to the post of legislative counsel in the Braunschweig delegation to the Reichstag. He was accordingly granted German citizenship as a civil servant. During his campaign for Reich president, Hitler sent 50,000 phonograph records of his speeches to local party leaders around the country to be amplified on street corners, at factory gates, and other gathering spots—a technique altogether novel in German politics. He likewise used the airplane as had no other politician before him, and led four or five rallies every day; in the final week of campaigning, he spoke before a total of fifty-four rallies. He came in second behind Hindenburg, trailing the ancient warrior by 6 million votes.

COMEDY PREMIERES, 1931–1932

PLAYWRIGHT(S)	PLAY TITLE	CITY and THEATRE	DATE
Achard, Marcel	*Zu Hilfe, Max*	Darmstadt Landestheater	11/25/31
Alkins, Joe	*kalifornische Nachtigall, Die*	Dresden Albert Theater	09/17/31
Angermayer, Fred Antoine	*Liebling der Kurve*	Leipzig Kleines Theater	03/12/32
Berstl, Julius	*Penelope*	Stettin Stadttheater	01/29/32
Beste, Konrad	*Glück ins Haus*	Hamburg Deutsches Schauspielhaus	01/16/32

Bonn, Ferdinand	*Politische Schuster*	Dresden Albert Theater	09/16/31
Brandley, John	*Kopf in der Schlinge*	Berlin Theater in der Stresemannstraße	11/10/31
Cammerlohr, Franz	*Tiefstapler, Der*	Berlin Theater in der Behrenstraße	06/02/32
Colantuoni, Albert	*Gebrüder Kuckelhorn, Die*	Düsseldorf Schauspielhaus	09/01/31
Dernburg, Jürgen	*eiserne Jungfrau, Die*	Berlin Rose Theater	06/15/32
Dierhagen, Paul Alfred	*Misthaufen, Der*	Frankfurt /M. Neues Theater	09/21/31
Espe, W. M.	*Fall Grootmann*	Berlin Renaissance Theater	02/12/32
Fajko, Alexei	*Mann mit der Mappe, Der*	Dresden Komödie	01/15/32
Fey, Nikolaus	*Aufwertung*	Würzburg Stadttheater	02/13/32
Frank, Bruno	*Nina*	Dresden Staatliches Schauspielhaus	09/03/31
Gero, Marcel	*Uli Witewup*	Leipzig Altes Theater	01/08/32
Glasenapp, Ewald von	*Mann aus der Pfefferland, Der*	Baden-Baden Städtische Schauspiele	10/20/31
Gottwald, Fritz, and Joe Gribitz	*Wiener Küche*	Brunn Schauspielhaus	11/08/31
Graff, Sigmund	*Mary und Lisa*	Gießen Stadttheater	11/20/31
Grant, Neil	*Mutter muß heiraten*	Bremen Stadttheater	05/04/32
Gruebel, Joachim	*Dollardämmerung*	Leipzig Komödienhaus	03/05/32
Gurster, Eugen	*Wetter für morgen veränderlich*	Berlin Tribüne Theater	03/24/32
Halbe, Max	*Gineova*	Munich Residenztheater	06/07/32
Harich, Walther	*Sie sollen platzen*	Königsberg Schauspielhaus	10/10/31
Holm, Fritz	*Beinah Vadder*	Kiel Schauspielhaus	10/15/31
Impekoven, Toni,	*Stanker, Der*	Berlin Theater am Nollendorfplatz	05/13/32
Impekoven, Toni and Carl Mathern	*Wie heißt das Stück?*	Frankfurt /M. Schauspielhaus	05/21/32
Irmler, Karl	*Scherz oder Ehe*	Dortmund Stadttheater	04/19/32

Kaufman, Arthur	*Knockout durch Tizian*	Düsseldorf Städtische Bühne	11/30/31
Lekisch, Hermann and Kurt Sellnick	*Himmelstürmer*	Wiesbaden Staatstheater	05/06/32
Lenz, Leo	*Mann mit der grauèn Schlafen*	Berlin Theater in der Behrenstraße	12/03/31
Lernet-Holenia, Alexander	*Kapriolen*	Munich Schauspielhaus	09/25/31
Lernet-Holenia, Alexander	*Liebesnächte*	Berlin Komödie	03/16/32
Lichtenberg, Wil-helm	*Eva hat keinen Papa*	Hamburg Thalia Theater	09/19/31
Lunzer, Fritz	*Max, der Sieger*	Baden Stadttheater	12/26/31
Mantler, Philip	*Was fang' ich mit ihr an?*	Kassel Kleines Theater	07/27/32
Maurer, Honorio	*Juliette kauft sich ein Kind*	Gießen Stadttheater	01/27/32
Mayer-Exner, Karl	*Karriere*	Teplitz-Schönau Kammerspiele	01/31/31
Moeller, Philip	*Sie und er*	Leipzig Schauspielhaus	10/24/31
Müller, Hans	*Morgen geht's uns gut*	Berlin Lessing Theater	12/25/31
Munch, Peter	*Weltachse, Die*	Kaiserslautern Landestheater	12/27/31
Neander, Felix, and Horst Mann	*Goldmacher Tausendschön*	Altona Schiller Theater	11/13/31
Neumann, Siegmund	*Scheidung*	Berlin Kleines Theater	11/13/31
Ortner, Hermann Heinz	*Amerika sucht Helden*	MunsterTheater der Stadt	11/22/31
Osborn, Paul	*Ich weiß etwas, daß du nicht weißt*	Berlin Theater in der Stresemannstraße	10/10/31
Palitzsch, Otto Alfred	*Madamoiselle Docteur*	Hamburg Lustspielhaus	10/31/31
Pelzer, Franz Michael	*Rosenbraut, Die*	Berlin Deutsches Künstlertheater	09/08/31
Petersen, P. P.	*Kapitalisten, Die*	Schleswig Nordmark Landestheater	11/08/31

Pohl, Jules	*Geldbeutel, Der*	Nuremberg Schau-spielhaus	01/12/32
Preradovic, Peter von	*Verstehen wir uns?*	Gießen Stadttheater	01/12/32
Rehfisch, Hans- José	*Sprung über Sieben*	Hamburg Kammerspiele	11/26/31
Reimann, Hans, and Hans Spoerl	*beschleunigte Personenzug, Der*	Berlin Theater am Nollendorfplatz	09/18/31
Relovnik, Hermann	*Mrs. O.*	Baden-Baden Städtische Bühne	03/12/32
Rickelt, Gustav	*Reparationsagent, Der*	Guben Stadttheater	10/11/31
Romains, Jules	*Kapitalist, Der*	Berlin Deutsches Künstlertheater	10/22/31
Rosner, Karl	*vollkommene Adrian, Der*	Leipzig Schauspielhaus	10/03/31
Rossler, Carl	*verfluchte Geld!, Das*	Berlin Theater in der Behrenstraße	10/02/31
Salm, Stefan W.	*Mary treibt Politk*	Freiburg Stadttheater	03/30/32
Samson, Ralph	*Junge Liebe*	Berlin Lessing Theater	09/03/31
Schulenberg, Werner von dem	*Venus im ersten Haus*	Hamburg Thalia Theater	11/30/31
Steig, Friedrich	*Fortuna 28,003*	Bad Polzin Kurtheater	08/02/32
Stoskopf, Gustav	*doppelte Müller, Der*	Leipzig Komödienhaus	12/01/31
Stuart, Donald	*Rückkehr*	Berlin Komödie	09/25/31
Stubmann, Peter Franz	*Krieg über Sonia*	Hamburg Stadttheater	02/11/32
Sturm, Hans	*Mäuschen im Hause Frensen*	Bad Reinerz Kurtheater	07/29/32
Szomory, Desider	*Eine Frau mit sich allein*	Leipzig Altes Theater	02/13/32
Traut, Carl	*Auskunft streng vertraulich*	Baden-Baden Städtisches Schauspielhaus	09/05/31
Unruh, Fritz von	*Zero*	Frankfurt /M. Schauspielhaus	05/08/32
Wallace, Edgar	*Platz und Sieg*	Leipzig Schauspielhaus	04/16/32
Wäscher, Aribert	*Götter unter sich*	Berlin Rose Theater	02/14/32

Werner, Wilhelm	*Recht auf Sünde, Das*	Hamburg Deutsches Schauspielhaus	03/17/32
Wolf, Edmund	*Musik im Hof*	Mannheim National Theater	06/18/32

NOTES

1. The Cologne Schauspielhaus, Düsseldorf Schauspielhaus, and the Dumont-Lindemann Theater of Düsseldorf merged to form the Deutsches Theater am Rhein; in Breslau the municipal Schauspielhaus and the private Lobe Theater suspended operations simultaneously, then reemerged from bankruptcy as a unified organization. The Prussian government closed its state theatres in Kassel and Wiesbaden, and in Berlin Max Reinhardt relinquished the leases on all his Berlin theatres, while continuing to maintain the Deutsches Theater. His Reibaro cooperative arrangement with Viktor Barnowsky and Robert Klein failed to salvage their operations. Barnowsky's risky effort of the previous season to attract audiences, reducing all ticket prices by fifty percent, may have accelerated Reibaro's collapse.

2. Car production sank during the period from 1930 to 1931 to 76,000, about two-thirds of what it was the previous year, and all other economic indicators showed a continuing decline in output. Cash reserves, investment, wages, mining production, consumption, and profits all dropped precipitously. Taken together, companies in Germany posted losses totaling RM 1.06 billion in 1931, whereas in 1930 they posted overall profits of RM 511 million.

3. Reparations had been a bone of contention in the formulation of both domestic policy and foreign diplomacy throughout the Weimar Republic. As the economic situation worsened, reparations became a "political football," kicked around by several parties in hopes of scoring points with the German electorate. In his New Year's Eve speech of this season, President Hindenburg accused the Allies of injustice and called upon Germans to remember his victory over the Russians at Tannenberg in 1914 and bade his countrymen "co-operate faithfully with one another in unity and with a sense of shared destiny." The Nazis in the Thuringian provincial legislature manipulated the issue more blatantly, compelling school pupils in that province to memorize Paragraph 231 of the Versailles Treaty, which stipulated German payments to former enemies.

4. Bernauer and Österreicher's other notable comedies were *Der Garten Eden* (The Garden of Eden), which had been performed over 1,100 times from 1926 to 1930, and *Geld auf der Straße* (Streets Paved with Gold) during the 1928–1929 season. Bernauer himself, as already noted, was enormously successful as an actor, playwright, producer, director, and film exhibitor.

5. Herbert Ihering, review of *Konto X* in *Berliner Börsen-Courier*, July 16, 1930, n. p.

6. Yorck was the subject of a popular film during this season, starring Werner Krauß, which glorified German military exploits of the nineteenth century, as a series of films about Frederick the Great (starring Otto Gebühr) glorified Prussian victories of the eighteenth century.

7. Michael Balfour, *The Kaiser and His Times* (New York: Norton, 1972), 270.

8. Reichstag deputy Kurt Schumacher (SPD), denouncing the Nazi mania for uniforms, stated in his only speech before the Reichstag during this season, "The entire agitation of National Socialism consists in an appeal to the inner son of a bitch in every man. If we recognize something of ourselves in that appeal, then it confirms for the first time in German politics that the restless mobilization of human stupidity has been achieved." Quoted in Manfred Overesch and Friedrich Wilhelm Saal, *Die Weimarer Republik* (Düsseldorf: Droste, 1982), 580.

16

The 1932–January 30, 1933 Season

Bruno Frank's *Nina*, a vehicle for his mother-in-law, Fritzi Massary, continued its popularity during the last few months of the Weimar Republic and was the most frequently performed comedy until the Nazi takeover. *Nina* employed devices similar to those of other successful comedies of previous seasons. It satirized the film industry; its action centered around the title character(s); and it skillfully implemented discoveries, misunderstandings, reversals, and mistaken identities to propel the action toward a conclusion of seeming inevitability. The novelty playwright Frank implemented was the overt manipulation of Nina's identity, which, in fact, was shared by two characters.

Frank created them for Fritzi Massary (1882–1969), who began her career as an operetta performer in Vienna.[1] She arrived in Berlin in 1904 and played leading roles in works by Johann Strauß II, Franz Lehár, and Leo Fall at the Metropol Theater. By 1918 she was among the most popular musical performers in the city, known as much for her exuberant personality as for her superb singing voice. Julius Bab was one of many critics who hailed her as a "Goddess of the City," whose performances regularly sold out. By the time *Nina* premiered,[2] she was approaching age fifty and her career as a diva had begun to fade. So Frank wrote the play for her, and as Nina Gallas she recapitulated several of her familiar personae. As Nina's film double and stand-in Trude Mielitz, however, she embodied the brash impetuosity of the Berlin film industry itself.

In the play's first act, Nina decides to retire from films in order to spend more time with her devoted husband, a shy inventor. She proposes to the producer of her films, a suave Hungarian named Paul Hyrkan,[3] that her replacement be Trude Mielitz, who looks and sounds so much like Nina that she could easily become the studio's next diva. Hyrkan agrees to become Trude's Pygmalion, and the former stand-in rises from obscurity into full-blown, petulant stardom. She and Hyrkan travel to Hollywood for her first English-language film, and there Trude learns definitive lessons in flamboyant superficiality. She returns to Berlin in the final act with an aura of tawdry glitz and irresistible banality. Frank combined well-motivated exits and entrances for Nina/Trude, and his clever pacing allowed the contrasting personalities of both to emerge. This comedy also featured various recognizable comic stage types, such as the *gemütlich* Bavarian, the urbane film director, the officious secretary, and the obliging husband, all of whom prove foils for either Nina or Trude.[4]

As he had in his earlier successes (particularly *Sturm im Wasserglas*), Bruno Frank interlarded his comedy with political observation. This comedy was about the creation of an "image," and Frank was keenly aware of Adolf Hitler's success in manipulating the media and exploiting recent technological innovations in the creation of his own image as Germany's savior. Though his run for Reich president had been unsuccessful, Hitler had nevertheless made an enormous impact on the German electorate. The National Socialist German Workers' party was, by the time this season began, the largest party in the country and boasted the largest faction in the Reichstag.[5] Hitler was an ingenious innovator in the use of radio, film, air travel, the print media, and public relations in general. It seemed plausible to Frank, and to the thousands who saw his play, that conscientious effort dedicated to imagemaking could pay enormous dividends. If an unemployed, uneducated rabblerouser could become the country's best-selling author and leading political force, certainly a former stand-in for a star could become a star herself.

Under no circumstances, however, was *Nina* a protest against the rise of the Nazi movement. By the fall of 1932, Nazism had become much too powerful for a single play to impede its progress toward the takeover of power. The chancellor himself, Franz von Papen, stated in September that the ideal of the Weimar constitution, self-government by the people, was no longer possible. An authoritarian form of government, he said, was the only alternative for the German state. He made that statement as a feeble rationale for his own attempts to maintain power, but the eighth and last general election for the Reichstag before the Nazi takeover proved his observation accurate. The Nazis netted the most votes (11.74 million, or 33.1 percent of the entire electorate), with their closest rivals (the Social Democrats) getting 7.25 million, or 20.4 percent. There were the usual resignations from the Cabinet, but Hindenburg refused to appoint Hitler chancellor. Instead, he called upon Kurt von Schleicher to form a new government. Schleicher named barons, counts, and knights as ministers, all of whom were dedicated to keeping the Nazis out of power. Schleicher's aristocrats considered the Nazis similar to Trude Mielitz; they were flashy but crude.

Hindenburg himself considered Hitler a comical figure. On January 27, 1933 President Hindenburg assured army chief of staff General von Hammerstein, "You don't think I'm going name this Austrian corporal Chancellor of the Reich, do you?" The next day, Schleicher's government resigned, and rumors flew through the city that Schleicher and General von Hammerstein had ordered the Potsdam garrison to march on Berlin and arrest Hindenburg. In a panic, Hindenburg listened to his son Oskar argue that Hitler should lead the new government. At 11:00 a.m.

the next day, January 30, 1933, Hindenburg named Hitler chancellor and administered the oath of office to him. That afternoon, Hitler moved into the Reich Chancellery. As he entered the building, he is reported to have said, "No power on earth will bring me out of here alive." It was the last day of the Weimar Republic.

COMEDY PREMIERES OF 1932–JAN. 30, 1933

PLAYWRIGHT(S)	PLAY TITLE	CITY and THEATRE	DATE
Arnold, Franz	*Da stimmt etwas nicht*	Dresden Komödie	12/23/32
Billinger, Richard	*Lob des Landes*	Leipzig Altes Theater	01/25/33
Brennert, Hans	*Kolonne Immergrün*	Berlin Theater am Schiffbauerdamm	09/23/32
Giovanetti, Silvio	*Spazierstock, Der*	Berlin Tribüne Theater	10/13/32
Gräbke, Friedrich	*Mann, den es nicht gibt, Der*	Hannover Städtische Bühne	12/11/32
Hay, Julius	*neue Paradies, Das*	Berlin Volksbühne am Bülowplatz	12/03/32
Horváth, Ödön von	*Kasimir und Karoline*	Leipzig Schauspielhaus	11/18/32
Just, Peter	*Ein Mädel hat sich verlaufen*	Bremen Schau-spielhaus	10/18/32
Laszlo, Aladar	*ehrlicher Finder erhält . . .?, Der*	Hamburg Deutsches Schauspielhaus	09/09/32
Lekisch, Hermann, and Kurt Sellnick	*Gold!!!*	Wiesbaden Landes-theater	12/25/32
Loesch, Wilma von	*Traum in Blau*	Baden-Baden Städtische Schauspiele	10/28/32
Lutz, Josef Maria	*Zwischenfall, Der*	Rudolstadt Land-estheater	12/20/32
Müller-Schlösser, Hans	*Die Laus im Pelz*	Krefeld Stadttheater	01/13/33
Neal, Max, and Karl Bohrig	*Ein Amtsschimmel wird scheu*	Breslau Deutsche Bühne	12/25/32
Reck-Malleczewen, Percy	*Bomben auf Monte Carlo*	Liegnitz Stadttheater	11/18/32
Winsloe, Christa	*Schicksal nach Wunsch*	Berlin Deutsches Theater	09/09/32

NOTES

1. Bruno Frank was only five years younger than his mother-in-law, and she outlived him by a quarter-century. Fritzi Massary's husband, the comic actor Max Pallenberg, was killed in a 1934 plane crash. She accompanied Frank and her daughter first to England and later to Hollywood.

2. *Nina* premiered in Dresden at the beginning of the previous season with Alice Verden in the title role(s). It was a "tryout" production prior to the one with Massary in Berlin, which opened in November 1931 at the Deutches Künstlertheater. Frank used the Dresden production to "fine tune" the play before it opened in Berlin.

3. The "image" of the urbane film director was familiar to German audiences. The directors Ernst Lubitsch, Fritz Lang, G. W. Pabst, and Friedrich Wilhelm Murnau had well-established careers (both in Berlin and in Hollywood) by the time *Nina* premiered and were as well known as Fritzi Massary herself.

4. This season in New York saw a startlingly similar character, named Lili Garland, in Hecht and MacArthur's *Twentieth Century* on Broadway. Lili begins as a piano accompanist, becomes a Broadway musical star, and subsequently achieves movie stardom. The play was the basis for a successful film with Carole Lombard as Lili, and as a 1978 musical titled *On the Twentieth Century*, with music by Cy Coleman, starring Madeline Kahn as Lili.

5. The NSDAP had 1.3 million members in September 1932; its nearest competitor, the Social Democratic party, had 917,000 members. Hermann Göring had been elected president of the Reichstag in August, and other Nazi leaders had been named to head influential committees. Hitler himself had been offered the post of vice-chancellor, but he rejected it, demanding instead the full powers of state leadership.

Biographical Appendix

Useful information readily available in English about German playwrights is sparse in general, and the facts about most of them with connections to comedy in the Weimar Republic are rare indeed. This appendix attempts to remedy that circumstance by summarizing the careers of the most significant and influential contributors of plays covered in this book. Some were, of course, more significant than others; some had died by the time the Weimar Republic was declared (such as Franz von Schönthann and Adolf L'Arronge). Yet they appear here because their plays enjoyed a continued appeal among audiences. Others were substantial contributors in other genres and their association with comedy was only ephemeral (such as Hugo von Hofmannsthal and Bertolt Brecht), yet their importance to the period in general demands their inclusion. Several non-German playwrights are included as well—all of them had comedies performed in the Weimar Republic, and some (such as George Bernard Shaw, Avery Hopwood, Noel Coward, and Marcel Pagnol) were among the most popular playwrights on German stages.

A majority of the personalities and backgrounds covered in this appendix had close, functional bonds to practical theatre work. The experience of many successful comic playwrights in the Weimar Republic included stints as actors, directors, or dramaturgs; that partly explains the astounding commercial success of several plays with devices distinctively constructed for widespread commercial appeal and with a specific style of performance, or even a specific actor, in mind. Guido Thielscher, for example, played the central role in eight of the eleven comedies premiered by Franz Arnold and Ernst Bach between 1919 and 1933. The comedies of Toni Impekoven and Carl Mathern were often created for the ensemble of actors they had gathered in Frankfurt am Main.

Many observers of German drama were reluctant to grant serious consideration to a comedy if they detected any conspicuous commercial intent on the part of the comedy's creator(s). Most Berlin critics depreciated a play's intellectual value if it aimed at a wide audience. The same critics paradoxically dismissed it if they felt the same play could not achieve success when performed by any group of talented actors. Such criticism, like its counterpart today, overlooked the fact that comedies written initially for specific actors (such as *Der Hauptmann von Köpenick* for Werner Krauß or *Nina* for Fritzi Massary) went on to hundreds of performances in scores of other successful productions.

MARCEL ACHARD (1899–1974) was one of several French playwrights whose work enjoyed popularity on German stages during the Weimar Republic. Achard's theatrical pursuits began in 1919 with Jacques Copeau at Vieux-Colombier in Paris; his playwriting career began with Charles Dullin's successful production of his *Voulez-vous jouer avec moi?* (Do You Want to Play with Me?) in 1923; it premiered in Germany on December 31, 1926, at the Düsseldorf Schauspielhaus under the title *Wollen Sie mit mir spielen?* Achard was strongly influenced by Luigi Pirandello and used characters from the *commedia* tradition to explore the instability of the modern world. He had numerous other successes in the Parisian theatre, but only one other was premiered in Germany. He emigrated briefly to Hollywood, California in the 1930s, but he returned to France in 1938.

LEONHARDT ADELT (1881–1945) attended university in Berlin and later worked as a newspaper editor in Vienna and Hamburg. During World War I he was a battlefield correspondent for the *Berliner Tageblatt*, and after the war he held various other editorial jobs in Vienna and Munich. His output as a comic playwright was substantial though undistinguished. His comedies that premiered during the Weimar years included *Die Dohle* (The Jackdaw, 1920), which concerned a newly rich businessman who buys an ancient palace to transform it into a showplace for himself. Along with the palace he unknowingly has bought its resident talking jackdaw (hence the title). The bird has mystical powers and possesses the spirit of a woman who died in the palace years earlier. The entire play is an attempt at comic metaphor, with the palace symbolizing the "good old days" gone by; the businessman represents the new, insensitive mercantile class running the Weimar Republic. Other comedies by Adelt included *Falsche Karten—Redlich Spiel* (1926), *Villa Robinson* (1929), *Kathrin bleibt jung* (1929), and *Mabels Baby* (1932).

FRANZ ARNOLD (1878–1960) was perhaps the most commercially successful playwright in the Weimar Republic. Arnold was born in Znin near Bromberg and studied acting with Arthur Kraußneck in Berlin. He debuted as an actor in 1897 at Eberswald and had subsequent engagements in Wismar, Leignitz, Beuthen, and Magdeburg, and finally by 1907 in Berlin. There he acted in comic roles at the Friedrich-Wilhelmstädtisches Theater, achieving his "breakthrough" as Giesecke in *Im wießen Rößl* (The White Horse Inn) by Franz von Schönthann and Gustav Kadelburg. He started working in 1909 for the Lustspielhaus, a theatre wholly devoted to comedy production. There he met Ernst Bach, under whose direction he acted and with whom he frequently performed. Their first great triumph written together was *Die spanische Fliege* in 1913, in which Arnold played the central character Klinke and Bach played his imaginary son Gerlach. Their collaboration was interrupted by the war's outbreak, and Arnold acted and directed in an army theatre in 1917 and 1918 on the western front. After the war, he returned to Berlin and again began writing plays with Bach, directing them himself. Their procedure was usually to vacation in Bavaria together and to write a play each season. Their partnership was so successful that together they became known as "the firm of Arnold and Bach." In every season, except 1923–1924, their plays were among the most often performed during the lifetime of the Weimar Republic. After Bach's death in 1929, Arnold could not continue in the same way; he emigrated to England in 1933.

ERNST BACH (1876–1929) was Franz Arnold's partner, although he was an established director and producer in his own right. Their phenomenal success as playwrights enabled him to run the Munich Volkstheater throughout the Weimar years and earn extraordinary profits. He was born in Bohemia, and after finishing high school in Vienna he began acting in Vienna's Raimund Theater. For the 1903–1904 season he was engaged at the Berlin Residenztheater under director Siegmund Lautenberg; that theatre specialized in French farces, which Bach studied closely as an actor. In the fall of 1905, Bach was engaged by the Lustspielhaus in Berlin, where he began directing. In 1908 he was named principal director at that theatre, and a year later he began working with Franz Arnold. In 1914 Bach was drafted into the Austrian army, and upon his discharge took over codirectorship of the Munich Volkstheater. In 1923 he became that theatre's principal director. He ceased acting altogether after the war and concentrated on his work with Arnold; Arnold usually premiered their plays in Berlin, and Bach followed with his own production in Munich throughout the Weimar years until his untimely death in 1929. Among the more successful comedies he and Arnold wrote were *Zwangseinquartierung* (1918), *Der keusche Lebemann* (1921), *Der kühne Schwimmer* (1922), *Die vertagte Nacht* (1923), *Der wahre Jakob* (1924), *Stöpsel* (1926), *Hurra—ein Junge!* (1927), *Unter Geschäftsaussicht* (1928), and *Week-end im Paradies* (1929).

HERMANN BAHR (1863–1934) may best be described as a prophet without honor in his own country. His profession was that of journalist, and he remained one most of his life because he never earned enough money in his literary pursuits to support himself otherwise. His collected works total 120 volumes, including forty plays, ten novels, five collections of novellas, nine published volumes of diaries, eight volumes of theatre criticism, and forty-eight volumes of essays. He was among that group of writers in the decaying Habsburg world who were sensitive, melancholy, and skeptical. His comedies dealt with the erotic adventures of eccentric people whose psychoses drive them to thrillseeking. His comedies were most often performed in Germany at the beginning of the twentieth century, although his *Das*

Konzert (1910) was performed frequently during the Weimar Republic years.

ERNST BARLACH (1870–1938), the son of a doctor in Holstein, studied in Dresden and trained as a graphic artist and sculptor in Paris and in Hamburg. In Berlin he later taught ceramics while created remarkable sculptures in wood. His best writing for the theatre he completed after the age of forty and was awarded the Kleist Prize in 1924. He is generally known as an Expressionist playwright, although the characters he created are earthy and rooted in distinct motivation.

RUDOLF BERNAUER (1880–1953) was one of the most energetic personalities in the history of twentieth-century German theatre. He was born in Budapest but completed high school in Berlin. At the University of Berlin he studied philosophy while an apprentice at Deutsches Theater under Otto Brahm. He subsequently worked as a full-time actor for Brahm, performing with fellow actor Max Reinhardt, with whom he collaborated on premieres at the Schall und Rauch cabaret. He was among the first actors Reinhardt hired in 1903 at the Neues Theater in Berlin, and later Bernauer became Reinhardt's personal assistant at the Deutsches Theater. In 1901 he began working with Carl Meinhard (1886–1949) on their cowritten parodies of then-current Berlin theatrical triumphs, and with Meinhard he took over the lease of the Berliner Theater in 1907. In 1911 they added the Theater in der Königgrätzerstraße and in 1913 the Komödienhaus; they later became owners of the Theater am Nollendorfplatz. Even after he became wealthy as a theatrical entrepreneur and retired to Italy in 1924, Bernauer continued to write libretti for operettas, comedies, burlesque reviews, and screenplays; he also returned to Berlin occasionally to direct and produce. In 1931 he opened an elaborate movie house in Berlin, where Lewis Milestone's *All Quiet on Western Front* premiered, which earned him the enmity of the Nazis. When they came to power, Bernauer was arrested and later forced to auction his Berlin properties at a considerable loss. He emigrated to London in 1934, where he wrote screenplays. In the last years of the Weimar Republic, Bernauer formed a writing partnership with Rudolf Österreicher, and together they wrote some of the most successful comedies of that period. Their *Der Garten Eden* (1926), *Das Geld auf der Straße* (1928), and *Konto X* (1930) were performed hundreds of times in scores of productions.

GEORGES BERR (1867–1943) was a frequent collaborator with Louis Verneuil in Parisian boulevard comedies. Berr and Verneuil had one success in Berlin, *Maître Bolbec et son mari* performed in German under the title *Dr. Bolbec und seine Gatte* (Dr. Bolbec and his Wife). It premiered one year after its 1926 Paris premiere at Berlin's Renaissance Theater. Its subject matter was the postwar increase in the number of women lawyers. Dr. Bolbec in the title is forced to become a "house husband" and must make appointments to see his wife, as do all her other clients.

JULIUS BERSTL (Gordon Mitchell, 1893–1975) was born in Bernburg/Saale (now in the Czech Republic) and studied in Göttingen and Leipzig. He began his theatrical career at the Kleines Theater in Berlin from 1909 to 1913 and from 1913 to 1916 for Viktor Barnowsky at the Lessing Theater. After military service Berstl returned to Barnowsky and worked simultaneously for a Berlin publisher. His comedies *Dover-Calais* (1926) and *Scribbys Suppen sind die Besten* (Scribby's Soups are the Best, 1929) enjoyed substantial runs in Berlin but not in provincial theatres. In 1936 he emigrated to London, where he wrote radio dramas in English for the British Broadcasting Corporation.

BERNHARD BLUME (1901–1974) was born in Stuttgart and studied in Munich, Tübingen, and Stuttgart. During the 1925–1926 season he was dramaturg at the Oberschlesisches Landestheater, and after 1926 he worked as a freelance writer in Stuttgart. He left Germany in 1936 and taught at Mills College in California until 1945, when he became Professor of German Art and Culture at Ohio State University. He remained there until 1966, when he accepted a teaching post at the University of California at San Diego. His Weimar comedies were *Feurio* (1928) and *Gelegenheit macht Liebe* (Opportunity for Love, 1931).

OSCAR BLUMENTHAL (1852–1917) was born in Berlin and died even before the Weimar Republic was declared, yet the popularity of his plays through the Weimar years remained considerable. He studied in Leipzig, where he earned a doctorate at the age of twenty. In 1873 he became an editor in Leipzig, and a year later he moved to Dresden where he edited and published a monthly journal of poetry and criticism. In 1875 he returned to Berlin to become the drama critic of the *Berliner Tageblatt*, from which he exercised considerable influence. Blumenthal gave up daily journalism in 1887 to take over the directorship of the Lessing Theater in Berlin. In this theatre he staged comedies he had written himself. In 1898 he retired from active practice in the theatre, largely because his playwriting efforts had made him wealthy. Thereafter he devoted himself to freelance writing in Berlin. His most popular plays were written with Gustav Kadelburg (1851–1925); among them were *Großstadtluft* (Big City Airs, 1891); *Hans Huckebein*, 1897; and their most successful, indeed one of the most successful and popular of all German comedies, *Im weißen Rößl* (The White Horse Inn, 1897). This particular comedy was enormously popular during the Wilhelmine period, and through the war years it remained in the repertoires of most theatres through the life of the Weimar Republic. Many actors got their start performing roles in it at provincial playhouses, and it was frequently revived at private theatres in larger cities.

CURT BOIS (1901–1992), who was born in Berlin, was a child actor there from 1908 to 1914 at the old Thalia Theater. From 1914 to 1921 he worked as a dancer at cabarets and clubs in Germany, Austria, Hungary, and Switzerland; from 1921 to 1923 he worked with Rudolf Nelson and Rosa Valetti in their cabaret act; and from 1923 to 1925 he performed in operettas at Theater am Kurfürstendamm in Berlin. From 1925 to the end of the Weimar Republic, he wrote plays (most notably *Dienst am Kunden*, or Serve the Customer, with Max Hansen), was popular as a comic actor in various Berlin and Viennese theatres, and worked in radio and film. Bois emigrated to Vienna in 1933 and in 1934 to New York, where he appeared in a 1935 English-language production of Friedrich Wolfs *Cyanide*. From 1937 to 1950, he worked as an actor in several Hollywood films, most notably Warner Brothers' *Casablanca* in 1942. In 1950 he returned to East Berlin to work with Bertolt Brecht and Helene Weigel at the Berliner Ensemble. He also worked in the Federal Republic of Germany with Fritz Kortner, under whose direction he went from comic to character parts at the Schiller and Schloßpark Theaters in West Berlin. By the time of his death at ninety-one, he had received numerous prizes, awards, and honors in both German republics. His last acting assignment was a featured role in Wim Wenders's 1989 film, *Wings of Desire*, with Peter Falk.

FERDINAND BONN (1861–1933) studied law in Munich, but in 1885 he became an actor, taking private lessons from actors at the Residenztheater in Munich and getting his first job at the Stadttheater Nuremberg. There followed a series of engagements, because Bonn became popular with audiences as a leading man. He was most popular at the prestigious Burgtheater Vienna, where he worked until 1896. He then moved to Berlin and the Lessing Theater. In 1905 he opened Ferdinand Bonns Berliner Theater on Charlottenstraße, where he presented an entire repertoire of plays he had written himself. After this business collapsed (Berlin critics reacted negatively to his work, although the kaiser and his sons regularly attended the productions), he successfully toured provincial theatres. He was particularly popular in his adaptation of Arthur Conan Doyle's *The Hound of the Baskervilles*, in which he played the role of Sherlock Holmes. He returned to Berlin shortly before World War I in a production of Shakespeare's *Richard III* on horseback for the Busch Circus, to vituperative condemnation by critics. He continued acting and wrote two comedies during the years of the Weimar Republic.

EDOUARD BOURDET (1877–1945) wrote both comedies and plays with serious subject matter that were popular mostly in Berlin during the Weimar Republic. His *Le Prisonnière* (*Die Gefangene*, or The Female Inmate, 1926), for example, was a study of lesbianism. His comedies also treated sexuality, but as satirical comedies of manners with unusual psychological insights. His *Le Sexe faible* (*Das schwache Geschlecht*, or The Weaker Sex, 1920), for example, portrays prosperous "emancipated" women in a posh Paris hotel, where the cynical maître d'hôtel arranges encounters for them with attractive young men. It is a world in which social and sexual norms of the prewar world are reversed.

BERTOLT BRECHT (1898–1956) was born in the Bavarian town of Augsburg, where he grew up and attended school. He served briefly in a medical ward at the close of World War I and then attended university in Munich. Brecht became one

of the twentieth century's most influential theorists, and one of its most successful playwrights and directors as well. He wrote plays in the Weimar period which he termed "comedies" (such as *Trommeln in der Nacht*, or Drums in the Night and *Mann ist Mann*, or A Man's a Man), but his most successful effort was *Die Dreigroschenoper* (The Three Penny Opera) in 1928, a collaboration with Kurt Weill and Elisabeth Hauptmann based upon John Gay's *The Beggar's Opera*. During the 1928–1929 season it was one of the most frequently performed musical plays on German-language stages.

NOEL COWARD (1899–1973) began his theatrical career in London at the age of twelve, and by age twenty-three he was already a successful playwright in the West End. In the 1925 London season alone, he had five comedies running simultaneously. His comedies were likewise popular throughout Germany during the Weimar period; his first hit was *Hay Fever* (under the German title *Week-End*) in 1927–1928. During the 1931–1932 season, *Private Lives* (under the title *Intimitäten*, or Intimacies) was one of the most frequently performed of any comedy in Germany. Coward himself was an extraordinarily versatile theatre artist; in addition to his skills as a playwright, he was a gifted song writer and librettist. He was also a talented actor in his own plays and in his musicals, which he often staged himself. His success as a playwright continued well into the 1940s, when his *Blithe Spirit* had a record run in London with nearly 2,000 performances. He also wrote, directed, and starred in the popular patriotic film *In Which We Serve* in 1944. He was knighted in 1970.

JACQUES DEVAL (1894–1972) created comedies which structurally resembled those of Franz Arnold and Ernst Bach, Toni Impekoven and Carl Mathern, Bruno Frank, Max Reimann and Otto Schwartz, and that of his Parisian colleagues Marcel Achard, Georges Birabeau, Sacha Guitry, and Louis Verneuil. What set Deval apart was his choice of difficult subject matter. The best example is *Etienne*, which was popular both in Paris and in Berlin in 1930. The eponymous hero is a teenager who seeks to mediate between his bombastic, philandering father and his diffident, anguished mother. The play at first seeks to treat Etienne's emotional development, but it descends into caricature, much to the delight of audiences. "If a play has a happy ending," Deval once wrote, "it is because it would be too depressing for it to have an unhappy one."

GEORG ENGEL (1866–1931) was born in Greifswald, the son of a business executive. He was for a short time editor of the *Berliner Tageblatt*, but for the most part he worked as a freelance writer, and most of his plays were performed in the Wilhelmine years. His last play, and the only one done in Weimar years, was *Die Diplomatin* (The Lady Diplomat) in 1924.

OTTO ERLER (1873–1943), born in Gera, Thuringia, was the son of a peasant family. He studied in Berlin and Marburg, where he completed a dissertation on medieval French mystery plays. He lived as freelance writer in Dresden during the Nazi period and saw himself as the successor to Heinrich von Kleist and Friedrich Hebbel. His most successful effort during the Weimar period was *Der Galgenstrick* (The Scalawag) in 1925, but among the Nazis he found favor with *Thors Gast* (Thor's Guest) in 1937.

PAUL ERNST (1866–1933) studied political science in Göttingen and earned a doctorate at Berlin. The son of a miner, he was active in Social Democratic party politics and wrote Naturalist plays during the Wilhelmine period; he later began to write in a neoromantic style, then in a neoclassical style. He then became a confirmed Christian believer and gave up politics and playwriting altogether, even though his comedies found favor among Nazi critical circles.

HERBERT EULENBERG (1876–1946) was a successful playwright among Wilhelmine audiences from about 1902 to 1912, and his comedies continued to be premiered during the Weimar years. By that time, however, his work had fallen in critical esteem. In 1901 he got the attention of Ferdinand Bonn, who hired him as a dramaturg at the Berliner Theater. Luise Dumont, who as an actress with director Otto Brahm until 1904, liked his play *Münchhausen* and employed him as her dramaturg in Düsseldorf from 1906 to 1909; during that period, Eulenberg also edited Dumont's in-house literary journal, titled *Die Masken*.

RENE FAUCHOIS (1882–1962) was an actor as well as a successful Parisian playwright. He is best remembered for a 1932 play that was notable first in French (*Prenez garde à la peinture*), then in German (*Achtung, frisch gestrichen!*), and in English as *The Late Christopher Bean*. It was based loosely on the life of Vincent van Gogh. Fauchois's other success in the Weimar years was *Der sprechende Affe* (*Le Singe qui parle*, or The Ape Who could Talk), which premiered at the Berlin Komödie in 1925.

LION FEUCHTWANGER (1884–1958) was born into an orthodox Jewish family in Munich, where he attended university; in Berlin, he completed a doctoral thesis on Heinrich Heine. Berlin also saw the beginning of his career that included editorial work, founding his own literary journal and ultimately writing several novels with Jewish themes. He was interned in Italy at the outbreak of World War I, but he escaped to enlist in the German army. Feuchtwanger lived in Berlin during Weimar years and was a close friend and advisor to Bertolt Brecht. Feuchtwanger and Brecht collaborated in 1924 on the adaptation of Christopher Marlowe's *Edward II*. He is perhaps best known as author of the novels *Jud Süß* (Jew Suess, 1925) and *Erfolg* (Success, 1929). The latter recounts the revolutionary events in Bavaria in the early 1920s, when several Jewish politicians were killed or imprisoned for their participation in the short-lived "Bavarian Soviet Republic." *Jud Süß* is based on an earlier novelle (1828) by Wilhelm Hauff (1802–1827). Feuchtwanger's version, like the earlier one, treats the historical figure Josef Süß-

Oppenheimer (1698–1738), financier to the corrupt and extravagant Duke Karl Alexander of Württemburg. Süß satisfied the duke's increasing demands for money to pay for his luxuries by oppressive taxation, the sale of public offices, and extortion. When the duke desired Süß's daughter Naemi as his mistress, Süß turned secretly against his patron and betrayed his political plans. The duke died, and long-restrained popular hatred of Süß resulted in his trial, conviction for high crimes, and public execution in Stuttgart amid general rejoicing. Paul Kornfeld's stage treatment appeared in 1930, and the Nazi film with Werner Krauß came out in 1940. Feuchtwanger collaborated with Brecht in the 1950s in a stage version of his novel *Simone*, which became *Die Gesichte der Simone Machard.*

MARIELUISE FLEISSER (Marieluise Haindl, 1901–1974) was born and died in Ingolstadt to an established family in the ironware business. She was educated at a convent school and briefly at the University of Munich. In the early 1920s, she became acquainted with Lion Feuchtwanger and through him with Bertolt Brecht. Brecht convinced Moritz Seeler to do her play *Die Fußwaschung* (The Foot Washing) under the auspices of Die junge Bühne in 1926 at the Deutsches Theater; Brecht not only directed it but retitled it *Fegefeuer in Ingolstadt* (Purgatory in Ingolstadt). The critic Alfred Kerr said it sounded like it had been mostly written by Brecht, too. Her only comedy in the Weimar era, *Pioniere in Ingolstadt* (Pioneers in Ingolstadt), was likewise directed by Brecht, and the production contributed to a rift between the two.

BRUNO FRANK (1887–1945) was born in Stuttgart and studied in Tübingen, Munich, Straßburg, and Heidelberg, where he earned a doctorate. One of the most successful of all playwrights in the Weimar years, he lived in Munich as an independent playwright and translator. He achieved his first successes with his translations from French farces and later in his own plays Perlenkomödie (Pearl Comedy), *Sturm im Wasserglas* (Tempest in a Teacup), and *Nina* (written for his mother-in-law, the distinguished operetta performer Fritzi Massary). *Sturm im Wasserglas* was the most performed play of the 1930–1931 season, and *Nina* was leading all other titles by the time of the Nazi takeover in January 1933. Along with Max Mohr, Georg Kaiser, and Carl Zuckmayer, Frank was among the most popular of individual comedic playwrights in the Weimar period.

FULDA, LUDWIG (1862–1939), the son of a wealthy Jewish family, studied in Berlin and Heidelberg, where he earned a doctorate. He lived in various German cities until 1896, when he settled in Berlin and became an influential figure in the Reich capital's literary circles. Fulda was a prolific essayist, translator (of Molière, Edmond Rostand, Henrik Ibsen, and Spanish playwrights), and comic playwright, especially in the Wilhelmine era. His *Der Talisman* was to have won the 1903 Schiller Prize, but Kaiser Wilhelm II vetoed the award; Fulda then left for America, but returned in 1906. Fulda's Weimar comedies include *Das Wundermittel* (1919), *Des Esels Schatten* (1922), *Höhensonne* and *Die Durchgängerin* (1925), and *Frau*

Fräulein (1929).

HENRI GHEON (1875–1943) was a leader of the modern revival of religious drama in France; he converted to Roman Catholicism as a result of his experiences in World War I, in which he served as a surgeon. His plays were written after Paul Claudel's but performed before them. His only play to be performed in the Weimar years was *Le Comédien et la grâce*, titled *Das Spiel vom Gehenkten* (The Condemned Man) in German. It premiered at the Berlin Komödie in 1925 and enjoyed a thriving run, but it did not do well in provincial theatres.

JEAN GIRADOUX (1882–1944) was a novelist and playwright who had discovered an interest in the German language and culture during his student days. His first successful play was *Siegfried*, based upon a novel he had begun in 1922. It premiered in France under the direction of Louis Jouvet in 1928. Its subject was a French soldier who is wounded on a World War I battlefield and is reeducated as a German. It did not do well on German stages. His *Amphytrion 38*, on the other hand, did well in Berlin and Hamburg in 1931. It is the thirty-eighth retelling, according to Giradoux's reckoning, of the old legend in which Jupiter comes to Earth disguised as the Theban general Amphitryon in order to seduce the latter's wife, Alcmena (whose main preoccupation is fidelity to her husband). Jupiter succeeds in disguise, but when he reveals himself to her he fails as a lover. S. N. Behrman did a successful adaptation which ran on Broadway in 1937–1938 with Alfred Lunt and Lynn Fontanne; Brooks Atkinson described it as a bedroom farce pure and simple, a "theatre prank," but "the bedroom joke has never had such a polished telling." A musical version, called *Olympus on My Mind*, ran off-Broadway in a production featuring Lewis G. Staedlen at the Lambs' Theatre in 1990.

CURT GOETZ (Kurt Götz, 1888–1960) was born in Mainz into a Protestant businessman's family; he emigrated to Switzerland in 1933, then to the United States in 1939. He worked as an actor beginning in 1920 in Rostock and Nuremberg, then with Viktor Barnowsky at the Lessing Theater in Berlin. Goetz became "the German Noel Coward," appearing in plays he had written for himself, doing several runs in both private and subsidized theatres throughout the later years of the Weimar Republic. His ensemble always included his second wife, Valerie von Martens, and his most profitable undertaking was *Hokuspokus* in 1926. The production staged by Barnowsky at the Lessing ran in Berlin for more than 350 performances. Less successful was *Der Lügner und die Nonne* (The Liar and the Nun) of 1930, although it became the basis of a popular motion picture. After Goetz and Valerie von Martens left Europe, they traveled throughout the United States and ultimately settled in Hollywood, California, where Goetz worked under contract as a screenwriter for the Metro-Goldwyn-Mayer studio.

HEINZ GORDON (1871–perished in a concentration camp sometime between

1933 and 1945) was born in Tarnowitz, Upper Silesia, and began his acting career in Milwaukee, Wisconsin, as a member of the German Theater Company at the Pabst Theater. He began writing comedies for that company, and when he returned to Berlin in the mid-1890s his plays appeared on several Wilhelmine stages. His most successful comedies during the Weimar period were *Der ehemalige Leutnant* (The Former Lieutenant, written with Gustav Kadelburg) and *Die Rutschbahn* (The Roller Coaster, written with Curt Goetz).

SIGMUND GRAFF (1898–1979) was born in Franconia to a small-town mayor's family. He enlisted in the German army in World War I and rose to officer rank. Graff became a journalist after the war and later was an active member of the Nazi movement. He wrote numerous comedies in the Third Reich; his Weimar comedies included *Etappe* (1927) and *Mary und Lisa* (1931). During the Weimar period, he was best known for (and most successful with) a play titled *Die endlose Straße* (The Eternal Road), written with Carl Ernst Hintze in 1926. It, along with Sheriff's *Journey's End* and Stallings and Anderson's *What Price Glory?*, was among the most notable "war comrade" plays of the period. *Die endlose Straße* was rejected by theatres throughout Germany, and only after it had attracted big audiences in London during the 1929–1930 season did a German theatre (the Stadttheater Aachen) agree to premiere it in 1930. It had over 5,000 performances thereafter in numerous theatres, including small provincial towns and cities, until it was banned in 1936; it also was extremely popular in South America.

SACHA GEORGES ALEXANDRE PIERRE GUITRY (1885–1957), the son of an established French actor, Lucien-Germain Guitry, was born in Saint Petersburg, Russia, where his father had gone to run a theatre. Sacha Guitry was the author of over 100 plays and was also an actor, who appeared first in Saint Petersburg under his father's management and later at the Renaissance Theatre in Paris, again under his father. He was well established as an actor and playwright by 1906. He was extremely popular in London, where he performed, as he did in Paris, the leading role in his own plays. He also starred in over thirty films, which he usually directed and for which he customarily wrote the screenplay.

WALTER HASENCLEVER (1890–1940) was born in Aachen and studied law in Oxford, Lausanne, and Leipzig. In World War I he served in Belgium and on the eastern front, where he was severely wounded. He was discharged in 1917 and recuperated in Dresden, where he became closely acquainted with Oskar Kokoschka. After the war Hasenclever worked as a newspaper correspondent and lived in the United States and France from 1924 to 1930. His was a remarkable literary and theatrical career. He is probably best known for his Expressionist play *Der Sohn* (The Son), which he wrote before the war (1914); it was premiered in Prague in 1916 and enjoyed numerous productions after the war in Germany and abroad. Hasenclever won the Kleist Prize of 1917 and wrote a version of *Antigone* that year in the form of a passionate antiwar grievance. His career entered a new and lucrative phase in 1926 with the publication and premiere of the comedy *Ein besserer Herr* (A Better Sort of Gentleman); after its initial staging in Frankfurt am Main, it enjoyed scores of other productions and hundreds of performances around the country for the next six years. His second comedy, *Ehen werden im Himmel geschlossen* (Marriages Made in Heaven, 1928), was popular, although it was not as well received nor as frequently performed as *Ein besserer Herr*. He emigrated to Yugoslavia in 1933, and in 1936 the Propaganda Ministry banned both publication and performances of his work, while the Foreign Ministry stripped him of German citizenship. In 1939 he was arrested and twice interned in France, but he was released through the intervention of Jean Giradoux. He was arrested again in 1940 and placed in a French prison camp, where he committed suicide.

BEN HECHT (1894–1964) and CHARLES MACARTHUR (1895–1956) were originally journalists in Chicago when they turned their hands to playwriting and, later, to screenwriting. Hecht was born in New York City and attended high school in Racine, Wisconsin. After graduation he worked on newspapers in Chicago from 1910 to 1923, where he met and began collaborating with MacArthur. Their partnership was prosperous for both, though not nearly so prolific as those of their German counterparts Franz Arnold and Ernst Bach or Toni Impekoven and Carl Mathern. Their two most noteworthy comedies were the hugely successful *The Front Page* (1928) and *Twentieth Century* (1932), both of which were made into motion pictures; the former has in fact experienced numerous film interpretations, and the latter was the basis for a successful Broadway musical. MacArthur was born in Scranton, Pennsylvania, and collaborated with other notable playwrights, including Edward Sheldon and Sidney Howard, before working with Hecht.

OTTO ERNST HESSE (Michael Gesell, 1891–1946), the son of a schoolteacher, studied in Freiburg, Munich, and Leipzig, where he earned a doctorate. He later taught at the University of Königsberg, was feuilleton editor for a Königsberg newspaper, and in 1925 he accepted a similar position with the prestigious *Vossische Zeitung* in Berlin. His comedies included *Der Bigamist* (1921); *Kinder des Augenblicks* (1921); *BGB § 1312* (1923); *Klinkutsch* (1925); *Komödianten* (1926); *Die Maske* (1925); *Die Liebeslehre* (1925); *Das Privileg* (1921); he continued writing comedies throughout Third Reich.

HUGO von HOFMANNSTHAL (1874–1929) was the scion of a wealthy Jewish silk-manufacturing family in Vienna raised to the nobility in 1835. He attended the University of Vienna, where he studied law, but he earned a doctorate in Romance literature and languages. He served as a reserve officer in the Austro-Hungarian army during World War I and later was a diplomat. He had residences in France and Italy but lived primarily in Vienna where he wrote lyrical poetry and narrative fiction. He is best known as the librettist for the Richard Strauß operas *Elektra* (1909), *Der Rosenkavalier* (1911), *Ariadne auf Naxos* (1912), *Die Frau ohne Schatten* (1919), and *Die ägyptische Helena* (1928). He was also closely associated with Max Reinhardt and the Salzburger Festspiele, for which he wrote *Jedermann* (1911) and *Das Salzburger große Welttheater* (1928). His comedies written and performed during the Weimar years, *Der Schwierige* (1921) and *Der Unbestechliche* (1923), were moderately successful in Berlin. Scholars have often referred to von Hofmannsthal as a "Viennese neo-Romantic," though he is also regarded as a "classicist" because of his attempts to revive Greek tragedies; some of these were produced by Reinhardt, including *Elektra, Ödipus und die Sphinx* (premiered at Deutsches Theater 1905), *König Ödipus* (1907), and *Alkestis* (1909).

ARTHUR HOPKINS (1879–1950), who was born in Cleveland, Ohio, was originally a journalist. He entered show business as a publicity agent in vaudeville and then became an extremely successful Broadway director in the 1920s, using many of the techniques he had seen used in Berlin. His most notable premiere productions were Anderson and Stallings' *What Price Glory?* in 1924 and the comedy he wrote with George Watters in 1927, *Burlesque*. These productions he staged at the Plymouth Theatre in New York, the Shubert-owned facility he had leased in 1918. He had contracted John Barrymore as his principal actor and Robert Edmond Jones as his designer for these productions, which included Alexei Tolstoy's *The Living Corpse* (also a hit in Berlin at the time) and the enormously successful *Richard II* by William Shakespeare. Hopkins was greatly impressed with Max Reinhardt's work and wanted to employ similar techniques in New York; his 1921 production of *Macbeth* (starring Lionel Barrymore) was influenced more by Leopold Jessner and Jürgen Fehling, however, and it was extremely controversial. His 1922 production of *Hamlet* established John Barrymore as a classical actor, and that production toured to London. He also presented Ethel Barrymore in numerous productions (she made her Broadway debut in Gerhart Hauptmann's *Rose Bernd*), and later premiered Eugene O'Neill's *Anna Christie* and *The Hairy Ape* on Broadway. *Burlesque* featured Barbara Stanwyck and Oscar Levant on Broadway; it became *Artisten* in Germany, premiering at Reinhardt's Deutsches Theater in 1928, where it enjoyed a substantial run.

AVERY HOPWOOD (1882–1928) was, like Arthur Hopkins, born in Cleveland, Ohio. After graduating from the University of Michigan, he worked as a reporter in Cleveland and wrote his first play with the New York press agent Channing Pollock in 1906, titled *Clothes*. It had a modest success on Broadway and he proceeded to write numerous other farces and mysteries in the prewar years. His most successful (in terms of popularity among German audiences) was *Fair and Warmer*, written in 1915 and given the German title *Der Mustergatte*. It appeared in several German theatres through the war years and continued to play frequently during the Weimar Republic years, and served as a star vehicle for such outstanding German comic actors as Max Adalbert, Max Pallenberg, Hans Waßmann, and most important, Heinz Rühmann. Rühmann first captured national attention among German critics, in fact, with his performance in *Der Mustergatte* in 1927 at the Munich Kammerspiele. Hopwood's most successful efforts on Broadway were written with Mary Rinehart Roberts; their *The Bat* (1920), based on her story, became a huge Broadway hit. He wrote *Getting Gertie's Garter* in 1921 with Wilson Collison and it, too, did well on Broadway, though it never achieved much distinction on German stages.

ÖDÖN von HORVÁTH (1901–1938) was the son of a Habsburg diplomat of Hungarian descent; thus his name Ödön, the Hungarian equivalent for Edmund. Horváth grew up in various central European cities where his father was posted and later studied in Munich. His "comedies" (they are best understood as social satires containing brutal character portraits) are noteworthy because they animate the familiar *Lokalstück* format with contemporary social consciousness, and they infuse characters with a nihilistic modernism. The characters in *Geschichten aus dem Wienerwald* (Tales of Vienna Woods, 1931), *Italienische Nacht* (Italian Night, 1931), and *Kasimir und Karoline* (1932) are indeed parodies of their more naïve counterparts in the nineteenth century, for they appear completely adrift amidst ominous social and political currents, over which they have no control and of which they have little understanding. They therefore speak in catch phrases and repeat clichés heard in political propaganda or in advertising. The characters nevertheless epitomize their environment, both in the local geographical sense (usually Austria or Bavaria) and within in the immediate political context of the early 1930s. Horváth was a more ascerbic observer of contemporary life than were Carl Zuckmayer or Marieluise Fleisser, the other playwrights active in the Weimar Republic whose work reflects the influence of nineteenth century *Lokalstück* tendencies. Some critics have furthermore judged Horváth a positive antidote to the attributes of commercial, more widely popular playwrights in the Weimar era because his plays have the potential to present disturbing social and political commentary within entirely familiar dimensions. He was not successful in his own lifetime, though Heinz Hilpert (the director of many Zuckmayer productions) premiered his plays at Max Reinhardt's Deutsches Theater in the early 1930s.

ANTON "TONI" IMPEKOVEN (1881–1947) was born in Cologne and began his theatrical career in the Berlin suburb of Rixdorf in 1900 as an actor. He was consistently cast as a young comic type and found steady work; in 1904 he was engaged by the newly formed Lustspielhaus in Berlin as both an actor and director, while also assuming responsibility for some design areas. While working there he met Franz Arnold and Ernst Bach; the three of them worked together until the outbreak of World War I, after *Die spanische Fliege* had opened in 1913 to popular acclaim. During this period, he studied the techniques Arnold and Bach used, and in 1914 Impekoven left the Lustspielhaus for an engagement with the Frankfurt Stadttheater. There he met Carl Mathern, and the two of them wrote *Junggesellendämmerung* (Twilight of the Bachelors), the first in a series of successful comedies patterned on the success of Arnold and Bach; they wrote thirteen in all. Their most popular was *Die drei Zwillinge* (The Three Twins), which had a place in the repertoires of most German theatres throughout the 1920s. Their plays remained popular through the Third Reich, and they continued writing until 1942. Toni Impekoven remained in Frankfurt for the rest of his life, principally as an actor and later, after 1930, as a director. He became Intendant of the Frankfurt Stadttheater shortly before his death.

HANNS JOHST (1890–1978) was a well-established playwright of both comedies and straight plays during the Weimar Republic, but his notoriety rests upon the fact that he was personally acquainted with Adolf Hitler and became Hitler's favorite playwright during the "years of struggle" before the Nazis assumed power. His comedies, which included *Wechsler und Händler* (Money Changers and Traders, 1923), *Der Ausländer* (The Foreigner, 1925), and *Komödie am Klavier* (Comedy with Piano Accompaniment, 1928), had moderate success but were overshadowed by the playwright's straight plays. The first of these was *Der Einsame* (The Lonely One, 1917), which had a profound effect on the young Bertolt Brecht. Brecht subsequently claimed to have written *Baal* in response to it. Johst's *Thomas Paine* attracted little attention when it premiered in 1926, but Nazi theatre critics later hailed the eponymous hero as "the American Horst Wessel." His last, and most important, play was *Schlageter*, written at Hitler's request and premiered on Hitler's birthday in 1933. Its hero was "the first soldier of the Third Reich," Albert Leo Schlageter, who was executed by the French in 1923 for guerilla activities against occupation troops in the Ruhr region. After 1933, Johst became an officer in the SS and an official in the Propaganda Ministry.

GUSTAV KADELBURG (1851–1925) was born in Budapest and trained as an actor in Vienna. After engagements in Leipzig and Halle he began work in 1871 at the Wallner Theater Berlin, playing roles of the "dandy" or "young gentleman" type. In 1875 he began directing at the Wallner, which presented mostly comedies and operettas. He began writing comedies and libretti for the theatre at the age of twenty-one, though he did not achieve lasting success until his work with Oscar Blumenthal began in 1891 with the musical comedy *Großstadtluft (Big City Airs)*. In 1897 came his greatest success with Blumenthal, *Im weißen Rößl (The White Horse Inn)*, which premiered at the Lessing Theater and remained an audience favorite for decades thereafter. He wrote only one comedy during the Weimar Republic (*Der ehemalige Leutnant*, with Heinz Gordon in 1919); it enjoyed moderate success.

GEORG KAISER (1878–1945) was one of the most prolific and successful of all German playwrights in the twentieth century. He wrote more than fifty plays, forty-five of which were produced before 1933. Kaiser first became known to German audiences for his Expressionist dramas written mostly before World War I but abundantly performed with the lifting of censorship in 1918. In 1923 he began to concentrate on comedy and enjoyed a second wave of popularity. His comedies were as cynical as his Expressionist dramas had been abstract. In some ways they became emblematic of devalued middle-class aspirations which had come in the wake of the economic chaos of 1923. Kaiser seemed to recognize that audiences had changed after that year, and his comedies were written to take financial advantage of that fact.

GEORGE S. KAUFMAN (1889–1961) was born in Pittsburgh, Pennsylvania, and worked for newspapers in Washington, D. C., and New York City before he began his career as "the Great Collaborator" with other playwrights in the 1920s. His successes in the Broadway theatre with playwrights Marc Connelly, Edna Ferber, Ring Lardner, Morris Ryskind, and Moss Hart resembled the successes of Franz Arnold and Ernst Bach, Toni Impekoven and Carl Mathern, Max Reimann and Otto Schwartz, Rudolf Bernauer and Rudolf Österreicher, and others on German stages. Kaufman's only German success came with *The Royal Family* (written with Ferber in 1927).

PAUL KORNFELD (1889–1942) was born in Prague but was educated in Frankfurt. He worked as a dramaturg at the Frankfurt municipal stages, the Hessische Landesbühne in Darmstadt, and the Deutsches Theater in Berlin. During World War I Kornfeld wrote plays in the Expressionist style and also authored essays that described the importance of Expressionism as a "new departure" in German playwriting. During the 1920s he wrote comedies that were popular in Berlin but were seldom performed elsewhere. He also wrote the semibiographical play *Jud-Süß* (Jew Suess), which premiered in 1930 and formed the basis of the anti-Semitic film of 1940 starring Werner Krauß. He emigrated to Prague in 1933 and was arrested there in 1941; Kornfeld was murdered a year later in the Lodz concentration camp.

CURT KRAATZ (1856–1925), who was born in Berlin, attended school in Danzig and Königsberg and later studied pharmacy at the University of Berlin. After becoming a registered apothecary he began his theatrical career as an actor at age twenty-seven. His first engagements were in Görlitz and Frankurt an der Oder. He began his career as a playwright in Mainz, where he was working as an actor and where he met Carl Laufs and Wilhelm Jacoby. Under their tutelage, he began to write comedies that were produced throughout the Wihelmine years. He became resident playwright of the Residenztheater in Wiesbaden in 1897 and in that theatre most of his work was premiered. He wrote over forty plays, mostly with other playwrights. His most successful effort was *Hochtouristen* in 1903, written with Max Neal. While they never achieved the popularity of Franz Arnold and Ernst Bach or Toni Impekoven and Carl Mathern, his comedies were performed frequently during the Weimar Republic; six of them premiered between 1921 and 1930.

EUGÈNE LABICHE (1815–1888) studied law and became a journalist in Paris, but then he became an extraordinarily prolific and influential author of comedies intended for middle-class audiences. Between 1838 and 1877, he wrote, or cowrote, more than 150 plays, most of which were produced at the Palais Royal in Paris. His most well known were farces usually depicting a bourgeois beset by a series of comical predicaments. His most famous was *Le Chapeau de paille d'Italie* (The Italian Straw Hat, 1851), which portrayed a wealthy young landlord on his wedding day. Early on the morning of that fateful day, his horse ate a lady's hat, and the predicament of replacing the hat sets off a chain of events, complicated by sudden reversals, recognitions, and misfortunes. This and other Labiche works provided prototypes for several comedies popular both in the Second Reich and in the Weimar Republic. Labiche's comedies contained songs, however, most of which were popular tunes of the day; they also had a generally wholesome tone.

ADOLF L'ARRONGE (1838–1908) was born in Hamburg and received a musical education. He became a conductor in Cologne and in Berlin in the 1860s, but he became most prominent in Berlin's theatre history as a playwright and theatre manager. He wrote *Mein Leopold* in 1873, a play that remained extraordinarily popular with German audiences throughout the Wilhelmine period. In the Weimar era it remained an audience favorite, appearing regularly in the repertoire of several German theatres. L'Arronge became wealthy enough on the proceeds of that one play to purchase the Friedrich-Wilhelmstädtisches Theater in 1881, which he subsequently renovated and renamed the Deutsches Theater.

ALEXANDER LERNET-HOLENIA (1897–1976) was born in Vienna, the son of aristocrats with a castle in Carinthia. He lived and wrote in Berlin during most of the 1920s and cultivated the image of himself as a lazy patrician. "I myself have never had an original idea, because almost nothing ever occurs to me," he once said when accused of plagiarism. Yet for his efforts he was awarded the Kleist Prize in 1926. That is when his "real" writing career began, he said, when he was able "to distinguish between what I stand for, and what I take money for." He enjoyed a string of comedies that were popular in Berlin (though infrequently performed in other locations) between 1927 and 1932, producing on average one play per year. They ranged in style from a conversational comedy of manners (*Österreichische Komödie*), to a comedy of intrigue (*Ollaportrida*), to a bedroom farce (*Tumult*). All of them possessed an "optimistic nihilism" in which moral values were turned on their heads and written, according to one critic, with "an irresistible talent for words and stageworthiness."

FREDERIC LONSDALE (Frederick Leonard, 1881–1954) began his career in London as a librettist for musicals in 1915. They included *Betty*, *High Jinks*, and *The Maid of the Mountains*, which in 1917 ran for over 1,300 performances. He turned his hand to comedy in the early 1920s; his ability to create amusing situations and effective dialogue made his comedies immediately popular with audiences who delighted in their lack of subtlety. They were popular in Germany, too. His "criminal comedy" titled *The Last of Mrs.Cheyney* (under the German title *Mrs. Cheyneys Ende*) was one of the most frequently performed plays in

Germany during the 1926-1927 season. Other Lonsdale comedies premiered in Weimar period, though less successful than *Mrs. Cheyney*, were *Spring Cleaning* (*Die Flucht aus Ägypten*, premiered in Bad Godesberg), *Aren't We All?* (*Sind wir das nicht alle?*, premiered in Hamburg), *On Approval* (*Zur gefallenen Ansicht*, premiered in Nuremberg), and *Canaries Sometimes Sing* (*Vogel, die am Morgen singen*, premiered in Berlin).

RUDOLF LOTHAR (Rudolf Spitzer, 1865–1933) was born in Budapest and studied in Vienna, Jena, Rostock, and Heidelberg, where he ultimately earned a doctorate in literature. He was employed as a newspaperman until his death but enjoyed success as a playwright working independently and with collaborators throughout the Wilhelmine and Weimar years. He wrote or cowrote, beginning in 1891, over sixty comedies, straight dramas, and libretti; among his collaborators were Hans Bachwitz, P. G. Wodehouse, Lucien Benard, Wilhelm Lichtenberg, and Fritz Gottwald.

CARL MATHERN (1887–1960) was born in Bad Homburg and worked at various undistinguished jobs until, at age twenty-seven, he landed a job with a Frankurt am Main newspaper. There he began to write columns about local life, and by 1920 his had become one of the most popular features in the newspaper. During these years he also began writing playlets, which came to the attention of actor Toni Impekoven. Impekoven and Mathern became an extremely successful playwriting duo, second only to Franz Arnold and Ernst Bach in popularity among audiences during the Weimar Republic. Mathern gave up his regular employment in 1930 and lived on his abundant royalties. He remained in the Frankfurt area through the Third Reich and continued writing for the next thirty years, though he never again realized the success he had enjoyed with Impekoven.

W. SOMERSET MAUGHAM, (1874–1965) was born in Paris and attended Heidelberg University; he later trained as a physician at Saint Thomas Hospital, London. He became a remarkably popular playwright in the British capital during the Edwardian period; in 1908, for example, he had four plays running concurrently. His plays were in the tradition of Oscar Wilde's comedies of manners, with epigrammatic dialogue and well-structured plots. His popularity in Berlin, New York, and London continued well into the 1920s; in the 1928–1929 season, his *The Constant Wife* (*Finden Sie, daß Constance sich richtig verhält?*) was the second most often performed comedy on all German stages. In the 1930–1931 season his *The Breadwinner* was also very popular. He ranked with George Bernard Shaw, Frederic Lonsdale, and Noel Coward as the most eminent of contemporary English-language playwrights to be translated and performed in Germany, and by 1933 he had written twenty-nine comedies, nearly all of them successfully produced in London, Germany, or New York.

MAX MOHR (1891–1944) was born in Würzburg and studied medicine in

Munich. He became a practicing physician and wrote comedies as a sideline. He wrote one of the most frequently performed comedies of the Weimar period (it had nearly a thousand performances in the 1922–1923 season alone): *Improvisationen im Juni* (Improvisations in June), which premiered at the Munich Residenztheater on March 24, 1922. His other comedies, such as *Sirill am Wrack* (Cyril Surveys the Wreckage) and *Der Arbeiter Esau* (The Workman Esau, both 1923), *Die Karawane* (The Caravan, 1924), and *Die Welt der Enkel* (The World of the Grandchildren, 1930) were popular but did not match Mohr's initial success.

FERENC MOLNAR (1878–1952) was born in Budapest and studied law, but he became the most well- known Hungarian playwright of the twentieth century. He began his career writing comedies which were frequently performed on German stages during the Wilhelmine era and in the Weimar period; he is best remembered for his fantasy romance *Lilliom*, though it failed in its premiere production in Budapest. It was extremely popular in New York and became the basis for Richard Rodgers and Oscar Hammerstein's musical *Carousel* (1945). His most important success during the 1920s was not in Europe at all but in New York with *The Guardsman*, produced by the Theatre Guild in 1924 as a vehicle for Alfred Lunt and Lynne Fontanne.

HANS MÜLLER-SCHLÖSSER (1884–1956) was a native of Düsseldorf who remained in that city all his professional life. He wrote short stories, essays, and numerous comedies in the 1920s that premiered at the Schauspielhaus in Düsseldorf, an institution with which he was closely associated over three decades. His most successful comedy was *Schneider Wibbel* (Wibbel the Tailor, 1913), which had nearly 120 performances in over twenty theatres during the 1919–1920 season. It continued to play well through the 1920s. His best play was *Eau de Cologne*, which premiered at the Düsseldorf Schauspielhaus in 1920. It closely resembled the successful works of Max Reimann and Otto Schwartz, Franz Arnold and Ernst Bach, Toni Impekoven and Carl Mathern, Max Mohr, and Bruno Frank, but it did not attract the national attention of those comedies, nor of his own *Schneider Wibbel*. Müller-Schlösser continued to work and write in Düsseldorf through the Nazi years, and he was director of the Kleines Theater there from 1945 to 1948.

ROBERT MUSIL (1880–1942) was born in Klagenfurt, Austria to a family elevated to the nobility in 1917. Musil was primarily a writer of fiction and an essayist whose chief preoccupation was the decline of the Hapsburg world in which he grew up. In this way he resembles Hugo von Hofmannsthal, Alexander Lernet-Holenia, and other Austrians whose comedies periodically appeared on German stages during the Weimar Republic. The work for which he is best known is his novel *Der Mann ohne Eigenschaften* (The Man Without Qualities), the first volume of which appeared in 1930; the second volume was published posthumously in 1943. The characters in that novel, as in most of his other writings (as well as his plays), are keenly aware of their estrangement from the society into which they were born; the characters experience various shadings of reality, which Musil described in both unusual prose and in stylish dialogue. The two comedies he wrote in the Weimar years were *Die Schwärmer* (The Enthusiasts, 1920, for which he won the Kleist Prize in 1923, but which did not premiere until 1929) and *Vinzenz und die Freundin bedeutender Männer* (Vincent and the Girlfriend of Important Men, 1923). Neither of these plays attracted much attention nationally, and Berlin critics were divided in their opinions. Herbert Ihering praised it, but Alfred Kerr said it was less a play and more "a bundle of humorous proceedings." Ludwig Sternaux was closest to the mark when he called it an "intellectual harlequinade."

MAX NEAL (1865–1941) was born in Munich to a painter's family, but as an adolescent he attended a military school. He joined the Wilhelmine army as a lieutenant but resigned his commission in 1892 to pursue a career in journalism. He worked for a series of newspapers in Würzburg and Munich before he became editor for many years of the *Münchener Zeitung*. His greatest theatrical success came with the comedy *Hochtouristen* (written with Curt Kraatz)in 1903, which continued to be popular throughout the Weimar years. Over the span of his career, Neal wrote more than 140 plays and screenplays.

MARCEL PAGNOL (1895–1974), who was born near Marseilles, France, became an instructor at various schools before coming to Paris in 1922. There he began to write popular comedies, achieving his first real success with *Jazz* in 1926. His most popular play in Paris and in the Weimar Republic was one based upon his experiences as a school instructor, *Topaze* (1928). It played in Germany under the title *Das große ABC* and was among the most frequently performed comedies on German stages in the early 1930s. His comedies, straight plays, and fiction drew on his personal background as a native of the south of France; his work could thus be compared to writers of *Volkstücke* in German. He worked almost exclusively in the French film industry from 1933 to 1955, when the popularity of his stage work waned. He founded the French journal of film commentary, *Cahiers du film*, and in 1947 Pagnol was elected as one of "the immortals" to the French Academy.

HUGO PHILLIPP (1889–1969) attended school in Dortmund and university in Berlin. He later studied acting and music at the Stern Conservatory in Berlin and made his debut as an opera basso in Detmold. He sang operatic engagements throughout Germany before World War I, but he turned to theatre directing in the 1920s at the Albert Theater in Dresden. There he wrote several comedies, although only one, *Der glühende Einmaleins* (That Wonderful Once Upon a Time, premiered November 17, 1922 at the Mainz Stadttheater) was successful.

RUDOLPH PRESBER (1868–1935), son of the writer Hermann Presber, studied in Freiburg and Heidelberg. Presber began working, after completing doctoral studies in Heidelberg, as a newspaper editor in Frankfurt am Main but moved to

Berlin in 1898. There he worked as an editor of journals and magazines while also writing plays, several of which were performed in the prewar years. His greatest success, however, came with the historical comedy he cowrote with Leo Walter Stein, *Liselotte von der Pfalz* (Liselotte of the Palatinate), which premiered Christmas Day 1918 in Stuttgart. This play was one of the most frequently performed in theatres throughout the Weimar Republic, with over 200 productions from 1919 to 1933. During that period, many well-known actresses used the play as a touring vehicle, among them Lucie Mannheim and Käthe Dorsch. The production at the Berlin Staatliches Schauspielhaus with Mannheim and Gustaf Gründgens was the most well known, running for over 100 performances in the 1930–1931 season.

HANS-JOSÉ REHFISCH, (pseud. Hans Turner, 1891–1960) studied in Grenoble and in Heidelberg, where he earned a law degree. He worked subsequently as a lawyer and judge in Berlin, while writing comedies and historical dramas. Among the latter, his most notable was *Die Affäre Dreyfus* in 1929; his most successful comedy was *Wer weint um Juckenack?* (Who Weeps for Juckenack?), among the most performed of all comedies during the 1924–1925 season. His *Nickel und die 36 Gerechten* (Nickel and the 36 Righteous Men) opened in thirteen different theatres during the same week of the 1925-1926 season, in anticipation of similar success; but *Nickel* never attained the same popularity. Rehfisch later ran a film company, and with Erwin Piscator he ran the Central Theater in Berlin from 1931 to 1933. Rehfisch was imprisoned briefly in 1933 due to his Jewish family background and his association with Piscator. He was able to emigrate to Vienna and remain there until 1938, when he escaped to London, where he remained throughout the war. By 1945 he was working with Piscator again, this time in New York at the Drama Workshop of the New School for Social Research until 1950, when he returned to Germany. He began working actively in the German Democratic Republic in 1957, staging his own plays and directing new plays on East German radio.

MAX REIMANN (1875–1943) was born in Danzig (now Gdansk in Poland) and began his theatrical career as an actor at the age of seventeen. He worked in various theatres, most importantly at the Wallner in Berlin. In 1901 he began a decade-long engagement at the Frankfurt Stadttheater, where he regularly played comic roles. During this period, he came to know the playwright and composer Otto Schwartz, with whom he wrote his most successful comedies. Their *Die Familie Hannemann* (The Hannemann Family, 1917) was popular throughout the Weimar period, and their *Willys Frau* (Willy's Wife) was among the most performed of all comedies in the 1919–1920 season. Their *Der Sprung in die Ehe* (The Leap Into Marriage) was the third-most frequently performed comedy of the 1923–24 season, and their *Der Meisterboxer* (The Boxing Champion) was nearly as popular the following season. After that season, Reimann virtually retired from playwriting to concentrate on producing. He had helped cofound the Neues Theater in Frankfurt in 1911 (with

Arthur Hellmer), and in 1920 he took over the administration of the Nuremberg Intimes Theater with Hans Merck. Both of these were private, nonsubsidized theatres, and their survival was due in large part to the plays of Reimann and Schwartz.

LOTHAR SACHS (1889–1944) was one of the more frequently produced playwrights in the Weimar Republic, although his comedies were often imitations of more successful endeavors by other, more well-known playwrights. His works enjoyed numerous productions in urban, commercial venues; among touring companies; and in provincial, subsidized houses.

FRANZ von SCHÖNTHANN (1849–1913) was born in Vienna to an aristocratic Habsburg family; he completed schooling and joined the Austro-Hungarian navy in 1867. After four years of military service he resigned to study acting. He was unsuccessful as an actor, although he received numerous short-term engagements in small Austrian and German theatres before he moved to Berlin in 1878 to work at the Residenztheater. A year later, he began working at the Wallner Theater, where he met Gustav Kadelburg. Kadelburg's influence proved to be extraordinarily beneficial, for in 1884 the Wallner premiered Schönthann's *Der Raub der Sabinerinnen* (The Rape of the Sabine Women). The comedy's central character is a schoolteacher named Martin Gollwitz, who dreams of fame and fortune as a playwright. He has written a play based on early Roman history titled *Der Raub der Sabinerinnen.* One day the head of a touring theatre troupe comes to town and offers to produce the play. Gollwitz is delighted but must hide the fact from his wife, who is very much opposed to any theatrical activity on moral grounds. When Gollwitz finally sees his play produced he is disgraced, because even he must acknowledge that the play he wrote is awful. He also perceives that his wife has been right all along—the theatre is a waste of time. A subplot features a love affair between Gollwitz's daughter and an actor in the company; the affair ends happily when the actor agrees to give up his artistic ambitions and to settle down with a steady job. This comedy proved to be among the most successful of all comedies ever written in German. It ran in scores of theatres through the Wilhelmine and Weimar periods. Schönthann wrote more than forty other plays, both by himself and with collaborators, but few equalled the popularity of *Raub*.

GEORGE BERNARD SHAW (1856–1950) had an astounding career as a prosperous playwright in both Imperial Germany and in the Weimar Republic, due to the efforts of his translator and longtime champion, Siegfried Trebitsch (1868–1956). In 1902 Shaw granted Trebitsch exclusive rights to negotiate with any German-language theatre on his behalf; although there was never a written contract between them, Trebitsch had a free hand to translate Shaw's plays as he saw fit and to oversee all contractual affairs with producers. Shaw's plays were popular in Germany before the war, especially *The Devil's Disciple*, his first play in German. It premiered in Vienna at the Raimund Theater in 1903. By 1926, the year he received the Nobel Prize for Literature, Shaw was regarded as indispensable to a prosperous season in Germany, whether in a provincial theatre or in Berlin. Nearly all his full-length plays were given careful, fully realized productions. That was not the case in France; in 1926 Shaw became embroiled in a literary feud with the popular French playwright Henri Bernstein (1876–1953), when Shaw said the cool reception of his plays in France was due to the "provincialism" of Paris. Bernstein felt compelled to defend France's honor by reporting that Shaw had laughed at his own mother's cremation. Shaw replied that Bernstein was "a romantic Jew" attempting to exploit French patriotic feelings. Bernstein then accused Shaw of anti-Semitism, to which Shaw replied he had no need of sensitivity to Jewish feelings because he was an English playwright, and England was a country relatively free from anti-Semitism.

LEO WALTER STEIN, (1866–1930) was principally an actor and director, although his writing for the stage with Rudolf Presber was in one instance enormously successful. *Liselotte von der Pfalz* (Liselotte of the Palatinate), which premiered in late 1918, capitalized on anti-French sympathies throughout the first years of the Weimar Republic. Though it was nominally a costume drama about the noble families of France and the Rhineland Palatinate in the seventeenth century, Presber and Stein fashioned its characters on distinctly bourgeois patterns and created situations for them that were transparently comic. As noted above, the play became a profitable vehicle for several female stars in the 1920s.

CARL STERNHEIM (1878–1942) was born in Leipzig the illegitimate son of a wealthy Jewish banker. Sternheim grew up in Berlin and studied at Göttingen, Leipzig, Jena, and Berlin. His first comedy was *Auf Dorfkrug* (On the Bummel) in 1902, and Sternheim went on to write several satirical comedies through the Wilhelmine years. They were infrequently performed due to police censorship in most localities, and when they were performed it was in abridged versions. Yet his plays won a wide readership, and Sternheim was considered among the most important of Wilhelmine playwrights. His work experienced extensive production in uncut renditions throughout the Weimar years. *Bürger Schippel* (Citizen Schippel), for example, was one of the most frequently performed plays of the 1923–1924 season.

ERNST TOLLER (1893-1939) was born in Samotschin, West Prussia, and graduated from high school there; his university studies at Grenoble were interrupted by the outbreak of World War I. He enlisted and served on the western front until 1917, when after his experience at the battle of Verdun he was mustered out. In 1918 he studied at Heidelberg but left the university to join the communist-led takeover of the Bavarian government in that year. He was imprisoned soon thereafter in Eichstädt, and his experiences (both as a soldier and as an activist) made him a politically committed playwright. He wrote most of the plays for which he is best known from his prison cell, including *Die Wandlung* (The Transformation, 1919), *Masse Mensch* (Masses and Man, 1922), *Der deutsche Hinkemann* (The German Disabled Veteran, 1922), and *Die Maschinenstürmer* (The Luddites, 1922). His best comedy, *Der entfesselte Wotan* (Wotan the Mighty, 1923), was a satire on Adolf Hitler and premiered in Moscow. His other comedy, *Die Rache des verhöhnten Liebhabers* (The Revenge of the Aggrieved Lover, 1928) was unusual, even for the antiestablishment, leftist agitator Toller. A sexual fantasy written in rhymed couplets, it is based upon a story by Cardinal Giuseppe Bandello depicting Venetian characters of the mid-sixteenth century. The characters vaguely resemble *commedia* types, but the principal action concentrates on the young Lorenzo's desire to avenge himself (hence the title) on Giuseppe, a powerful local politician who resembles the bourgeois capitalists of Germany. Toller emigrated to the United States after 1933 and worked for the Metro-Goldwyn-Mayer film studio. He committed suicide in his New York City hotel room in the fall of 1939.

FRITZ von UNRUH, (1885–1970) was born in Koblenz to a military family (his father was a general) which traced its lineage to Charlemagne. Unruh himself entered the German military during the Wilhelmine period as a career officer; he resigned his commission in 1911 to devote himself to playwriting. At the outbreak of World War I, he reentered the army and assumed command of a cavalry unit on the western front. He was severely wounded there, and the experience transformed him into a pacifist. During his convalescence he returned to playwriting, and he wrote in the Expressionist style. Several of his plays were produced immediately after the war; they espoused an exalted tone of apocalyptic revelation. He wrote two comedies near the end of the Weimar Republic, one of which (*Phaea*, 1930) was a satire on the German film industry and proved very popular among Berlin audiences. When the Nazis assumed power, he emigrated and arrived in the United States with the help of Albert Einstein. He supported himself in America as a painter and lived on Long Island.

CARL ZUCKMAYER (1896–1977) was born in the Rhine village of Nackenheim and grew up in the nearby city of Mainz, where he attended high school. He enlisted (while still a school pupil) in a cavalry regiment at the outbreak of World War I and attained the rank of captain by 1917. After the collapse of the western front, he wandered back to Mainz and attended university classes in Frankfurt. There he began writing plays; his first effort, written in the ejaculatory style of Expressionism, was staged in Berlin at the Staatliches Schauspielhaus under Leopold Jessner. It played only five performances. After that he left the university and worked sporadically in provincial theatres; in Munich he met Bertolt Brecht who, in 1924, secured jobs for both of them at Max Reinhardt's Deutsches Theater. His second play, written while working with Brecht, met with even worse reviews than had the first. Zuckmayer remained determined nonetheless to write plays with broad audience appeal. He achieved that goal at the end of 1925 with *Der fröhliche Weinberg* (The Merry Vineyard), one of the more successful comedies in the Weimar era. It was performed in scores of theatres throughout the 1920s, and

Zuckmayer continued to write other plays, the most successful of which premiered in 1931. This was *Der Hauptmann von Köpenick* (The Captain of Köpenick), perhaps the best of all comedies written between 1919 and 1933 and the one most frequently performed during the 1931–1932 season. He emigrated to Austria in 1933 and remained there until 1938; he settled in the United States in 1940, where he became a citizen and remained until 1946. His *Des Teufels General* (The Devil's General), written on a farm he had rented in Vermont, generated intense controversy and was the most frequently performed drama in Germany during the immediate postwar period. He settled in Switzerland in 1958 and continued to write plays until his death, though he never again attempted to write comedy.

Bibliographical Essay

GENERAL STUDIES

The history of the Weimar Republic remains a fascinating topic, and studies of its culture will doubtless continue to appear for years to come. Several recent books in English have augmented an already substantial literature. Premiere among them is John Willett's *The Theatre of the Weimar Republic* (New York: Holmes and Meier, 1988), which complemented that outstanding scholar's *Art and Politics of the Weimar Period* (London: Thames and Hudson, 1978). Detlev Peukert's *The Weimar Republic,* translated by Richard Deveson (New York: Hill and Wang, 1992), provides superb analysis of the "crisis of classical modernity" besetting the Weimar Republic's culture and its theatre in particular. Michael Patterson's *The Revolution in German Theatre*, 1900–1933 (London: Routledge and Kegan Paul, 1981) includes some appraisal of pre-World War I trends, while Walter Lacquer's *Weimar: A Cultural History* (New York: Putnam, 1974) asserts that "Weimar culture" predates the Weimar Republic by at least ten years. Peter Gay's *Weimar Culture* (New York: Harper and Row, 1968) likewise indulges somewhat in generalities, but the author's gift for aphoristic metaphor remains unmatched. The Weimar Republic, he notes, was "too successful to satisfy its critics, but not successful enough to satisfy its well-wishers." Ronald Taylor's *Literature and Society in Germany*, 1918–1945 (Totowa, N.J.: Barnes and Noble, 1980) extends its coverage beyond the Weimar years, so its evaluations are relatively less extensive.

Among the finest German-language studies of the Weimar Republic's theatre was Günther Rühle's volume of newspaper reviews, which he titled *Theater für die Republik* (Frankfurt: Fischer, 1967); it remains an indispensable resource. Manfred Overesch and Friedrich Wilhelm Saal's chronicle *Die Weimarer Republik* (Düsseldorf: Droste, 1982) is, like Rühle's book, a compendium rather than an analytical study, but also like Rühle it is extremely helpful as a reference guide to productions, personalities, and events. Combining both compendium and analytical characteristics was the catalogue of the University of Cologne's 1977 exhibition in Berlin and in Bonn, published under the title *Theater in der Weimarer Republik* (Berlin: Kunstamt Kreuzberg, 1977). Volker Klotz's *Bürgerliches Lachtheater* (Munich: DTV, 1980) is a study of bourgeois theatrical entertainment; its focus remains primarily on the nineteenth century, but it nevertheless is extremely valuable for any reader interested in popular German comedy. Even more valuable is Bernd Wilms's 1969 dissertation completed at the Free University of Berlin, "Der Schwank: Dramaturgie and Theatereffekt, Deutsches Trivialtheater 1880–1930," which to date, remains inexplicably unpublished. Jost Hermand and Frank Trommler's *Die Kultur der Weimarer Republik* (Munich: Nymphenburger, 1978) is particularly valuable for its examination of the changing nature of audiences for comedy during the later Weimar years.

Among several essays with important insights on the Weimar theatre is Reinhold Grimm's "Neuer Humor? Die Komödienproduktion zwischen 1918 und 1933" in *Die deutsche Komödie im zwanzigsten Jahrhundert*, edited by Wolfgang Paulsen (Heidelberg: Lothar Stiem, 1976), 107–133. Grimm is one of the rare scholars willing to probe the work of Curt Goetz and Bruno Frank. Walther Kiaulehn's "Die Berliner Kritik war jüdisch" in *Porträts deutsch-jüdischer Geistesgeschichte*, edited by Thilo Koch (Cologne: DuMont Schauberg, 1961), 205–227, probes the impact of German Jews on the Weimar theatre. Most Berlin newspaper critics were Jewish, as were many of the city's producers. E. B. Natan likewise provides a wealth of information on Jewish contributions to Weimar culture in his "Der demographische und wirtschaftliche Struktur der Juden," in *Entscheidungsjahr 1932*, edited by W. E. Mosse (Tübingen: Klett, 1965) 87-131.

PLAYS

As noted earlier, most of the outstanding comedies of the Weimar Republic have never been translated into English. Many of them appeared only as stage manuscripts and were never officially published in German. They were regarded as disposable items of industrial entertainment, and even the playwrights themselves made little effort to preserve their work. There are of course notable exceptions, especially when the plays were considered to have some literary merit. Georg Kaiser's plays have appeared in several anthologies and even in collections dedicated to him alone—but rarely have the collections included his comedies. Of Carl Zuckmayer's comedies, only *The Captain of Köpenick* has been published in English. It appears in *German Drama* between the Wars, edited by George Wellwarth (New York: Dutton, 1972), translated by Richard Mueller. Four translations of Ödön von Horváth's plays are contained in *Four Plays by Ödön von Horváth* (New York: PAJ, 1986), with a valuable introductory essay by Martin Esslin. Walter Hasenclever's plays, like Kaiser's, appear in numerous collections but to date remain largely untranslated into English. Of the leading comedies of the Weimar Republic, few are easy to locate. The Library of Congress and the New York Public Library own several, but the collection of the Theatre Museum of the University of Cologne in Porz is the most extensive. Its holdings have been edited by Roswitha Flatz and published under the title *The Play Book Collection of the Theatre Museum of the University of Cologne* (New York: Saur, 1990).

ANALYSES OF PLAYS

The paucity of published comedy scripts produced in the Weimar Republic is reflected in the dearth of meaningful analyses of the plays and of the playwrights. Few students of the German theatre have undertaken studies of Franz Arnold and Ernst Bach, Toni Impekoven and Carl Mathern, Bruno Frank, Rudolf Bernauer, Max Mohr, and others. There have, however, been valuable examinations of Georg Kaiser's work. Among them are Ernst Schürer's *Georg Kaiser* (Boston: Twayne, 1971), which devotes an entire chapter to Kaiser's comedies, titled "Retreat from Utopia." Peter K. Tyson's *The Reception of Georg Kaiser* (Bern: Peter Lang, 1984) totals 1,042 pages in two volumes and is extremely useful for examining all of Kaiser's plays. John Henry Antosh completed an excellent doctoral dissertation at Indiana University in 1977, titled "Georg Kaiser's Comedies of the Twenties." Burghard Dedner's *Carl Sternheim* (Boston: Twayne, 1982) is one of the better evaluations of Sternheim in English, while Manfred Linke's *Carl Sternheim* (Hamburg: Rowohlt, 1979) is a *Bildbiographie* featuring abundant photos and personal information, along with valuable discussions of the subject's work. Miriam Raggam's *Walter Hasenclever* (Hildesheim: Gerstenberg, 1973) contains no photographs but does include some discussion of the playwright's shift to comic playwriting in the later 1920s.

AUTOBIOGRAPHIES AND DIARIES

There is a wealth of personal accounts and observations by German theatre artists which provide unique, if somewhat unreliable, details of production and performance. Carl Zuckmayer's *Als wär's ein Stück von mir* (Frankfurt: Fischer, 1966) is the most complete of his many autobiographical accounts. It was so popular in its first edition that Fischer authorized an English version, titled *A Part of Myself*, soon after its initial publication. In both versions he recounts experiences and personalities who influenced him on his way to becoming one of the Weimar Republic's most popular and most often-performed playwrights. Fritz Kortner's *Aller Tage Abend* (Munich: Kindler, 1969) is on a par with Zuckmayer's autobiography. It is a more impassioned account, although it tends also to be more self-serving and selective. The autobiographies of fellow actors Alexander Granach, *Da geht ein Mensch* (Munich: Herbig, 1973), and Tilla Durieux, *Meine erste neunzig Jahre* (Munich: Herbig, 1971), were likewise fascinating, though predictably subjective.

Most fascinating of all for the purposes of studying comedy in the Weimar years is Rudolf Bernauer's *Das Theater meines Lebens* (Berlin: Blanvalet, 1955). In it, one of the real adventurers in Berlin theatre paints that city's life in bright colors with broad strokes. He describes the Wilhelmine years (when he got his start and established himself with his partner Carl Meinhard) in vivid detail. During the Weimar years, he continued in the old paths, he says, though by that time the audience had become jaded and was no longer interested in "real" art. Ferdinand Bonn's *Mein Künstlerleben* (Munich: Huber, 1920) is a surprisingly self-effacing account of one "artist's life" (as the title implies) in the German theatre. Many have disputed his status as "artist," since most of his plays were comic puffery or melodramatic private detective exploits. The most objective account of the Weimar years is found in the diaries of Count Harry Kessler, whose *Tagebücher, 1918–1937* (Frankfurt: Insel, 1982) is often quoted in histories of the Republic for his witty, often sardonic eye-witness accounts. Count Harry had access to the corridors of power and to personalities at the center of the action, and his descriptions are flavored with the "old school" manner for which he has become celebrated.

Index

About the Author

WILLIAM GRANGE is Associate Professor in the Department of Performing Arts, Marquette University. An actor and director as well as a widely published scholar, he is the author of *Partnership in the German Theatre* (1991).

ISBN 0-313-29983-8

90000>

EAN

9 780313 299834

HARDCOVER BAR CODE